NEBRASKA GOVERNMENT AND POLITICS

*Politics and Governments of*
*the American States*

Founding Editor

DANIEL J. ELAZAR

Published by the University of Nebraska Press
in association with the Center for the Study of
Federalism at the Robert B. and Helen S. Meyner
Center for the Study of State and Local
Government, Lafayette College

# Nebraska Government and Politics

SECOND EDITION

EDITED BY ROBERT BLAIR,
CHRISTIAN L. JANOUSEK, AND JEROME DEICHERT

UNIVERSITY OF NEBRASKA PRESS

LINCOLN

The University of Nebraska Press is part of a land-grant institution with campuses and programs on the past, present, and future homelands of the Pawnee, Ponca, Otoe-Missouria, Omaha, Dakota, Lakota, Kaw, Cheyenne, and Arapaho Peoples, as well as those of the relocated Ho-Chunk, Sac and Fox, and Iowa Peoples.

♾

Library of Congress Cataloging-in-Publication Data
Names: Blair, Robert, 1949– editor. | Janousek, Christian L., editor. | Deichert, Jerome A., editor.
Title: Nebraska government and politics / edited by Robert Blair, Christian L. Janousek, and Jerome Deichert.
Description: Second edition. | Lincoln: University of Nebraska Press, [2025] | Series: Politics and governments of the American states | Includes bibliographical references and index.
Identifiers: LCCN 2024024767
ISBN 9780803230491 (paperback)
ISBN 9781496242402 (epub)
ISBN 9781496242419 (pdf)
Subjects: LCSH: Nebraska—Politics and government. | BISAC: POLITICAL SCIENCE / American Government / Local | HISTORY / United States / State & Local / Midwest (IA, IL, IN, KS, MI, MN, MO, ND, NE, OH, SD, WI)
Classification: LCC JK6616 .N43 2025 | DDC 320.9782—dc23/eng/20241118
LC record available at https://lccn.loc.gov/2024024767

Set in Minion Pro by Lacey Losh.

This book is dedicated to Andrew Blair, a fourth-generation Nebraskan whose determination, resilience, and practicality reflect the nature and culture of the state.

# CONTENTS

## Part 2. Government and Administration

# ILLUSTRATIONS

# Acknowledgments

The authors would like to acknowledge the work of the late Robert D. Miewald, professor of political science at the University of Nebraska–Lincoln and editor of the first edition of this volume. His personal and scholarly contributions to the study of Nebraska politics and government are held in high regard. We would also like to recognize the late Daniel J. Elazar, founding editor of this series, for his seminal and unparalleled study of political culture in the U.S. states. His work has influenced and informed all subsequent analyses in this area, including our current endeavor. Finally, we would like to thank the contributing authors, John Bartle, Diane Duffin, Carol Ebdon, James Harrold, Peter Longo, and Anthony Schutz, for their dedication and expertise.

A special thanks to the staff of the University of Nebraska at Omaha Center for Public Affairs Research and the Office of the Dean of Public Affairs and Community Service for their contributions, including Erin Skoog and especially the outstanding editorial and copy work and assistance from Melanie Kiper, without whom this book would not have been possible.

# Introduction

*Robert Blair, Christian L. Janousek, and Jerome Deichert*

The most discernible and conspicuous institution representing the diversity of the American populace is the state. The fifty U.S. states, each embodying a uniqueness of origin and composition, exemplify a unified yet viable assortment of governmental entities formulated from a vast collection of histories, cultures, and geographic influences. Beginning with the first colonial settlements, states have exhibited contrasting differences in social structures, political orientations, economics, and societal progressions. Researchers have examined the U.S. states from numerous perspectives, attempting to identify and categorize the core features and attributes contributing to the range of dissimilarities that span the American terrain. These distinctions of individual state identity derive in part from context, signifying a semi-autonomous component in the piecemeal conglomeration of the federal system. While all are fundamentally American in nature, each state possesses defining traits, events, and circumstances that have created a unique situational setting of politics and government.

According to Daniel Elazar (1972, 1994), esteemed political scientist and expert in American federalism, culture and context generate a specialized atmosphere of local values, beliefs, and customs, in turn representing formative determinants in the institutions of politics and governance. As Elazar suggests, the historical patterns of settlement and establishment as well as the environmental and topographical makeup of the land shape and inspire the development of systems and institutions. Elazar explains these regional separations in terms of political, social, and economic characteristics that have been fashioned by geographic setting, yielding a provincial "sectional-ism" emblematic of the complementary interrelatedness of specific locales.

In other words, political culture has a profound effect on institutional-ization, producing an overarching sentiment or paradigm of political and governmental philosophies that sustains a common and uniting perception shared by a majority of people in a country, region, or state. This collective and enduring set of political norms delineates implicit rules or guidelines by which public decisions are made, thus influencing the manner and expecta-tions of governance. Within the state setting, the manifestations of political culture may be witnessed in varying forms, comprising political viewpoints and affiliations, legislative and policy priorities, governmental and organi-zational configurations, and administrative practices and actions. In sum, a thorough comprehension of the uniqueness of a state's politics and govern-ment requires an understanding and appreciation of its political culture.

As part of Elazar's greater West section of the United States, Nebraska emerged from the original rural-land frontier to become the first territory to gain statehood following the Civil War. Originally inhabited by several Native American tribes and situated just west of the Missouri River, Nebraska, a Great Plains state near the geographic center of the continental United States, is emblazoned with evidence of its frontier heritage and traces of the pioneer spirit. Its political culture embodies these formative traits, with some institutions that are unique to the state and others that share charac-teristics with its neighbors. The remnants of Nebraska's colorful past and the vitality of its emerging present energize a host of evolving topics about the operation of the state's political and governmental practices that are worthy of examination.

Envisioning the Old West, the Oregon Trail, and the pioneer spirit of the grassland prairie, the symbolic imagery of Nebraska distinguishes the state in the annals of the American legend. Nebraska continues to embrace these foundational cultural properties as a gateway state to the West and an agricultural engine for the nation and the world. Yet over the years, popula-tion and economic shifts altered the political landscape, with the growing metropolitan clout on the eastern side of the state calling for transformations in the scope and obligations of government.

Nebraska has been described as "periodically populist" (Pierce and Hag-strom 1984), favoring trends of progressivism when consistent with private interests. This cultural mix of commonwealth and marketplace polities contributes to several distinctively Nebraskan political and governmental institutions, such as one-house (unicameral) nonpartisan elections, an all-public electric power structure, and a fierce protection of citizen control and independence.

This second edition of *Nebraska Government and Politics*, following the 1984 series precursor edited by the late Robert D. Miewald of the Political Science Department of the University of Nebraska–Lincoln, revisits these topics of state government and politics. At the time of the first edition, the authors raised the question of the future vitality of the American states in the reorganized constructs of the federal system. In this new edition, the authors employed political culture as an organizing theme. Faculty from the University of Nebraska at Omaha, Creighton University, the University of Nebraska at Kearney, and the University of Nebraska–Lincoln will attempt to shed new light on this query, resuming this important conversation as it pertains to Nebraska state government more than four decades later.

A wide audience will find this book interesting, enlightening, and a valuable source of information on the government and politics of Nebraska. College-level students will gain in-depth knowledge of the impact of culture on the formation of state political traditions and institutions. Younger students will learn about Nebraska's heritage and how history and culture affect current events. Elected and appointed governmental officials will be able to make more informed policy decisions based on enhanced understanding of Nebraska's institutional framework. People outside the state will be educated on the unique Nebraska governmental and political structure and history. The book will also be a source of information for researchers engaging in comparative state studies. Finally, *Nebraska Government and Politics* will help Nebraskans gain a greater appreciation of the uniqueness and character of their state. In sum, this book not only functions as a reference book on Nebraska government and politics but also serves as a story of Nebraska's "periodically populist" traditions and approaches to public issues and questions.

This second edition follows the primary themes of the prior books in this series of the University of Nebraska Press, Politics and Governments of the American States, touching on the aspects of federalism, constitutionalism, and the continuing American frontier with special attention to the effects and frameworks of political culture. This second edition includes topics of Nebraska's institutions and character, the state constitution and judiciary, political parties and electoral processes, financial administration, the state legislature, the governor and executive branch, the state bureaucracy, local government and intergovernmental relations, and tax and fiscal policy. We delve into the fundamental mechanisms of Nebraska politics and government, emphasizing facets of governance, public administration, public policy, and enduring issues in Nebraska state government. The remaining portion of this introduction provides previews of each of the chapters and topics discussed in this second edition of *Nebraska Government and Politics*.

### PART 1: CULTURE AND INSTITUTIONS

This section examines the cultural foundations and character of Nebraska's political institutions. An important factor that defines the state's political and social identity is Nebraska's heritage of periodic populism. This includes explorations of history, demographics, constitutional and legal designs, and political parties and elections.

Chapter 1, "Nebraska's Political Culture: Periodic Populism," presents an overview of the historical developments of the state with specific emphasis on how history and culture helped shape the traditions and institutions of Nebraska politics and government. Nebraska's distinct brand of political culture was contextualized by the Industrial Revolution, especially the railroads, and the reaction of the Reform era and the Populist movement of the late nineteenth and early twentieth centuries.

Chapter 2, "The Character of Nebraska: A People in Transition," provides a demographic profile of Nebraska, including rural and urban growth trends and a description of the changing structure of Nebraska's economic base. While agriculture continues to play a principal role in the economics of the state, technology and service industries are transforming the economic and demographic organization of Nebraska.

Chapter 3, "The Nebraska State Constitution: A Serviceable Document," discusses the historical and cultural factors that influenced the composition of the state constitution, which functions as the legal foundation for many of the governmental institutions in the state. While the tradition of direct democracy has resulted in extensive amendments, Nebraska boasts one of the oldest state constitutions in the country.

One of the defining dimensions of the Nebraska government is its custom of nonpartisanship. This characteristic, of course, has a major impact on the way political parties' function in the state. Nebraska also was an early proponent of methods of direct democracy, including the use of primary elections, which tend to decrease the influence of political parties. Chapter 4, "Political Parties and Voting: Nonpartisanship and Direct Democracy," will also track trends in public opinion and political ideology in the state.

PART 2: GOVERNMENT AND ADMINISTRATION

This section details the major governmental structures in the state with an emphasis on political and administrative relationships and enduring issues. This involves discussions of financial policies and procedures as well as the state's executive and legislative branches and the various arrangements of local government and intergovernmental relations.

Taxes and financial resources constitute the lifeblood of government activities. Chapter 5, "The Nebraska State Budget: Process, Politics, Priorities," explores the budgeting processes at the state level and for selected local governments. It also examines fundamental laws and institutions that affect financial management and administration, comparing the state to others in both of these areas.

Nebraska retains the only one-house legislature in the United States. This unique legislative assemblage, coupled with nonpartisanship and based in part on tenets of prairie populism and progressivism, greatly impacts the policymaking process in the state. The enactment of this anomalous lawmaking body is examined in chapter 6, "The Unicameral Legislature: Uniquely Nebraska," along with the associated traits and challenges inherent to this distinct legislative model.

The governor of Nebraska, when compared to other states, has significant institutional powers and the potential to play a key role in the policy process, but tradition, unicameralism, and nonpartisanship affect gubernatorial activism and administration. Chapter 7, "The Executive Branch: Efficiency vs. Responsiveness," also discusses the various offices and agencies that constitute the state's executive branch and the nature and administrative qualities of the state bureaucracy and government.

Chapter 8, "Nebraska Local Government: A Reflection of its Political Culture," investigates the multitudinous layers of local government in Nebraska.

Because of its liberal and unique use of special districts, the state has one of the largest number of units of local government in the country. Specific topics addressed include the assorted tiers of local government entities, the functions and forms of municipalities, professional management, and state intergovernmental relationships and operations.

Tax policies are in a constant flux in most states, and they impact the policy development and implementation processes. Chapter 9, "Tax and Fiscal Policy: The Price of Local Control," compares Nebraska to other states in the structure and level of taxes and examines the history of state fiscal policy. Recent policy changes and their implications for the future of taxation are also explored.

Using the movement to abolish the death penalty in Nebraska as a case study, chapter 10, "The Controversy over Capital Punishment: A Case Study of Political Culture," illustrates the application of Nebraska's state institutions and political culture. This effort intermingles the functions and roles of each of the main themes presented throughout the book and demonstrates Nebraska politics and government in action.

### REFERENCES

Elazar, Daniel. 1972. *American Federalism: A View from the States.* 2nd ed. New York: Thomas Y. Crowell.

———. 1994. *The American Mosaic: The Impact of Space, Time, and Culture on American Politics.* Boulder CO: Westview Press.

Pierce, Neal, and Jerry Hagstrom. 1984. "Nebraska: Periodically Populist." In *The Book of America: Inside 50 States Today,* edited by N. Pierce and J. Hagstrom, 578–84. New York: W. W. Norton.

NEBRASKA GOVERNMENT AND POLITICS

## PART 1

# Culture and Institutions

# CHAPTER ONE

# Nebraska's Political Culture

## PERIODIC POPULISM

*Robert Blair, Christian L. Janousek, and Jerome Deichert*

### INTRODUCTION

American federalism permits states to develop their own political system, consistent with the U.S. Constitution. Political culture, in turn, creates the foundation for the structure of these political institutions and tenets. Historical events shape a state's values and beliefs, helping fashion its distinctive political culture. Nebraska's political culture, described by Daniel Elazar, an expert on the subject, as individualistic with a strong element of moralism results in what has been labeled "periodically populist." Located in the middle of the country, far from the coasts and large cities, and protective of their traditional values, Nebraskans "sometimes wait decades to resurrect their populism" to address critical policy concerns in their "conservative and nonideological" and practical manner (summarization of statements from Benes 2019; Elazar 1972; Luebke 1988; Pierce and Hagstrom 1984).

A misunderstood and confusing term, *populism* refers to a variety of movements that appeal to ordinary people who feel that their concerns are disregarded by established elites. Populism, therefore, may have progressive, liberal, conservative, or even reactionary objectives, "channeling popular disdain for established governing norms, forms, ideas and values" advocating the power of the people (Maskovsky and Bjork-James 2022, 1).

This chapter describes the impact of Nebraska's political culture on the formation and operation of governmental institutions and governance structures within the state. First, a discussion of key historical events, circumstances, and actors in Nebraska outlines the nature and origins of the state's political culture. Next, the general concept of political culture and its role in the development of governmental institutions is examined, followed by a description of Nebraska's political culture. The chapter ends with an illustration of some of the state's most important cultural symbols and examples of Nebraska's distinctive contemporary political culture trends and values.

Native American tribes have lived in the land that become Nebraska for thousands of years. Over the centuries, people occupied and then left the area due to climate fluctuations, which ranged from long periods of drought to times of adequate rainfall. This continual migration of people shaped a diverse mixture of Native American languages and cultures. Several Native American language groups could be found in Nebraska, including the Arapahos, who spoke Algonquian, and the Arikaras, with Nebraska being their traditional home. At least fifteen tribes have been identified as hunting or occupying the area at some point in time.

In the eighteenth century, the Omaha, Ponca, and Oto tribes entered eastern Nebraska and lived near the Missouri River. The Lakotas, Arapahos, and Cheyennes migrated west about that time. About forty thousand people of various Native American tribes lived in Nebraska in 1800. By the 1850s, however, the Pawnees, Omahas, Oto-Missouris, Poncas, Lakotas, and Cheyennes were the main Great Plains tribes living in what is now the state of Nebraska (North 2016).

Much of the land of the Omaha tribe was ceded to the United States in the Treaty with the Omaha, 1854, and the Omahas relocated to a reservation in northern Nebraska. The Ponca tribe moved to Oklahoma's Indian Territory in 1877 by an order of the United States government. Ponca leaders, however, returned to their Nebraska homeland and then sued the U.S. government. The Supreme Court, in the landmark case of *Standing Bear v. Crook* (1872), established the fact that the Constitution provided certain rights to Native Americans. Subsequently, the government awarded land in Nebraska to the Poncas. The U.S. government, however, terminated the Ponca tribe in 1966 and dissolved their land and holdings. In 1990 Poncas would regain recognition, but they do not have a reservation in Nebraska (Ponca Tribe of Nebraska n.d.).

The Winnebagos moved to their current location in Nebraska from South Dakota, though central Wisconsin and northern Illinois constitute their ancestral lands. The treaties of 1865 and 1874 established the Winnebago Indian Reservation by taking half of the Omaha reservation. Many of the dispossessed Winnebagos, under cover of darkness, traveled down the Missouri River to rejoin their tribe in Nebraska. By 1913 the General Allotment Act of 1887 reduced the size of the reservation by about two thirds. As a result, the Winnebago tribe experienced a significant loss of population and economic opportunities through the 1960s (Winnebago Tribe of Nebraska n.d.).

The Santees, the "frontier guardians of the Sioux Nation," roamed from their traditional home in modern Minnesota, across the plains, to the northern Rocky Mountains and south through the northwestern part of Nebraska. Following severe punishment by the U.S government for the Santee Uprising of 1862, a reservation in northeastern Nebraska was created. The reservation originally consisted of 115,075 acres, but the Dawes Severalty Act of 1887 significantly reduced the tribe's total acres (Nebraska Indian College n.d.).

The land that became the state of Nebraska was acquired by the United States in 1803 as part of the Louisiana Purchase. Nebraska became a territory in 1854 under the Kansas-Nebraska Act as part of a compromise between slave and free states. The Nebraska Territory consisted of the current state of Nebraska and included parts of the states of North and South Dakota, Colorado, Wyoming, and much of the current state of Montana. According to the Kansas-Nebraska Act, settlers in the two territories would vote on whether to permit slavery, under the principle of popular sovereignty. Opposition to the Kansas-Nebraska Act inspired the formation of the Republican Party as an antislavery party, leading to the outbreak of the Civil War in 1861.

In the period prior to and following the Civil War, Nebraska functioned mostly as a highway to the West. Few settled in what explorer Stephen Long called "the great American desert" (Nebraska Studies n.d.). Nebraska, however, played a role in several momentous events of the western expansion of the United States, including the Louisiana Purchase, the Lewis and Clark Expedition, the mass migration of pioneers on the Mormon and Oregon Trails, and the building of the transcontinental railroad along the Platte River Road.

Congress granted Nebraska statehood in 1867, the first state admitted after the Civil War, with the politics of its founding tied to the sectional conflicts of the time. Nebraska became a state around the time of the completion of the transcontinental railroad across the state, opening the area to development. The extension of the railroads across the state figured prominently in the development of Nebraska after statehood. The state's first communities functioned as railroad service centers, determining settlement patterns and influencing the early growth of Nebraska. The railroads encouraged settlements to expand their markets and help protect their lines from Indian raids. Railroads continue to be an integral part of the state's economy by providing thousands of jobs, as the main lines of Union Pacific and BNSF railroads crisscross Nebraska.

Settlement slowed in the 1870s because of drought, plagues of locusts, and a deep national depression, but when prosperity and rain returned in the 1880s, the population swelled, in part due to immigration from Europe. Throughout the decade, the state's farmers and ranchers prospered, exporting their products to world markets, but drought returned in the 1890s, as did the effects of overproduction. Hard economic times returned, and Nebraska's growth virtually ceased.

To help jump-start the stagnant economy in the state, and inspired by the Chicago World's Fair in 1893, yet undaunted by the reality that only major cities held such large and expensive events, Omaha business leaders raised funds locally, regionally, and nationally for the Trans-Mississippi and International Exposition. Held in Omaha from June 1 to October 31, 1898, the event celebrated the city's role as a center of industry west of the Mississippi River, signaling its emergence as an energetic American city. Spread across 184 acres at the northern edge of the city near the Missouri River, the exposition hosted some 2.5 million visitors, including President William McKinley. Built in Renaissance style, ivory-white in color with gray-green roofs, the exposition's European-style structures contrasted with the image of Omaha, still regarded by many as a rough-and-tumble frontier town. An important and unique feature of the Trans-Mississippi and International Exposition was the addition of the Indian Congress, representing twelve Native American tribes. The exposition also included Buffalo Bill Cody's Wild West Show. True to Nebraska's political culture, the Trans-Mississippi and International Exposition was the only world's fair at the time that opened on schedule and within budget.

The boom-bust cycle of the late nineteenth century, however, generated a move for political change that made Nebraska the center of that reform effort. In 1892 the People's Party, or the Populists, met in Omaha to nominate a candidate for president and draft a declaration of principles known as the Omaha Platform. Decrying a government that they believed put corporate and financial interests above the general welfare, the Populists called for a reorientation of politics to put people first. Measures advocated included government ownership of transportation systems and a more liberal monetary policy. Both measures resonated with Nebraskans, where railroads dominated state politics and whose farmers suffered in the economic downturn. In 1896 a young Nebraska congressman, William Jennings Bryan, won the Democratic presidential nomination on the reform platform that reflected many of the Populists' demands.

The reform tradition continued in the early twentieth century with Progressives, such as Senator George Norris, who championed the benefits of publicly owned electric utilities and helped create a more streamlined and responsive one-house (unicameral), nonpartisan legislative structure in Nebraska. The reform movement ended with the Great Depression. Most Nebraskans did not support the New Deal, and the state transitioned to and has remained strongly Republican.

Despite the end of the reform movement, tenets of populism continued to be an important element of Nebraska's political culture and are reflected in the structure of several state institutions.

### POLITICAL CULTURE AND STATE INSTITUTIONS

The set of values and moral beliefs that reflect basic political perceptions and attitudes of a collection of people exemplifies the concept of political culture. These values and beliefs, shared by a large percentage of people in a state or region, constitute a sustained collection of political ideals, expectations, and principles. Political culture establishes the rules, procedures, and norms of governance; in other words, it shapes how people relate to and connect with their government and public institutions.

Culture greatly affects the policymaking process, mainly by framing how citizens view and depict issues and by determining how the public addresses its problems (Gray, Hanson, and Kousser 2017; Moon, Pierce, and Lovrich

2001). In turn, political culture influences citizen expectations from government and the public and nonprofit sectors, producing a standard and guide for public affairs and operations. In summary, political culture influences the nature of the collective actions of the state and region. While political culture evolves over time, change typically occurs at an extremely slow and deliberative pace.

Regional similarities among U.S. states create grouping generalizations, providing for classification by geographical location such as the Northeast, the Southwest, and the Midwest. Such geographical divisions represent a common categorization of the U.S. states. Daniel Elazar (1971), who presents a description and categorization of the types of political culture most prevalent within the U.S. states, defines these regional separations in terms of political, social, and economic characteristics shaped by geographic setting, migration, and settlement patterns, creating structures of regionalism or sectionalism that signify the nature and personality of specific locales.

Elazar designates regional distinctions involving both geographical and cultural elements, which represent familiarized social and environmental features that extend across state lines. These political subcultures define the relationships, sentiments, and motives of the regional populace in relation to political systems and conventions. Elazar identifies three dominant U.S. political subcultures: moralistic, individualistic, and traditionalistic. While the traditionalistic subculture is principally found in the southern U.S. states, the moralistic and individualistic subcultures are more widespread and interspersed.

In the scope of Elazar's political subcultures, Nebraska displays a mixture of the moralistic and individualistic political cultures, exhibiting both a communal regard of nonpartisan politics as well as a tendency for specialized government and individual independence.

Moralistic political culture focuses on the commonwealth, a construct denoting the overall health and well-being of the whole. The realization of the public good acts as a measure of government in this culture, with the expectation that government accepts a responsibility for communal interests and assumes a positive role in society. In this public-regarding spirit, political participation of citizens constitutes civic duty, and public service represents a stature of obligation and selflessness. Issue-oriented, moralistic culture signifies both a pragmatic and a communal strategy to problem solving.

In this way, loyalty to political parties has less importance than the public good, and nonpartisanship in political institutions allows for an expansion of access and discourse among those of the community. While most evident within the New England states, the moralistic political culture also exists in the upper Midwest region in states such as Wisconsin and Minnesota and is common in many states of the greater West, including Nebraska.

The individualistic political culture, on the other hand, displays a businesslike approach to government with an overarching focus on private interests. Elazar describes this type of political culture as economically based with government assuming a secondary role as a necessary but restrained facilitator of the marketplace. The individualistic culture conveys a private-regarding ethos, subservient to individual needs and efficient government. From this perspective, it views community intervention as cumbersome, an obstacle of the marketplace, and political participation of citizens should be limited toward productive ends. In addition, the individualistic political culture recognizes government as a business with an expectation to operate as such, favoring the professional practice of public service in a system of specialization and marketplace competition. This likewise contributes to a charged partisan environment of enterprise and public demands. This type of political culture flourishes mostly in the lower midwestern states, such as Illinois and Ohio, and in many states of the greater West, such as Nebraska.

The fusion of these two subcultures produced a distinctive character in the state. As noted by Elazar, the individualistic culture in Nebraska tends to be more prevalent, with moralistic underpinnings. This combination of the two regional subcultures influenced the formation of Nebraska's institutions and is representative of the state's unique political culture.

## NEBRASKA'S POLITICAL CULTURE

Political institutions vary from state to state. As described above through Elazar's categorizations, culture and history affect the operation of these institutions (Dincer and Johnston 2017). Nebraska's political culture, based on its unique history, distinguishes the state's political and governmental institutions from other midwestern states. Nebraska, for example, played an important role in the Westward Expansion movement and was the first state admitted to the Union after the Civil War. The Oregon, California, and Mormon Trails passed through Nebraska, bringing an array of ethnic settlers and cultures to the state. Immigration patterns, then, left a deep impression on the personality of Nebraska's political culture, encompassing various ideals, customs, and values of the settling populations.

Initial settlers of the late 1800s, mostly of German, Czech, and Scandinavian descent, consisted of European migrants and pioneers of the western frontier, bringing with them political views that were quintessential of the pioneer mentality and ethos. This was, in many ways, a community-based culture, founded on agrarian principles and commonwealth connections. Willa Cather, arguably the state's most well-known author, includes these traits in her Nebraska-based pioneer novels. These traits defined the American pioneer spirit, exuding a rugged individualism and placing importance on independence, localized control, and the voice of the people. These traits, noted in Elazar's assessment of Nebraska's political culture, reflect an observable confluence of moralistic and individualistic subcultures, with individualistic elements as the more dominant. This characterization describes the progressive and populist baselines of Nebraska's political systems and ethos, lending support to many of the modern manifestations of these governmental philosophies, values, and institutions.

In general, Nebraska's political culture, primarily conservative with a nonideological basis, emphasizes an economical and practical approach to government enterprise. This perspective reflects pragmatism with strong regard for the individual, meaning that government involvement and expansion into private interests should be limited. The rural history and orientation of the state likewise maintains a localized focus, wary of big business and government overreach and intent on autonomy and self-reliance. These views may be most noticeable at the local level, such as the ninety-three county governments, the large number of special districts, and advocacy for increased autonomy among municipalities. Yet this mixture of moralistic and individualistic subcultures also contributes to enduring cultural conflicts within the state, as individual rights contrast with broader ideals, the growing urban population diverges from the state's rural past, and the growth of nonagricultural related business challenges Nebraska's agricultural identity.

Nevertheless, Nebraska's political culture remains stubbornly true to its foundations, still capable of occasional and periodic progressive reforms while solidly planted in the roots of populism. These intrinsic attributes of Nebraska's modern political culture are not incidental but rather a chrono-

logical outcome of past events, circumstances, and, perhaps most importantly, the actions of influential Nebraskans.

In the late nineteenth and early twentieth centuries, three Nebraskans
impacted politics on the national level and continue to shape the political
culture of Nebraska into the twenty-first century. J. Sterling Morton, founder
of Arbor Day, the first of several Nebraskans serving as the U.S. secretary of
agriculture, promoted agriculture as an industry, helping lay the foundation
for the modern agricultural economic system in Nebraska and the United
States. William Jennings Bryan, a three-time presidential candidate and
leader of the Populist Party that challenged the two-party structure, helped
form the core of modern liberalism by advocating a strong role for the
national government to improve the common good. And George Norris, a
long-time powerful member of Congress, "one of the most gifted legislators
of all time" (Pierce and Hagstrom 1984, 581) and a leader of the progressive
movement, advocated the benefits of publicly owned electric utilities.

Bryan and Norris provided a foundation that epitomizes Nebraska political culture today. Bryan's economic populism of the late nineteenth century
evolved into the progressivism of Norris in the twentieth century. Nebraska's
political culture begins with William Jennings Bryan. Because of Bryan,
Nebraska "may be forever linked to the idea and ideal of populism" (Berens
2004, 1). In general, populism rejects any hint of political or business elitism
and favoritism and supports the political belief that people should function
on a level plane. While the Populist Party is now a footnote in American
history, Nebraskans' support for Bryan's notions resulted in a political culture that continues to mold institutions and help shape public policy in the
state to this day.

Persistent populist legacies in Nebraska include a one-house, nonpartisan
legislature (the Unicameral, as it is popularly known in the state); liberal
use of initiative, referendum, and recall; and the only state with an electric
power system that is entirely publicly owned and operated. While these
institutional traditions appear progressive in nature, in fact, as pointed out
by Frederick Luebke, a notable Nebraska historian, they may actually "spring
from conservative, nonideological concerns about economic relationships"
(1988, 165) involving the monopolistic actions of railroads and other private
enterprises and reflecting the state's marketplace individualistic political
subculture. Luebke notes that the adoption of the unicameral legislature

and the statewide system of public power reflect the workings of Nebraska's political culture (163).

Nebraska's "periodically populist" (Pierce and Hagstrom 1984, 581) tendencies and institutional innovations understandably embody its approach of sensibility and practicality addressing public problems. The ongoing debate that began in the early 2010s over the construction of a transcontinental crude oil pipeline across the state graphically illustrates its periodic populism. Many Nebraskans expressed concern that a leak from the TransCanada Keystone XL pipeline could damage the Ogallala Aquifer, a major source of water for agriculture. Also, the protesters contested the eminent domain aspect of the pipeline, reflecting the individualistic dimension of the state's political culture. Nebraskans protesting the pipeline included a politically diverse coalition of conservative farmers and ranchers, Native American tribes, and liberal environmentalists. One observer noted that the pipeline protest shows that Nebraskans are "people who are willing to work to advance certain issues minus the unrelenting rancor of contemporary partisan politics can get the job done" (Benes 2019). This example shows how political culture enables Nebraskans to take a "prairie practical" approach to addressing public issues.

The theme of Nebraska's conservative and nonideological avenue to addressing public issues is particularly evident in later chapters of this book that describe in detail the designs, constructs, and variations of these institutional innovations in the state legislature, the state constitution, economic policies, and other materializations that permeate Nebraska's state and local governments.

### SYMBOLS OF NEBRASKA'S POLITICAL CULTURE

The state capitol building in Lincoln arguably serves as the most visible representation of Nebraska's political heritage and culture, "the preeminent symbol of the state to its citizens" (Luebke 2006, 163). A phrase inscribed over the capitol's main entrance reflects the political philosophy of Nebraskans: "The salvation of the state is watchfulness in the citizen." Hartley Burr Alexander, a Nebraska native and professor of philosophy at the University of Nebraska, selected this quote. Alexander contributed much to the thematic framework of the capitol's design and construction concepts.

Based on the architectural designs of Bertram Grosvenor Goodhue and including the works of sculptor Lee Lawrie and mosaicist Hildreth Meiere, the state capitol building stands as a tribute to the legacy of Nebraska's cultural foundations. As noted by Thomas Kimball, Nebraska native and architectural consultant to the state capitol commission, "The capitol of a state is the outward sign of the character of its people" (Office of the Capitol Commission 2006).

Begun on November 11, 1922, Armistice Day (later Veterans Day), the capitol building was completed a decade later. Since the Nebraska Constitution limits the state's ability to borrow, the legislature periodically needed to raise additional construction funds. This reflects Nebraska's political culture of fiscal responsibility.

The design of the state capitol building of Nebraska, including several distinct cultural symbols, representations, and emblems, reflects the political and historical influences of the state's central institutions. The independent pioneer philosophies of the state's original settlers inspired Goodhue's design of the building. As observed by architectural historian Eric McCready, "Life for the prairie farmer is not easy, especially when no natural shelter exists, and every step forward seems an endless battle against nature and her unpredictability. It is tempting to believe that the pioneering spirit of Nebraskans supplied at least part of the impetus for Goodhue to strike off in a new direction" (1974, 357). Aligned with Goodhue's vision, symbols of Nebraska history and culture emblazon both the interiors and exteriors of the building.

Sculptural depictions adorning the exterior of the main north entrance exhibit portrayals of pioneer life, including the Native American tribes of the area. The east and west entrances address the history of law, and the south entrance represents great historical documents and figures that include, among others, sculptures of Hammurabi, Moses, Julius Caesar, and Napoleon. Within each of these themes are multiple sculptural illustrations of historical events with significance to the progress of human law and justice, including the codification of Roman law, a vision of the ideal state as expressed by Plato in *The Republic*, and the Magna Carta. This also encompasses multiple references to the political foundations of the United States and Nebraska, such as the signing of the Declaration of Independence, the writing of the U.S. Constitution, the Louisiana Purchase, the Kansas-Nebraska Act, and the admission of Nebraska as a state.

*The Sower*, a bronze statue standing nineteen feet tall atop the capitol dome, depicts a figure hand-sowing seed, a testament to the role of agriculture in the state's past and present. Hartley B. Alexander also felt that

*The Sower* represented "the fact that the chief purpose of men in forming societies is to sow for nobler modes of living" (Zabel 1981, 364). The capitol's interior likewise displays an assemblage of culturally significant structures. Mosaics and murals of European and Native American art ornament the halls, rotunda, and chambers, symbolizing life on the western plains with various connections to the elements of nature and society.

The west chamber, dedicated to the settlement of Nebraska, contains artistic renditions of the Lewis and Clark Expedition and the movement of the homesteaders into the Nebraska Territory. The Nebraska state legislature convenes in the west chamber, named for George W. Norris, "the U.S. Senator from McCook largely responsible for the formation of the Unicameral" (*Nebraska Life* 2012, 29). On the main floor, the Nebraska Hall of Fame includes a gallery of busts and statues of important figures in Nebraska's history, such as poet laureate John Neihardt, showman Buffalo Bill Cody, Ponca chief Standing Bear, author Mari Sandoz, and Boys Town founder Father Flanagan. Omaha native and leading figure of the civil rights movement Malcolm X was inducted in 2022. (See the "Suggested for Further Readings" chapter for a full listing of all members of the Nebraska Hall of Fame.) The Memorial Chamber at the top of the capitol tower contains a number of painted murals by Omaha artist Stephen C. Roberts dedicated to virtuous ideals and tribulations of Nebraska history and culture, including freedom, peace, heroism, and self-determination.

In addition to the state capitol, many other lasting symbols of Nebraska political culture are present throughout the state. Two national monuments—the Homestead Monument of America near Beatrice and the Scotts Bluff Monument near Gering—memorialize the passage of settlers across the western plains. The Chimney Rock National Historic Site near Bayard, an iconic landmark of Nebraska heritage, preserves the memory of the Oregon, California, Mormon, and Pony Express Trails. Fort Robinson State Park, in western Nebraska, served as a frontier military outpost for the safeguarding of western expansion. The homes of Willa Cather in Red Cloud, Buffalo Bill Cody in North Platte, George Norris in McCook, and J. Sterling Morton in Nebraska City demonstrate the impact of famous Nebraskans on the state's image and character. Together, these symbols of Nebraska's history typify events and people that shaped the state's political culture and continue to influence Nebraska politics and government.

CONTEMPORARY POLITICAL CULTURE

Nebraska can be described as one of the more conservative, Republican, and deep-red states in the Union. Since the 1970s or earlier, Nebraska consistently supported Republican candidates in national presidential elections. The *Omaha World-Herald*, the state's major newspaper, endorsed a Democrat for president only three times since 1932. From 1996 to 2021 the proportion of registered Republicans hovered around 50 percent of the total voters registered, while the percentage of Democratic registrations decreased from 38 percent to approximately 29 percent. The percentage of Independents and other registered voters correspondingly increased from 12 percent to 21 percent during the same time period. In 2021 Nebraska had a Republican governor, lieutenant governor, secretary of state, and attorney general, and in the 2021 state legislature, more than 65 percent of state senators identified as Republican.

Nebraska's political culture, with distinguishable remnants of the state's populist tradition and a likewise marked moralistic dimension, impacts many of the state's political institutions and elections. Nebraska's unicameral legislators and municipal officials, for example, are elected on a nonpartisan basis. The chairs of committees in the state legislature include both registered Republican and Democratic senators. Rooted in a general distain for big business and government and intrusive, overbearing national political party directives, Nebraska voters tend to prefer a pragmatic approach to government that demonstrates preference for the individual rather than their party affiliation.

Several notable contemporary Nebraska politicians displayed the nonpartisan character and traditions of Nebraska politics. These include Bob Kerrey (Democrat), former governor and U.S. senator; Ben Nelson (Democrat), former governor and U.S. senator; Chuck Hagel (Republican), former U.S. senator and secretary of defense in the Obama administration; Mike Johanns (Republican), former governor, U.S. senator, and secretary of agriculture in the second Bush administration; and Ed Zorinsky (Democrat), who switched parties and was elected as U.S. senator. State senator Ernie Chambers, a registered Independent, is the longest-serving state legislator in Nebraska history. Chapter 4 discusses Nebraska party politics in more detail.

An important illustration of Nebraska's independent and localized political culture is the distribution of Electoral College votes for national presidential elections. Beginning in 1992 Nebraska altered the allocation of its five electoral votes, providing that the winner of the popular vote receive two electoral votes, with one electoral vote assigned to the winner of each of the state's three congressional districts. Only two states, Maine being the other, utilize this method for electoral votes as opposed to the general winner-take-all approach.

Nebraska's electoral votes split for the first time during the 2008 U.S. presidential election. Republican candidate John McCain won the state with nearly 60 percent of the popular vote. However, Democratic candidate Barack Obama won the second congressional district, which includes the city of Omaha and surrounding metropolitan areas, by a margin of just above 1 percent, thus awarding him the electoral vote from that district. In the subsequent 2012 U.S. presidential election, Republican candidate Mitt Romney, running against then President Obama, solidly won the popular vote as well as all of the state's congressional districts, collecting all five of Nebraska's electoral votes. In 2016 and 2020 Republican presidential candidate Donald Trump won nearly 60 percent of the votes in the state; however, Democrat Joe Biden won the second district and its electoral vote by 4 percent in 2020.

Nebraska's political culture also remains recognizable at the local government level, revealing several traces of populist tendencies for citizen-based governance and a preference for professionalized local government administration. Professional management of Nebraska municipalities illustrates the individualistic dimension of the state's political culture, with its need for efficiency. More than fifty municipalities in the state, nearly 90 percent of the larger cities in the state (excluding Omaha and Lincoln), currently utilize some form of professional management, either a city manager or city administrator (League of Nebraska Municipalities 2021) (chapter 8 includes an extensive discussion of local government in Nebraska). Nebraska has many units of local government, including ninety-three counties, one of the highest numbers of county governments among all states despite its relatively low population. In addition, Nebraska ranks high in the number of special districts when compared to other states.

Taken as a whole, Nebraska's political culture continues to comprise several unique attributes, rejecting any means of definitive classification or standardization. The contemporary nature of Nebraska politics and government displays progressive tendencies while likewise retaining an unyielding foundation in the cultural traditions and history that demarcate the state's formative past. Each of the following chapters of this book explores the enduring influence and presence of Nebraska's political culture in its approach to government operation and public administration, both past and present. As suggested by Daniel Elazar, political culture "like all culture is rooted in the cumulative historical experiences of particular groups of people" (1971, 89), and changes in the political culture of a state are often slow to materialize. Nebraska is no exception to this rule and may serve as a testament to the endurance of the state's political culture.

## REFERENCES

Benes, Ross. 2019. "Nebraska's Hidden Progressivism." *American Prospect.* January 23, 2019. https://prospect.org/environment/nebraska-s-hidden-progressivism/.

Berens, Charlyne. 2004. *Power to the People: Social Choice and the Populist/Progressive Ideal.* Lanham MD: University Press of America.

Dincer, Oguzhan, and Michael Johnston. 2017. "Political Culture and Corruption Issues in State Politics: A New Measure of Corruption Issues and a Test of Relationships to Political Culture." *Publius* 47 (1): 131–48.

Elazar, Daniel. 1971. *American Federalism: A View from the States.* 2nd ed. New York: Thomas Y. Crowell.

———. 1994. *The American Mosaic: The Impact of Space, Time, and Culture on American Politics.* Boulder CO: Westview Press.

Gray, Virginia, Russell L. Hanson, and Thad Kousser. 2017. *Politics in the American States: A Comparative Analysis.* 11th ed. Washington DC: CQ Press.

League of Nebraska Municipalities. 2021. *2021 Nebraska Directory of Municipal Officials.* Lincoln: League of Nebraska Municipalities.

Luebke, Frederick C. 1988. "Time, Place, and Culture in Nebraska History." *Nebraska History* 69 (Winter): 150–68.

Maskovsky, Jeff, and Sophia Bjork-James. 2022. *Beyond Populism: Angry Politics and the Twilight of Neoliberalism.* Morgantown: West Virginia University Press.

McCready, Eric Scott. 1974. "The Nebraska State Capitol: Its Design, Background and Influence." *Nebraska History* 55 (3): 325–461.

Moon, David C., John C. Pierce, and Nicholas P. Lovrich. 2001. "Political Culture in the Urban West: Is It Really Different?" *State and Local Government Review* 33 (3): 195–201.

Nebraska Indian Community College. n.d. Website. Accessed February 7, 2023. http://www.thenicc.edu/index.php/en/santee-sioux-nation.

*Nebraska Life*. 2012. "Guide to the Nebraska State Capitol: A Journey through Nebraska History."

Nebraska Studies. n.d. "Homestead Act Signed." Accessed February 7, 2023. https://www.nebraskastudies.org/en/1850-1874/homestead-act-signed/.

North, Irene. 2016. "American Indians of Western Nebraska." *Scottsbluff Star Herald*. October 28, 2016.

Office of the Nebraska Capitol Commission. 2006. *Guide to the Exterior Art and Symbolism: Nebraska State Capitol*. Lincoln: Office of the Capitol Commission.

Pierce, Neal, and Jerry Hagstrom. 1984. "Nebraska: Periodically Populist." In *The Book of America: Inside 50 States Today*, 578–84. New York: Warner Books.

Ponca Tribe of Nebraska. n.d. Website. Accessed February 7, 2023. http://www.poncatribe-ne.org.

Winnebago Tribe of Nebraska. n.d. "Tribal History." Accessed February 7, 2023. https://winnebagotribe.com/tribal-history.

Zabel, Orville H. 1981. "History in Stone: The Story in Sculpture on the Exterior of the Nebraska Capitol." *Nebraska History* 62 (3).

# CHAPTER TWO

# The Character of Nebraska

## A PEOPLE IN TRANSITION

*Jerome Deichert, Christian L. Janousek, and Robert Blair*

### INTRODUCTION

As described in chapter 1, the history of Nebraska is one of transition. This transition began with the movement of Native American tribes during the centuries before the land that became Nebraska was part of the Louisiana Purchase. Later, Nebraska was an integral component of the migration of European settler and other pioneers on the Mormon and Oregon Trails and the development of the transcontinental railroad. Shortly after statehood many Nebraska communities transformed to function as railroad and agricultural service centers. As technology and the need for these activities diminished, the population in these communities and their surrounding rural areas also declined. As this chapter illustrates, transition continues to be a defining aspect of Nebraska's character.

This chapter focuses on aspects of Nebraska's demographics, employment, agriculture, income, education, and public health. Over the past several decades, notable demographic and economic transitions have contributed to related changes in Nebraska's state profile.

### NEBRASKA'S GEOGRAPHY

Like many Great Plains states, Nebraska occupies a large area of land near the geographic center of the continental United States yet is lightly populated. According to the 2020 Census, Nebraska's population of 1,961,504 ranks thirty-seventh in total population (U.S. Census Bureau n.d.b.). Stretching more than 400 miles from east to west and about 200 miles from north to south, Nebraska's area of 77,358 square miles ranks sixteenth in size when compared to other states. Because of the state's population of fewer than 2 million inhabitants, Nebraska ranks forty-third in population density, with 24.9 persons per square mile. For comparison, New Jersey, which ranks first in population, has 1,263 persons per square mile.

Notwithstanding its strong agricultural base consisting of livestock raising and grain production and its rural community image, the majority of Nebraskans live in urban concentrations. More than half (56 percent) of the state's 2020 population resides in its three most populous counties (Douglas, Sarpy, and Lancaster), which are located in the Omaha and Lincoln metropolitan areas. In sharp contrast, twelve of the state's ninety-three counties have fewer than 1,000 residents. McPherson, the state's least populous county, has only 399 residents.

Omaha, the birthplace and corporate home of the Union Pacific Railroad, serves as headquarters to several Fortune 500 companies. With a diverse business base and a central location, Omaha functions as one of the main economic engines for the northern Great Plains. Warren Buffet, one of the wealthiest people in the world and considered one of the most influential individuals on Wall Street, calls Omaha home.

Lincoln, the state capital, contains the flagship campus of the University of Nebraska and the majority of state government offices. The vast open spaces in Nebraska, coupled with urban population concentrations, contribute to a simmering urban-rural rift that began in the early years of the state and continues to steer many state policy issues into the twenty-first century. This is not unique to Nebraska, as urban-rural challenges exist in many other states.

### DEMOGRAPHIC TRANSITIONS

The state of Nebraska faces challenges resulting from changing demographics. Three of the most significant transitions include an increasing concentration of residents in its larger communities while its rural areas are losing population; increasing racial and ethnic diversity; and a population that is aging.

In 2020 Nebraska contained parts of four metropolitan areas in twelve counties:

Omaha–Council Bluffs, NE-IA (Cass, Douglas, Sarpy, Saun-
   ders, and Washington),
Lincoln, NE (Lancaster and Seward),
Grand Island, NE (Hall, Howard, and Merrick), and
Sioux City, IA-NE-SD (Dakota and Dixon).

Figure 1 shows that Nebraska is primarily a metropolitan state, with 65.3 percent of its 2020 population living in metropolitan areas (U.S. Census Bureau n.d.b.). The eighty-one non-metropolitan counties reached their peak population in 1930. Since that time, they have steadily declined in population, with their 2020 population lower than in 1900.

Nebraska also is becoming more racially and ethnically diverse. As shown in figure 2, in 2020 non-Hispanic whites made up 75.7 percent of the state (U.S. Census Bureau n.d.b.). The state's non-Hispanic white percentage has decreased steadily over the past few decades. In 1990 it was 92.6 percent, decreasing to 87.3 percent in 2000 and to 82.1 percent in 2010. Between 2010 and 2020 Nebraska's non-Hispanic white population declined 1.0 percent. The non-Hispanic white population is much older with relatively more persons forty-five or older and fewer younger than forty-five.

The next largest racial/ethnic group in Nebraska is persons who are Hispanic or Latino (12.0 percent). Much of the growth of this population occurred during the 1990s as they moved to Nebraska to work in the meat packing plants. The percentages of the remaining non-Hispanic racial/ethnic groups enumerated in the 2020 Census were Black or African American, 4.8 percent; American Indian or Alaska Native, 0.8 percent; Asian, 2.7 percent; Native Hawaiian and other Pacific Islander, 0.1 percent; other races, 0.3 percent; and two or more races, 3.7 percent. Persons identifying as other or two or more races represent the fastest growing racial/ethnic groups in the state.

As the baby-boom generation ages, the number and percent of the state's older population is increasing and projected to continue to increase. In 2019 the population aged sixty-five or older totaled 312,458 persons, representing 16.2 percent of the state's population (U.S. Census Bureau n.d.a.). This amounted to an increase of 26.7 percent since 2010. By 2030 the number of persons aged sixty-five or older is projected to increase another 31.7 percent (Drozd and Deichert 2015). This aging population places pressure on sev-

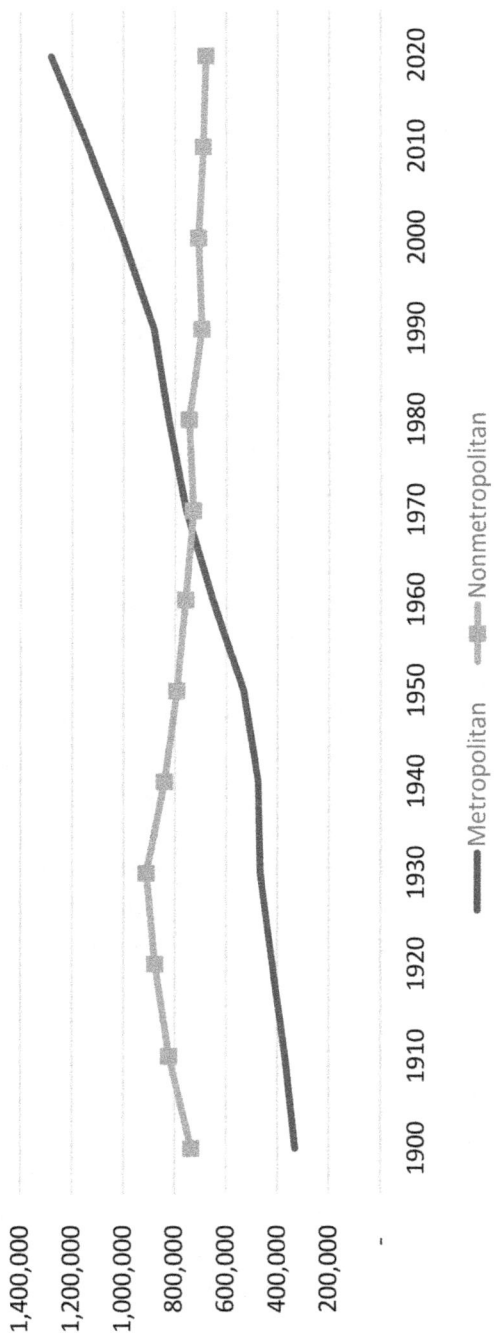

**Fig. 1.** Nebraska metropolitan and nonmetropolitan population, 1900–2020. Source: U.S. Census Bureau. Created by author.

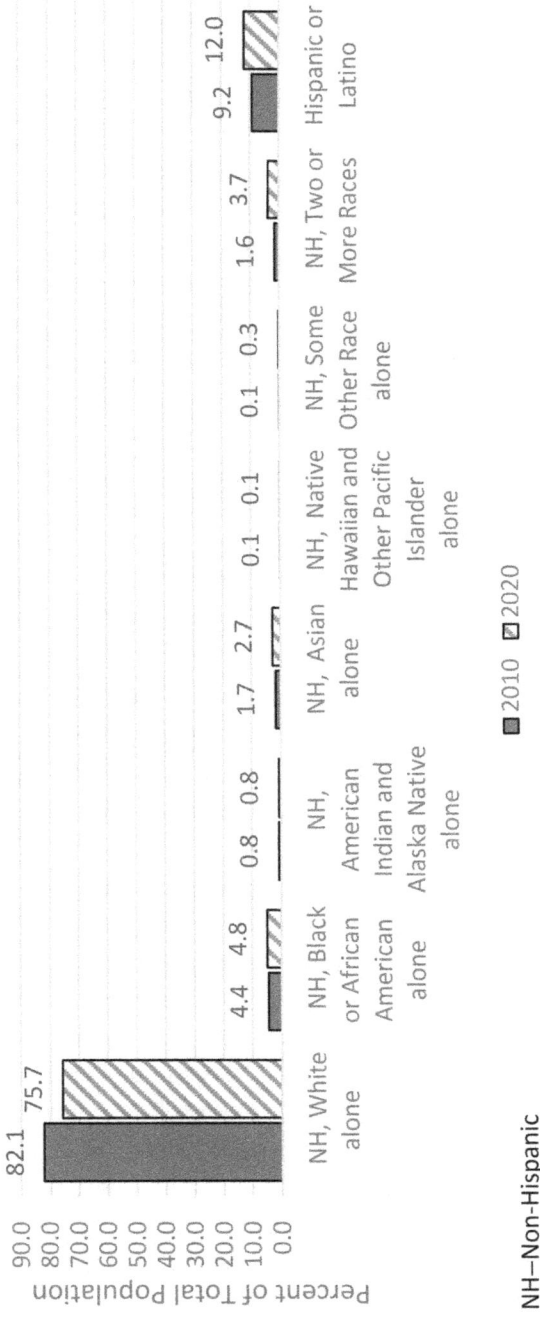

**Fig. 2.** Nebraska population by race and ethnicity, 2010 and 2020. Source: U.S. Census Bureau. Created by author.

eral Nebraska institutions. As the population ages and begins to leave the labor force, the workforce will decline, with resulting losses in incomes and income-related taxes. At the same time, an aging population will require additional government services, such as Medicaid.

## EMPLOYMENT AND LABOR FORCE

Historically, Nebraska has had one of the lowest unemployment rates and one of the highest labor force participation rates in the country. As a result, a large portion of Nebraska's children under the age of six have all their parents in the labor force. The low employment rate, high labor force participation rate, and aging population make it difficult for businesses and industries to find available workers. This is especially true in Nebraska's communities located outside the Omaha-Lincoln area.

This need for workers may be partially filled with new residents moving into the state. Between 2010 and 2019 Nebraska experienced a net in-migration of 14,903 persons, a gain was attributable to international migration as 35,100 persons moved to Nebraska from other countries. On the other hand, Nebraska recorded a net out-migration of 20,197 persons to other states (U.S. Census Bureau n.d.a.).

Much of this out-migration consists of young adults, many of whom have college degrees. In its 2021 annual report, the Nebraska Coordination Commission for Higher Education mentions that the out-migration of Nebraskans with at least a bachelor's degree continues to be a serious issue that must be addressed (118).

Unemployment is an important indicator of an area's economic well-being. Since 1980, Nebraska's unemployment rate has shown a pattern like the national rate but has consistently fallen below it (figure 3). The exception to this trend occurred in the 1990s, when the national rate rose between 1989 and 1992 and then fell steadily until 2000. In contrast, Nebraska's rate remained relatively steady until 1997 and then began to increase. Figure 3 shows that during economic downturns, Nebraska's unemployment rate increased much slower than the unemployment rate for the United States. In 2019 Nebraska's unemployment rate reached a low 3.0 percent but rose to 4.2 percent in 2020 only because of the pandemic. In contrast, the national unemployment rate more than doubled, growing from 3.7 percent to 8.1 percent (U.S. Bureau of Labor Statistics 2020).

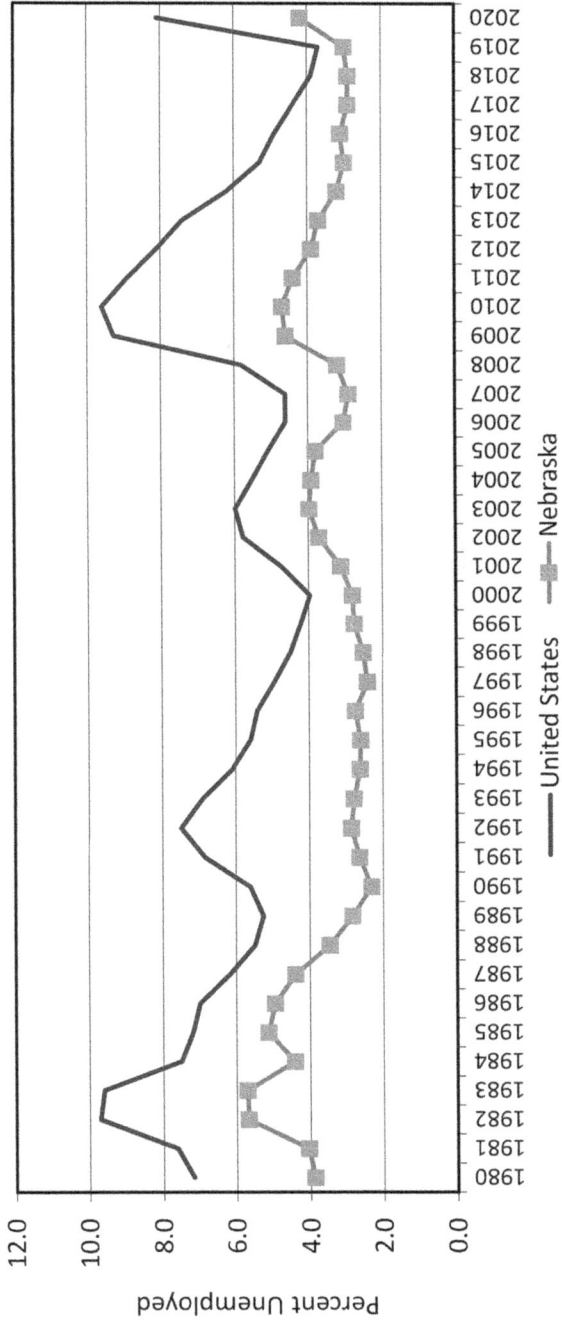

Fig. 3. Annual unemployment rates for Nebraska and the United States, 1980–2020. Source: U.S. Bureau of Labor Statistics. Created by author.

Much of the reason for Nebraska's relatively low unemployment rates can be explained by its economic structure. Employment information from the U.S Bureau of Economic Analysis shows that in 2020, compared to the nation, Nebraska's economy was relatively more reliant in agriculture, food processing, rail and truck transportation, data processing, insurance and finance, and nursing and residential care facilities. Economic ups and downs do not impact these industries as much as industries that are less important to Nebraska's economy (U.S. Bureau of Economic Analysis n.d.a.).

According to the 2019 American Community Survey, Nebraska's labor force comprised 69.1 percent of all Nebraskans and compares to a national rate of 63.6 percent (U.S. Census Bureau n.d.c.). As a result of this high participation rate, a large portion of Nebraska's children have working parents. In 2019, 76.2 percent of Nebraska's children under six years of age had all their parents in the labor force. This compares to the national average of 67.5 percent. Moreover, the percentage of children with all their parents in the labor force generally has been increasing during the past decade. In 2000 the comparable value was 69.8 percent (U.S. Census Bureau n.d.c.). Because a majority of Nebraska's young children have working parents, affordable childcare and early childhood education loom as ongoing issues the state must face.

### AGRICULTURE

Agriculture constitutes a major component of Nebraska's economy. Even though direct farm employment has steadily declined over the past decades, agriculture in Nebraska in 2017 accounted for an estimated 33 percent of the state's economy according to a report from the University of Nebraska–Lincoln (Thompson, Lubben, and Stokes 2020). Most of the impact is accounted for by activities such as food processing, transportation and warehousing, and agricultural support services, but farm production forms the basis of this activity.

The U.S. Bureau of Economic Analysis reported that Nebraska cash receipts from farm marketings in 2020 totaled $21.7 billion (U.S. Bureau of Economic Analysis n.d.b.), which ranked third nationally. Cash receipts from livestock and livestock products came to $11.8 billion, while cash receipts from crops amounted to $9.9 billion. Historically, cash receipts from livestock and livestock products have exceeded those from crops, but in 2012,

2011, and 2009, crop receipts exceeded those from livestock and livestock products. These were the only three years since 1980 when crop receipts exceeded those from livestock.

Payments from the federal government have long been an important source of farm income (figure 4). In 2020 the U.S. Bureau of Economic Analysis estimated that farm payments to Nebraska farmers were $2.4 million and accounted for 53.8 percent of net farm earnings of $4.5 billion (U.S. Bureau of Economic Analysis n.d.b.). Much of this assistance comes from payments to offset low commodity prices, compensation because of tariffs, and conservation programs assistance. Since 1980, government farm payments averaged nearly 40 percent of Nebraska's net farm earnings.

Agricultural diversity looks at the commodities produced in and exported from Nebraska. According to the Nebraska Department of Agriculture, in 2019 the top five agricultural commodities produced in Nebraska were cattle and calves, corn, soybeans, hogs, and dairy products. The five most important agricultural exports were soybeans and soybean products, beef, corn, pork, and ethanol. Nationally, Nebraska ranked sixth in the value of exports (Nebraska Department of Agriculture 2021).

Nebraska had 45,700 farms and ranches in 2019, with an average size of 982 acres, together utilizing 92 percent of the state's total land area. Similar to the state as a whole, Nebraska's farmers and ranchers also are older. According to the 2017 Census of Agriculture, the average age of the principal farm operator was 56.4 years (Nebraska Department of Agriculture 2021).

## INCOME, POVERTY, AND COST OF LIVING

The measures of Nebraska's income are slightly below the national average. In 2020 Nebraska had the nineteenth highest per capita personal income in the nation. During 2020 Nebraska's per capita personal income averaged $57,570 and was 3.3 percent below the national average of $59,510 (U.S. Bureau of Economic Analysis n.d.c.).

Figure 5 shows that between 1980 and 2008, Nebraska's per capita income generally fluctuated between 95 percent and 100 percent of the national average. Between 2009 and 2016, which were strong agricultural years, Nebraska's per capita personal income exceeded the national average. Since then, however, it has fallen into its long-term pattern mentioned earlier.

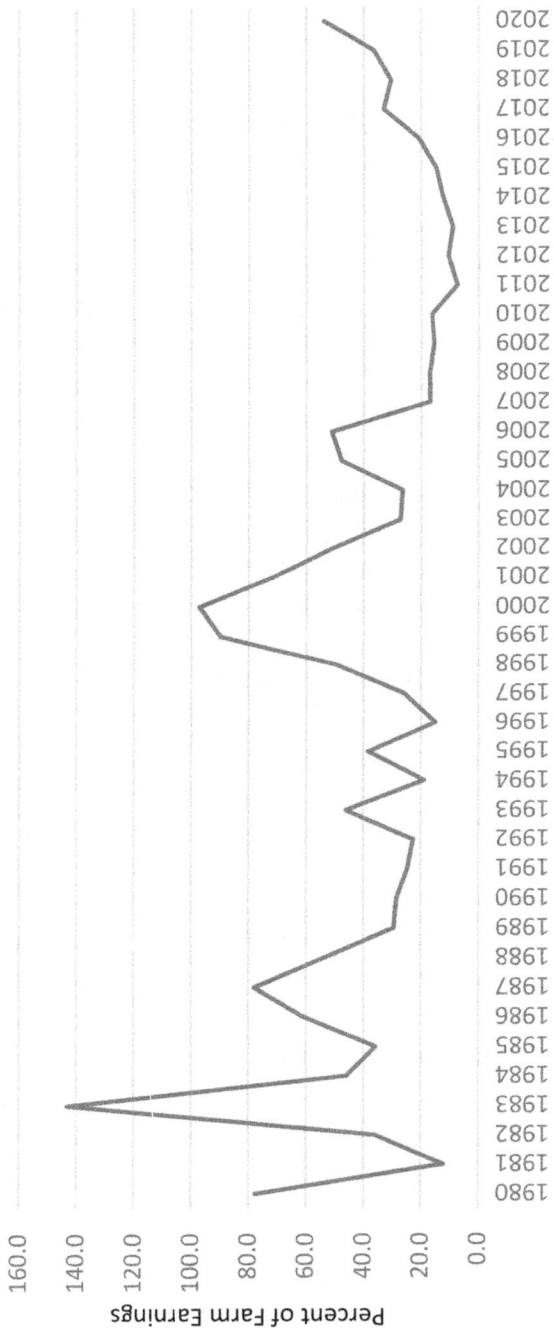

Fig. 4. Government payments to Nebraska farms, 1980–2020. Source: U.S. Bureau of Economic Analysis. Created by author.

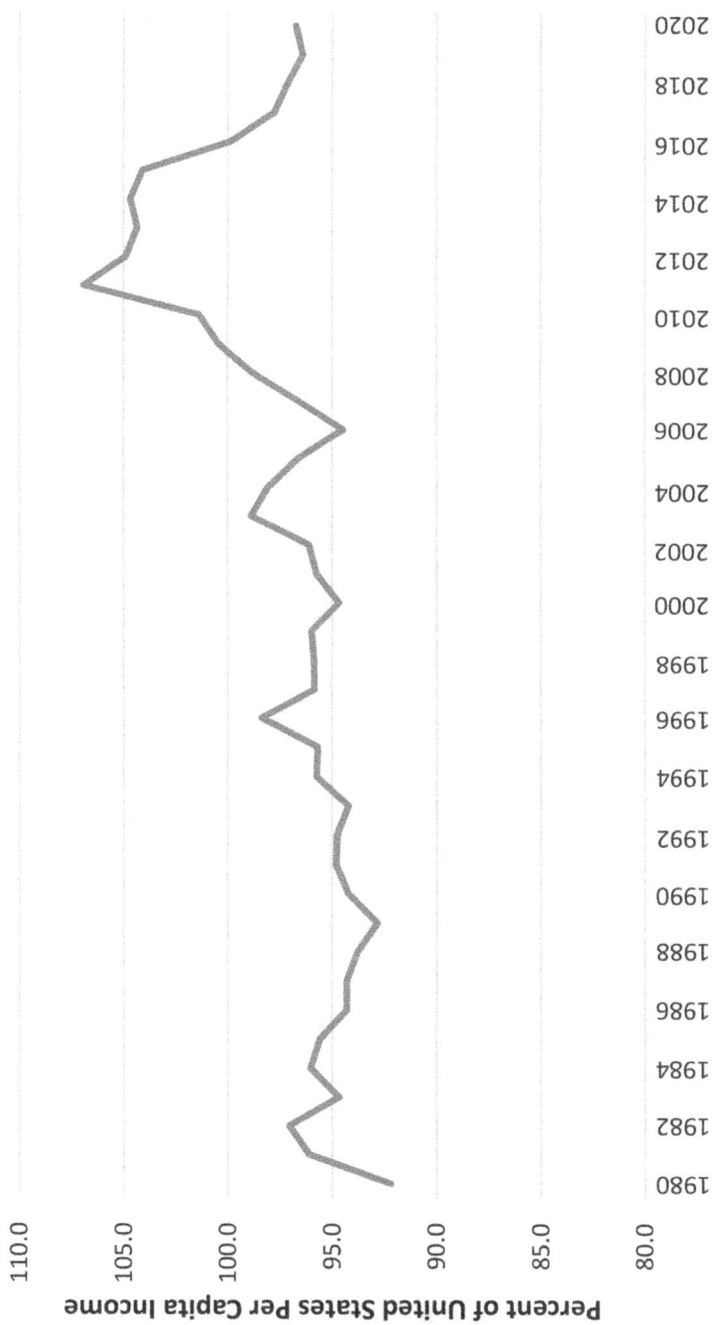

Fig. 5. Nebraska per capita personal income as a percentage of U.S. per capita personal income, 1980–2020. Source: U.S. Bureau of Economic Analysis. Created by author.

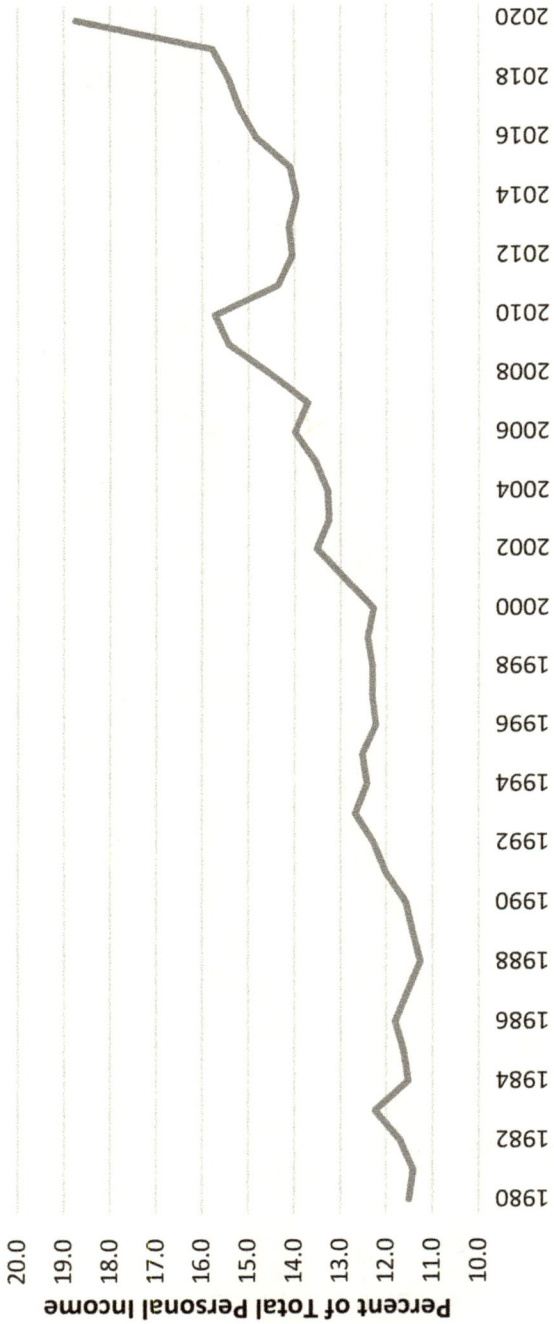

Fig. 6. Transfer receipts as a percentage of total personal income for Nebraska, 1980–2020. Source: U.S. Bureau of Economic Analysis. Created by author.

Nebraska is among the lowest states in the proportion of personal income received from transfer receipts to individuals from the federal government. Between 1980 and 2019 these payments have been increasingly important, rising from 11.5 percent to 15.8 percent of personal income over this period. These receipts consist of disbursements that are received as direct incomes to individuals, such as Social Security, or as expenditures that go to a third party as payment for services received by an individual, such as Medicare or Medicaid. Altogether, Social Security, Medicare, and Medicaid make up about three-fourths of the transfer receipts.

In 2020 transfer receipts from the federal government amounted to $20.9 billion, or somewhat less than $11,000 per Nebraskan. This represented 18.7 percent of the state's personal income, and that percentage ranked forty-second among the fifty states and District of Columbia (U.S. Bureau of Economic Analysis n.d.c.).

Another commonly used indicator of income is median household income. This measure is prepared annually by the U.S. Census Bureau. In 2019 the median household income amounted to $63,229 in Nebraska. This value ranked twenty-fifth nationally and fell slightly below the national average of $65,712 (U.S. Census Bureau n.d.d.). Since 2000, Nebraska's median household income has exhibited a growth rate about the same rate as the national rate, although there have been year-to-year fluctuations.

Although both per capita personal income and median household income are close to the national averages for these measures, Nebraska's cost of living is lower. The U.S. Bureau of Economic Analysis has prepared price comparisons by state since 2008. Since then, prices in Nebraska have averaged about 95 percent of the national value (U.S. Bureau of Economic Analysis n.d.d.). This implies that after accounting for cost-of-living differences, Nebraska's incomes have been slightly higher than the national average.

The relative cost of housing is another important indicator. Nebraska is among the most affordable states when looking at the value of housing compared to income. In 2019 Nebraska's median housing value was $172,700 (U.S. Census Bureau, n.d.c.). Dividing the median housing value by the median household income results in a ratio of 2.73. This means that in 2019 the median housing value equaled 2.73 times the median household income. Nationally, the median housing value of $240,500 resulted in a comparable ratio of 3.66. This difference in housing affordability is reflected in the fact that Nebraska has higher home ownership than the United States. In 2019 the respective home ownership rates were 66.3 percent and 64.1 percent (U.S Census Bureau n.d.c.).

While the state fares better than the nation in terms of poverty, Nebraska has consistently had a poverty rate significantly below the national rate. In 2019 Nebraska recorded one of the lowest poverty rates in the nation, with forty states having higher rates. During 2019, 9.9 percent of Nebraskans fell below the federal poverty level and ranked as the lowest rate since 2000. The national average totaled 12.3 percent. The poverty rate for Nebraska's children in 2019 amounted to 11.0 percent and compared favorably to the national value of 16.8 percent (U.S. Census Bureau n.d.c.). The sizeable increase in Nebraska's poverty rate between 2000 and 2014 was comparable to the national increase, with the gap between the United States and Nebraska widening since 2000.

### WORKFORCE QUALITY, TECHNOLOGY, AND INNOVATION

A quality workforce is one that can adapt and thrive in a rapidly changing economy. To adapt, Nebraska needs skilled workers to enhance its economic vitality and to compete in the global marketplace. Nebraska ranks high on the percentage of high school graduates but low on persons with advanced degrees and in science and engineering occupations.

In 2019 Nebraska exceeded the national high school graduation rate of 88.6 percent, as 92.0 percent of its population aged twenty-five years or older completed high school. Since 2000, Nebraska's percentage of high school graduates has been slowly increasing. One of the concerns for high school dropouts is future employment opportunities.

Nebraska also exceeded the national percentage of persons whose highest level of education was an associate degree in 2019. Nationally, 8.6 percent of the persons aged twenty-five years or older reported having an associate degree as their highest level of education; in Nebraska, the rate was 11.1 percent. Since 2000, Nebraska's rate of persons with an associate degree has been consistently higher than the national rate.

In 2019, 33.2 percent of the persons aged twenty-five years or older in Nebraska had completed a bachelor's degree. This was slightly above the national average of 33.1 percent. Since 2000, the percentage of persons with a bachelor's degree has increased steadily for both Nebraska and the United

States. Nebraska's rate generally has been within one percentage point of the nation's rate.

When looking at advanced degrees, Nebraska's rate has been picking up but still lags the nation. In 2019, 11.4 percent of Nebraskans aged twenty-five years and older had an advanced degree. This compares to 12.8 percent for the nation. Since 2000, however, Nebraska has steadily narrowed the gap with the United States, with the percentage of Nebraskans aged twenty-five years or older who have an advanced degree increasing from 7.3 percent to 11.4 percent.

In addition to a quality workforce, a state needs innovation to be economically successful. Top states for business prize innovation, nurture new ideas, and have the infrastructure to support them. One measure of this infrastructure is the share of a state's workforce that consists of science and engineering occupations. These occupations have been growing as a share of Nebraska's workforce. In 2019 they constituted 5.6 percent of the total workforce but were slightly below the national average of 6.4 percent (U.S. Census Bureau n.d.c.).

Many indicators of innovation and technology have been prepared by numerous organizations, but they often reflect the subjective view of the rating organization. The following are indicators from two institutions that are illustrative of these measures. CNBC prepares an annual study that measures all fifty states using more than eighty-five metrics. Using this scale, Nebraska ranks as the thirteenth best state for business but the thirty-seventh state for technology and innovation in 2021 (CNBC 2021). Using another study prepared by the Information Technology and Innovation Foundation, in 2020 Nebraska ranks thirty-first on their State New Economy Index (Atkinson and Footer 2020). This index quantifies the extent to which a state economy is "knowledge-based, globalized, entrepreneurial, IT-driven, and innovation oriented." Based on the previous metrics, it seems that Nebraska is behind many other states in technology and innovation.

### PUBLIC HEALTH

There are many areas of the state (particularly rural areas) that are dealing with additional demographic-related challenges that make it difficult to retain and attract residents. One of these challenges is related to measures of health. In 2019 Nebraska ranked better than the United States in the percentage of its noninstitutionalized population without health insurance, as 8.3 percent of the total population and 5.7 percent of children under aged eighteen years were uninsured. Comparable national numbers were 9.2 percent and 5.7 percent. Although most Nebraskans have health insurance, many rural areas are experiencing shortages of health-care professionals. The Rural Health Information Hub (2022) looks at professional shortage areas and shows that most of the counties in the western one-third of the state experienced shortages in primary care.

### SUMMARY AND IMPLICATIONS

This chapter illustrates how transition and adaptation have helped define aspects of Nebraska's character. Responses to these transition/adaptation cycles characterize Nebraska, contributing to its unique political culture, a fusion of individualism with moralism. While the individualistic culture tends to be more dominant, there are still strong moralistic underpinnings, creating tension between cultural values. These changes, it can be argued, contribute to competing features of the state, such as rural vs. urban, agricultural vs. industrial, and technology vs. tradition.

This chapter describes the people, demographics, and economic structure of Nebraska. The historical and demographic profile of the state can be summarized as a series of transitions and adaptations by its residents, often followed by another set of transitions and adaptations. Over the decades significant demographic characteristics of Nebraska evolved because of these transitions.

Cycles of transition began with the original peoples, as described in chapter 1. Long before Nebraska became part of the United States, Native American tribes in Nebraska adapted to changing climatic condition by migrating into and out of the area. Transition continued during the mass movement of European settlers and other pioneers on the Mormon and Oregon Trails across Nebraska. Some stayed in the state and adapted, while others kept moving westward.

The construction of the transcontinental railroad initiated another transition and adaptation cycle. Many communities were initially founded as railroad service centers. But as railroad technology advanced, fewer service centers were needed, which impacted the economic structure of many Nebraska communities. As the agricultural economy of Nebraska grew and flourished, many of the communities in the state transformed again, providing support to area farmers.

However, the seemingly endless cycle of rain and drought, as well as increased technical improvement in farming practices, affected the fortunes of the agricultural economy. Nebraska and its communities adapted again. While many communities declined, others thrived. In addition, this boom-bust cycle of the late nineteenth century generated a move for political change, making Nebraska the center of the widespread reform movement. Populism, a component of the reform movement, helped shape the enduring political culture of the state, as described in chapter 1.

Nebraska's demographics, employment, agriculture, income, education, and public health are discussed in this chapter. As noted, over the past several decades, demographic and economic transitions have altered the Nebraska's state profile. This includes the increasing racial and ethnic diversity of the state's population, the aging of its residents, the shrinking of its labor force, and the expansion of urbanization via the movement of people from rural locations to cities.

## Growing Diversity

Nebraska's population has become more diverse. In 2019, Census information indicated that 7.4 percent of the state's population was foreign born. Of that population, 64 percent came before 2010, showing recent growth in immigrants. More than half of the foreign-born population (52 percent) came from Latin American, 28 percent from Asia, 13 percent from Africa, and the remainder (7 percent) from other locations.

## Aging Population

Nebraskans are becoming older. The elderly tend to spend less, and there is greater dependence on transfer payments, such as Social Security income. In fact, by 2030 the number of persons over sixty-five years of age is projected to total nearly 420,000 persons and to make up 20.4 percent of the state's population.

## Shrinking Workforce

Because of a growing aging population and declining birth rates, there are fewer working-age people to make up the state's labor force. Nebraska has always had one of the country's lowest unemployment rates. As a result, the immigrant population has become a significant addition to the work force in the state.

## Urbanization

Nebraska's population is increasingly located in urban areas. While a solid red state, some urban areas seem to be becoming blue. District 2, for instance, in the Omaha metropolitan region, voted for Democratic candidates for president in 2008 and 2020. To address the growing urban-rural imbalance, Nebraska's state rural development policy has leveraged a significant portion of its development resources, most notably community development block grant funds, to some of the state's smallest communities (Blair, Deichert, and Drozd 2008). The urbanization of Nebraska may limit the ability of smaller and rural communities to provide health-care services to its population, resulting in closed hospitals and other health-care facilities.

These demographic trends have significant implications for the community and economic development strategies of the state's municipalities and counties. Smaller communities that depend on volunteers to staff fire protection and emergency services may be especially impacted because of an aging population. The tax base of many cities may be affected as sales taxes decrease because of less spending by older residents. In addition, the services needed by the elderly differ from a younger population. A community's labor force will be affected, too, by an aging population. Many local economic development efforts now focus on attracting workers for a range of jobs and professions. Finally, smaller communities may need to address issues pertaining to succession planning for local businesses and agricultural operations, as many of the heirs have moved away.

In its 2021 annual report, the Nebraska Community Foundation estimated that by 2030, the intergenerational transfer of assets of Nebraska families will approach $100 billion. As noted in the report, a significant amount of these assets from small and rural communities will migrate to larger urban areas, since many of the younger generation has moved to the cities (2022). Local community foundations, assisted by the Nebraska Community Foundation, are striving to maintain some of the assets in rural areas.

The topics and issues presented in this chapter lay the groundwork for this book. Subsequent chapters demonstrate how Nebraska's unique political culture, a combination of individualism with moralism, responds to these transitions and adaptations.

## REFERENCES

Atkinson, Robert D., and Caleb Footer. 2020. The 2020 State New Economic Index. Washington DC, Information Technology and Innovation Foundation. https://itif .org/publications/2020/10/19/2020-state-new-economy-index/.

Blair, Robert, Jerome Deichert, and David Drozd. 2008. "State Rural Development Policy: The Role of the Community Development Block Grant Program." *Journal of Public Budgeting, Accounting and Financial Management* 20 (1): 108–32.

CNBC. 2021. "America's Top States for Business 2021." July 13, 2021. https://www.cnbc .com/2021/07/13/americas-top-states-for-business.html.

Drozd, David, and Jerry Deichert. 2015. *Nebraska County Population Projections: 2010 to 2050.* Omaha: Center for Public Affairs Research, University of Nebraska at Omaha.

NCCPE (Nebraska Coordinating Commission for Postsecondary Education). 2021. *2021 Higher Education Progress Report.* Lincoln: Nebraska Coordinating Commission for Postsecondary Education. https://ccpe.nebraska.gov/sites/ccpe.nebraska.gov /files/PR_2021.pdf.

Nebraska Community Foundation. 2022. *2021 Annual Report.* Lincoln: Nebraska Community Foundation.

Nebraska Department of Agriculture. 2021. Nebraska Agricultural Fact Card, February 2021. Lincoln: Nebraska Department of Agriculture.

Rural Health Information Hub. 2022. "Health Professional Shortage Areas: Primary Care, by County, 2022." https://www.ruralhealthinfo.org/charts/5.

Thompson, Eric, Brad Lubben, and Jeff Stokes. 2020. *The 2017 Economic Impact of the Nebraska Agricultural Production Complex.* Lincoln: University of Nebraska– Lincoln, Department of Agricultural Economics and Bureau of Business Research.

U.S. Bureau of Economic Analysis. n.d.a. "SAEMP25N Total Full-Time and Part-Time Employment by NAICS Industry." Accessed February 17, 2023. https://apps.bea.gov/.

——. n.d.b. "SAINC45 Farm Income and Expenses." Accessed February 17, 2023. https://apps.bea.gov/.

——. n.d.c. "SAINC5N Personal Income by Major Component and Source and Earnings by NAICS Industry." Accessed February 27, 2023. https://apps.bea.gov/.

——. n.d.d. "SAIRPD Implicit Regional Price Deflators by State." Accessed February 27, 2023. https://apps.bea.gov/.

U.S. Bureau of Labor Statistics. 2020. "Local Area Unemployment Statistics, Over-the-Year Unemployment Rate for States, 2019–2020 Annual Averages." https:// www.bls.gov/lau/lastch20.htm.

U.S. Census Bureau. n.d.a. "2019 Population and Housing Unit Estimates." Accessed February 27, 2023. https://www.census.gov/programs-surveys/popest.html.

———. n.d.b. "2020 Census of Population and Housing." Accessed February 17, 2023. https://www.census.gov/programs-surveys/decennial-census/decade/2020/2020-census-main.html.

———. n.d.c. "American Community Survey." Accessed February 17, 2023. http://www.census.gov/programs-surveys/acs/.

# CHAPTER THREE

# The Nebraska State Constitution

## A SERVICEABLE DOCUMENT

*Robert D. Miewald, Anthony Schutz, and Peter Longo*

### INTRODUCTION

Political scientists have not been very fond of state constitutions. In general, the argument goes, these documents are relics of the past, hardly fit for the twentieth century, to say nothing of twenty-first century government. They are long and filled with arcane legalese, unintelligible to the average citizen. Even though they are supposed to be the fundamental law of the state, they are easily amended, and these changes are often slapped together in a haphazard fashion. They contain material more appropriately handled by statute, in many cases the result of special interest activity to enshrine an advantage as a constitutional principle. Most of all, they are negative things, with long lists of all that government may not do. The executive and legislative branches of state government are hamstrung by minute details, making effective governance almost impossible.

In several respects this indictment applies to the Nebraska Constitution. The current constitution was approved in 1875, making it the eighteenth oldest in the United States. Although it is shorter than the national average of twenty-seven thousand words (despite the addition in 1996 of several pages of fine print about term limits), it does not compare favorably with the remarkable brevity of the U.S. Constitution. The language is hardly inspiring, and few non-lawyers could define such words as *mesne* and *supersedeas*.

The preamble declares the constitution to be a "frame of government," but statutory material has been added over the years. The most notable example is the now unenforceable amendment in 1982 to Article XII concerning corporate farming, wherein one can learn of the special privileges of alfalfa producers and sod growers (Jones v. Gale, 470 F.3d 1261 [8th Cir. 2006]). When that amendment was challenged, the state supreme court concluded that there were few limits on the sort of material the people can put into their constitution (Omaha National Bank v. Spire, 223 Neb. 209, 1986). And one can expect future efforts to turn specific policies into the basic law. Other parts of the Nebraska Constitution deal with long-dead issues. Article X, for example, was aimed at checking the power of the railroads. While important in 1875, few people today, except perhaps those building pioneer museums, are overly concerned about railroad rolling stock or depots.

It certainly appears to be true that the Nebraska Constitution has not been regarded as a document for the ages and that citizens have few reservations about changing it. While the U.S. Constitution has been amended only 27 times in 234 years, the Nebraska version has been changed 236 times since its adoption. In all, 365 amendments have been presented to the voters, and 65 percent were accepted.

The basic negativity of the Nebraska Constitution is readily apparent, consistent with the state's mixture of individualistic and moralistic political cultures. The governor and the legislature are severely limited in their powers and in the procedures they must follow. The executive function is divided among several independent offices, and large parts of state government remain beyond the control of the governor. The legislature, in particular, is constrained in a variety of ways. For example, it was only in 1996 that voters permitted senators to suspend the requirement for a complete reading of all bills before a final vote, thus putting an end to the ludicrous spectacle of speed mumbling that had always gone on. The constitution also places numerous restrictions on the ability of the state and local municipalities to raise and spend money, including a limit on ordinary state debt of $100,000. (See chapters 6 and 7 for more information on the legislature and the executive branches of Nebraska state government.)

Although we can grant that state constitutions, including Nebraska's, are not the equal of the inspiring words of the U.S. Constitution, these documents, despite their deficiencies, have become the object of renewed interest among scholars. In the past three decades, state bills of rights have been reconsidered as additional protections for citizens. While an increasingly conservative federal judiciary was accused of curtailing parts of the U.S. Bill of Rights, some state courts were relying on their own constitution to extend some rights (Bowman and Kearney 2022). Whether this is a long-term trend is still in doubt, but legal commentators have been reevaluating the opinions of state supreme courts. In Nebraska this movement has gone beyond speculation, and the Constitutional Revision Commission noted that "few Nebraskans are aware of a heightened protection of their rights that the state's Supreme Court has said is possible in appropriate cases" (NCRC 1997, 8). The commission therefore recommended an amendment to the Nebraska Bill of Rights that makes explicit these extra protections (NCRC 1997, 7). The legislature did not submit the change to the people, but the principle remains a staple of state constitutional law, even if most people do not know it.

A second reason for a renewed interest in state constitutions is a revived emphasis on federalism. In 1995 the U.S. Supreme Court, for the first time since the 1930s, said there were limits to the power of Congress to set domestic policy for the states. And it followed suit in a series of cases, until it ran headlong into California's challenge to the Controlled Substances Act (Gonzalez v. Raich, 545 U.S. 1, 2005). More importantly, the shift of power to congressional Republicans has resulted in a dramatic change in federal attitudes toward the state. Perhaps the move is ideological or perhaps it is simply the desire of Washington politicians to shift the costs and responsibility for governance somewhere else. Whatever the reasons, states face huge challenges, and their constitutions are being reexamined in light of these added burdens. Can states cope? Answering that question must begin with a consideration of their rules for governing. Antiquated constitutions designed to protect old privileges or obsolete issues cannot meet modern conditions (Pew Research Center 2022).

But one can go too far in joining the professors who want to give flunking grades to state constitutions, including Nebraska's. The state endures, regardless of all the deficiencies, real or imagined, in its basic law. From the standpoint of the purist, one may deplore the numerous changes in what should be the fundamental rules of the game. But from another point of view, that is proof that the great game of politics, defined simply as "who gets what," is alive and well in Nebraska. A static constitution may not be a vital one. The real job of the political scientist is to total up the score to see who is winning and who is losing. That requires going back to the first inning.

NEBRASKA CONSTITUTIONAL HISTORY

The trouble with extending the game metaphor to Nebraska's constitutional development is that it is hard to keep track of the teams. That is, there are several reasonable explanations of who wanted to get what over the last 150-plus years. Constitutions, after all, are not the product of pure thought thinking about itself. They are human constructions and reflect the agendas of those who shaped them. In Nebraska there were many obvious teams competing on many fields. Geography, for example, played a large role in territorial and early statehood days, with battles between those living north of the Platte River and those on the south side. The urban-rural division is another continuing element in state politics. But there are several other interesting avenues to interpretation.

There is, first of all, that classification of political culture devised by Daniel Elazar (1984). Nebraska lies along the fault line of two major subcultures, the individualistic and the moralistic. The individualist sees politics as one means among many for personal advancement in terms of wealth or status. It is another way to make a living. One's self-interest is the overriding concern. The public in such a culture regards politics as a dirty business and expects a certain degree of corruption. Moralists, to the contrary, believe that government should be designed for the welfare of the larger community. Civic virtue is a powerful concept, and political activity should be directed toward promoting the public interest over narrow private interests.

In Nebraska the contest between elitists and populists comes naturally to mind. Elitists may be sincere democrats, but they also believe that one can have too much of a good thing. Government should be the business of those best qualified to handle public affairs, and citizens may need some tutelage in picking the right people. An elitist may even argue that there is a "science" of government that cannot be appreciated by the masses. The people, with their whims and passions, should not have unlimited access to government. The term *populist* implies more than the members of the People's Independent Party; it points instead to a whole political orientation that answers in the affirmative that old battle cry, "Shall the people rule?" If democracy is good, then more democracy is better, and we must have ways of tapping into the wisdom of common folks. Government belongs to be people, and the people should be able to do with it what they will.

Another category contains, first, those who regard government as a positive force by which citizens can solve their common problems. Whether progressive Republicans of 1910 or liberal Democrats of 1990, these people believe that good government by good people is a realistic goal. And through this, the community will be improved. Their counterparts may not have read their Hobbes, but they are suspicious that government and its operators are up to no good, especially if they are trying to make a lifetime career out of politics. To be sure, some level of government is necessary, but one cannot expect too much from it, especially if politicians are allowed to follow their natural inclinations to exploit the community rather than serve it. Government is inherently a negative element in society.

Finally, there is a set of contestants who may give Nebraska politics a unique flavor. It is rather hard to describe the differences here; it is not merely some sort of liberal-conservative division. While Nebraskans like to think of themselves as solidly conservative, conservatism may be too refined a term to apply here. Indeed, on most scales of policy liberalism, the state generally ranks somewhere in the middle range. So Nebraskans are not mindless opponents of progressive change; they would just as soon not have to pay for it. From early battles over statehood through the fight about pensions for professors at the university to the debacle surrounding the Commonwealth Savings scandal of the 1980s, Cornhuskers have generally been in favor of the right actions until someone shows them the price tag. One can even make the case that the unicameral legislature was not so much the result of enlightened statecraft as it was the simple calculation that one house would be cheaper than two. Whether this is only prudent frugality in a state that is by no means rolling in wealth or just petty cheapness, it is a factor that political leaders have had to face since territorial days. The counterpart to this considerable group of Nebraskans is harder to identify, but they are probably bearers of what Willa Cather described as the "wave of generous idealism, or noble seriousness" (1923, 238) that periodically sweeps across the state. To shift metaphors, the above are some of the threads running through the tapestry of Nebraska constitutionalism. One or another will stand out in this brief history of the present state constitution.

A political community requires, first, boundaries. So it is appropriate to look at how a place called Nebraska was carved out of the vast wilderness in the center of the North American continent. What was to become a state was governed by a succession of French and Spanish colonial administrators until the Louisiana Purchase of 1803. The area then became part of the Indiana Territory from 1804 to 1805 and the Louisiana Territory from 1805 until 1812, after which it was included in the Missouri Territory until Missouri became a state in 1821. After 1832 what was to become Nebraska was part of something called Indian Country. All these changes, of course, were largely irrelevant to the handful of whites within the area.

In 1834 Congress tried solving the question of what to do with Native Americans by designating a large part of the Trans-Missouri territory as off-limits to further settlement. The law had little effect on the westward push, and it was then that Nebraska's greatest advantage—its location—came into play. The Great Platte River Road was a natural path to the Pacific. To quote Cather again, the trail was "a highway for dreamers and adventurers; men who were in quest of gold or grace, freedom or romance" (1923, 236). Later, the pony express—and the railroads and truckers and tourists on I-80—would learn that Nebraska is the best route from here to there.

A few of these early transients, realizing that the land was not really part of a Great American Desert, decided to remain in small settlements along the Missouri River, thus becoming elements in what Addison Sheldon called "the idea of Nebraska" (1931, 230). That idea included grand notions such as Manifest Destiny and the fight over slavery as well as lesser motives such as the route of the transcontinental railroad and the need to remove the Indians from their land. Out of this stew emerged an omnibus solution: the passage of the Kansas-Nebraska Act of 1854.

The original Nebraska Territory was a huge area, including what would later become parts of the states of Colorado, Wyoming, Montana, North Dakota, and South Dakota. With a population of less than three thousand people, the territory was provided with a very basic governmental structure. But however crude the government, territorial politics was of intense concern to the inhabitants. Nebraska was not blessed with obvious natural resources such as oil and minerals. A commercially viable agriculture was still in the future. Thus, the most important source of a livelihood was the government. Positions in the territorial government were a stable source of income if one had the right patronage connections, and the location of public facilities might ensure the success of the numerous towns being platted by speculators known as "boomers." Playing politics was a matter of survival for territorial leaders who, as James Olson noted, "seem to have come to Nebraska in significant numbers for the express purpose of carving political careers for themselves in the new territory; others to use politics as one means of financial gain" (1966, 116).

The first attempt at statehood took place in 1860, stimulated in large part by the desire of various communities in the territory to reopen the question of the location of the state capital. An election was called in that year on the question of statehood and for the election of a constitutional convention. But the old patterns of federal patronage had been upset by the rapid emergence of the Republican Party. The Democrats could no longer count on the support of the national government or local voters. Moreover, there was considerable resistance to accepting the financial responsibility for running a state. Omaha was also opposed to the idea since it might jeopardize its possession of the capital. The proposal was defeated, and statehood was a dead issue for the next four years.

By 1864 national and territorial Republicans saw many advantages to bringing Nebraska into the Union, since that party had supplanted the Democrats as the dominant political force during the Civil War. The Democrats, conversely, were reluctant to add to the national strength of their opponents. And as usual, Nebraskans of both parties were not convinced that statehood was worth the added expense. Thus, the Enabling Act of 1864, which authorized Nebraskans to "form for themselves a constitution and state government," was not met with unanimous enthusiasm. Under the act citizens were to hold a convention to prepare a constitution for submission to the voters. Upon voter approval of such a document, the president was to proclaim Nebraska a state. A straightforward plan, but it was soon twisted out of shape by territorial politics.

The convention elected in 1864 to write a constitution was dominated by anti-statehood members, and its only act was to adjourn permanently. The Republicans, however, were not deterred for long, and in 1866 they came up with a plan for writing Nebraska's first constitution. This began a series of events that piled one irregularity on top of another. For conspiracy theorists who want to question the legitimacy of the present government, one might be able to make a good case that the state is still governed by the Kansas-Nebraska Act, because rarely has a constitution been presented with such dubious bona fides.

Ignoring the Enabling Act's requirement for an elected convention, the Republicans and other statehood advocates decided to write their own constitution. A small group of men, whose membership is not entirely known, put together a document and pushed it through the territorial legislature in a series of unorthodox maneuvers. These mysterious "founders" seem to have had at least one goal in mind: they were not going to discourage those frugal voters who were still wary of the costs of state government. The basic structure was taken from the Kansas-Nebraska Act and provided for minimal government at minimal expense. As a contemporary critic of the new constitution wrote of its promoters, "A respectable government would, they argued, frighten the people and they would reject the constitution. A cheap government of cheap men answered the purpose designed" (Sheldon 1931, 339).

In the subsequent election on the constitution, it was approved by a margin of one hundred votes. Both sides issued charges of electoral fraud, but the Republicans controlled the counting of ballots. Congress was notified that the conditions that had been set by the Enabling Act had been met and Nebraska was ready for admission as a state. The appropriate legislation was passed in 1866, but it became the subject of a pocket veto by President Andrew Johnson.

When the statehood question was brought up again in the next session of Congress, attention focused on an unusual provision: the right to vote was limited to whites. Congress, involved in the work of Reconstruction, found this offensive and passed a new act of admission that contained the "fundamental condition" that statehood was contingent on the recognition of a right to suffrage that did not deny the vote to anyone on account of race or color. President Johnson again applied the veto to the bill which was overridden by Congress.

Nebraska then had to contend with the fundamental condition. Although it was contrary to the provisions for amendment, the territorial legislature agreed to nullify the suffrage provision. Johnson then issued a proclamation of statehood on March 1, 1867. In an 1873 case, the Nebraska Supreme Court recounted all the questionable steps involved in constructing the constitution;

it was written by a group that had no authority to do so, it was approved in a possibly fraudulent election, and it was amended by another unauthorized group. The court decided, however, that admission was basically a political question to be decided by Congress and the 1866 constitution was valid (Brittle v. The People, 2 Neb. 198, 1873).

And so Nebraska had its government. It also had a corps of politicians who might serve as models for Elazar's individualists. The wheeling and dealing continued at a new pace at both state and local levels. Towns and villages irresponsibly issued a variety of bonds to attract railroads and industry, while state leaders bickered over the distribution of government facilities. The corruption reached a peak with the impeachment in 1873 of the first governor, David Butler, by a legislature probably no less larcenous than he. But even if the politicians of the time had been models of rectitude, they would have had difficulty in making the constitution of 1866 work. Its cumbersome structure and miserly pay almost insured ineffectiveness and corruption.

In the meantime, the composition of Nebraska was changing. The post–Civil War settlers were not just passing through. They soon learned that life on the plains was hard and that the construction of a viable agricultural economy was a long-term project. At the same time, as Olson noted, "the years in which Nebraska's state government was being established were characterized by gross public immorality in financial matters and an all-too-general practice of using public funds for private gain" (1966, 143). The growing moralist strain was made even more powerful by the awareness that only by community action could one cope with all the awful forces of nature on the Great Plains and that the individual farmer had little chance against the excesses of unbridled capitalism. It would take a few decades before these raw notions shaped the programs of the Populists and Progressives. But by 1870 many recognized that a more effective type of government was needed.

Agitation for a new constitution led to a call for a convention in 1871. The members used as a framework the 1870 Illinois Constitution. This was the so-called Granger Constitution that was widely emulated throughout the western states (although Illinois eventually abandoned this constitution, primarily because it was too restrictive). The major attraction of the Illinois model was its efforts to control the corporations and particularly the railroads. After two months of deliberation, the convention presented its constitution, which was resoundingly rejected by the voters.

But as more people moved into the state and the quality of public life continued to deteriorate, the pressure for constitutional change could not be ignored. By the mid-1870s it was more apparent than ever that effective government was essential for survival on the prairie. A second convention met in 1875, again borrowing heavily from the Illinois constitution. As in 1871, a well-founded mistrust in politicians and an obsession with economy produced a document with many limitations on government. At the same time it defined a clear role for government in the regulation of the railroads. Here again the Nebraska paradox had an impact: a public policy that was potentially helpful to many citizens was nullified by restrictions on the size of government, making it impossible to create effective regulatory mechanisms.

Voters in 1875 approved the constitution, and it remains the much-modified skeleton of the current document. It was this constitution that saw the state through its "time of troubles," beginning in the 1890s with the successes of the Populist movement. Oddly, despite the electoral victories of the Populist/Democrat fusion, there were no major attempts to overhaul the constitution, and populism, as a general political movement, had little impact on Nebraska constitutionalism. Part of this may be attributable to the near impossibility of amending the constitution, and changes were made only through creative counting or legal subterfuge.

As Nebraskans looked to the government for more and better services, the defects of the constitution became apparent. The limits on the executive branch were especially frustrating, but the constitution was clear that no more executive offices could be created; in fact, the attorney general was even prohibited from hiring a clerk. Little was done to change things, however, until the height of the progressive movement in the early decades of the twentieth century. The main political thrust was no longer the economic radicalism of the Populists but instead a program of reform of government structure, to lessen partisanship and to put public affairs on a more rational basis. Many of its supporters took as a model not the passions of the populist masses but instead the cool methods of the modern corporation or of what was regarded as the science of government.

By 1910 the Progressives had launched a campaign agitating for a new constitutional convention. Among the items they wanted considered were staples of the reform movement of the time: the short ballot, a merit system, a modern taxation system, and a unicameral legislature. While the impulse for reform was more elitist than populist, conservatives, concerned about such issues as the regulation of railroads and prohibition, resisted a convention.

In 1918, just as World War I was ending, voters approved the call for a new convention. The members elected in 1919 decided to submit only selected amendments rather than produce a completely new constitution. Among the major issues they confronted were the amending process, the scope and structure of the executive branch, and the authorization for a modern revenue system. In an act of real foresight, they approved three amendments that made clear that the state had the power to regulate Nebraska's water, its most precious natural resource. Eventually, forty-one amendments were recommended, and all were approved in 1920. Professor John Senning, later the partner of George Norris in the unicameral campaign, was not impressed with the changes, lamenting that the 1919 convention's work as "very conservative" and remarking that its structural changes "ignore entirely modern scientific principles of government" (1920, 426).

However, the results of the 1920 convention went a long way toward modernizing Nebraska government, and few amendments were voted on through the 1940s. However, the pace of change picked up in the 1960s, and the election of 1966 was especially alarming to many observers. In that year citizens used the referendum and initiative to repeal the newly imposed state income tax and to abolish the state property tax. In effect, the state was left without any significant source of revenue. One result of the concern of state leaders was the creation by the legislature in 1969 of a Constitutional Revision Commission. While the commission spent a great deal of time with minor revisions, one of its goals, which never reached the voters, was limiting the impact of direct democracy in matters of taxing and spending. In all, the commission recommended over a hundred changes to the legislature, which in sum referred forty-nine to the voters.

A mixture of motives could also be discerned in the most recent effort at a broad scale constitutional review. A second Constitutional Revision Commission, modeled along the lines of the first, was approved by the legislature in 1995. While the usual reasons were given for this move—the need to remove obsolete language, to eliminate unnecessary provisions, and to give greater flexibility to the governor and the legislature—the commission spent a considerable amount of time on the problem, as they perceived it, of the use or abuse of the initiative and referendum system. But was there a problem, or was it just the latest version of the ongoing struggle between elitists and populists? An answer to this question requires consideration of the ways in which the constitution can be and has been changed.

## CHANGING THE CONSTITUTION

The Nebraska Constitution has been amended 236 times since it was adopted in 1875, with over half of these changes occurring since the election of 1962. All amendments must be approved by a vote of the people. Originally, passage required a majority of all votes cast in an election, which meant that those who indicated no preference on an amendment were counted as voting "no." The "party circle law" was eventually adopted to make amending possible. Under this plan, political parties could endorse an amendment and all straight-ticket ballots were then counted in favor of the issue. The 1920 convention proposed the present method which only requires that an amendment receive a majority of those voting on the issue, so long as that number is at least 35 percent of the total vote.

There are three methods for proposing amendments to the voters. The constitutional convention is the least used, with the 1919–10 convention the only example. Based on this single instance, there appears to be two basic ingredients for a successful call for a convention. First, there must be serious flaws in the existing document. A second requisite is a determined organization of reformers with a clear agenda who are willing to keep the pressure on the legislature over a long period of time. In the earlier part of the century, the Nebraska Popular Government League and the Non-Partisan League fulfilled this function. At the present time, such a combination seems unlikely.

The most common way for proposals to appear on the ballot is through legislative action. By a three-fifths vote of its members, the legislature can propose amendments to the voters. All but 67 of 309 proposals have gone through this route. The two constitutional revision commissions fit within this category since their recommendations still must be approved by the legislature. One can argue that a serious drawback to this approach is that the legislature is unlikely to recommend changes in its fundamental features. So it was that the unicameral legislature as well as three term limit proposals came about through the initiative process.

And this brings us to the final and most problematic method for constitutional revision. The language of Article III, Section 1, on legislative

## Table 1. Nebraska constitutional amendments, 1882–2022

| YEARS | SUBMITTED | APPROVED | REJECTED | % APPROVED |
|---|---|---|---|---|
| 1882–90 | 8 | 1 | 7 | 12.5 |
| 1892–1900 | 14 | 0 | 14 | 0.0 |
| 1902–10 | 5 | 3 | 2 | 60.0 |
| 1912–20 | 12 (3) | 7 (1) | 5 (2) | 58.3 (33.3) |
| Convention | 41 | 41 | 0 | 100.0 |
| 1922–30 | 4 (1) | 1 | 3 (1) | 25.0 |
| 1932–40 | 13 (3) | 6 (2) | 7 (1) | 46.2 (66.7) |
| 1942–50 | 6 (3) | 1 (1) | 5 (2) | 16.7 (33.3) |
| 1952–60 | 37 (3) | 27 (1) | 10 (2) | 73.0 (33.3) |
| 1962–70 | 66 (3) | 49 (1) | 17 (2) | 74.2 (33.3) |
| 1972–80 | 59 | 40 | 19 | 67.8 |
| 1982–90 | 25 (4) | 17 (2) | 7 (2) | 70.8 (50.0) |
| 1992–2000 | 45 (9) | 28 (3) | 17 (6) | 62.2 (33.3) |
| 2002–10 | 22 (4) | 9 (2) | 13 (2) | 40.9 (50.0) |
| 2012–20 | 7 (1) | 5 (1) | 2 (0) | 71.4 (100.0) |
| 2022* | 2 (1) | 2 (1) | 0 | 100.0 (100.0) |

* Through general election of 2022.
Note: (#) indicates amendments proposed by citizen initiative included in adjacent number.
Sources: Nebraska Legislature, *2020–2021 Nebraska Blue Book* (Lincoln: Nebraska Legislature, 2020); Nebraska Secretary of State, *2022 Primary Canvass Book* (Lincoln: Nebraska Secretary of State). Compiled by author.

power is clear: "The people reserve to themselves the power to propose . . . amendments to the constitution and to enact or reject the same at the polls, independent of the Legislature." Without going into the details, the current procedure says that a proposal must go on the ballot after submission of a petition signed by 10 percent of registered voters (7 percent for referenda).

These signatures must also come from at least 5 percent of the registered voters in at least two-fifths of Nebraska's counties. Through this method, thirty-five proposals have been presented to the voters, and fifteen have been enacted. Some of the more important amendments by initiative include the unicameral legislature, the termination of the state property tax, a ban on corporate farming, the right to bear arms, a prohibition on affirmative action, the refusal to recognize same-sex marriage, the authorization of casino gaming, and numerous efforts at imposing term limits on various political offices.

For decades Nebraskans were proud of their initiative process. In one assessment, the process "represents the utmost in popular sovereignty and has proven a desirable and successful supplemental method of amending the state constitution" (Peterson, 1943, 44). The state seemed to have avoided the excesses of "cash-and-carry democracy" as practiced in California, where interests with enough money could hire petition circulators and then conduct expensive, if misleading, campaigns to get their very own constitutional provision. To be sure, some were uncomfortable in 1978 when the beverage industry conducted a fierce campaign to defeat a referendum on a version of the Oregon bottle bill. But the age of innocence really began to end in 1986, after three state senators and a powerful lobbyist were charged with violations of the relevant laws. Two years later the U.S. Supreme Court struck down state laws, including Nebraska's, prohibiting the hiring of petition circulators, and the Nebraska high court further suggested that people signing petitions did not even have to be registered voters in the state.

Ostensibly to clarify that last possibility, the legislature proposed an amendment that in turn only confused the issue while outraging the advocates of the initiative process. The Nebraska Supreme Court threw out the 1992 initiative on term limits because the petitioners had not collected enough signatures now that the requirements had been changed from 10 percent of "electors" to 10 percent of "registered voters." Although the senators who supported the change insisted they did not mean to make it harder to get issues on the ballot, populist suspicions were aroused, especially after the Nebraska court also voided a second term-limits amendment passed in 1994. One of the victims of this mistrust was Supreme Court Judge Lanphier, the author of the decision about numbers, who was ousted by the voters in 1996.

Friends of the initiative now claimed that because of the higher numbers needed, even the noblest cause could not rely on dedicated volunteers. To stop petition circulation from becoming a minor industry, the legislature required that circulators be registered Nebraska voters. When that provision was overturned in 1996 by a federal judge, Secretary of State Scott Moore said that the ruling "makes it so anybody can circulate petitions. Carpetbaggers, convicts, Californians, and children can circulate petitions in Nebraska" (*Omaha World-Herald* 1996, 10). The fact that some circulators were interested less in good government than in getting their hands on some quick cash was confirmed when county clerks noted some strange signatures, including a few from people whose last known address was the local cemetery. By July 1997 three people had been prosecuted for petition fraud. The evils of Californication had come to the heartland.

To restore some degree of purity to that "first power reserved by the people," several suggestions have been made. Believers in the value of direct democracy still suspected that some of the efforts were simply designed to make the process harder in order to thwart the will of the majority, a feeling exacerbated by numerous court challenges to term limits, the greatest bane of the political elite. Moreover, they argued, the dollars spent on petition drives were no more pernicious than the money lavished by lobbyists on the legislature. Their solution was a return to a smaller requirement of signatures, a measure that was proposed by initiative and defeated by the voters in 1996.

The 1997 Constitutional Revision Commission worried that the "increased and increasing political power of interest groups combined with the rise of the paid petition circulation industry prompts concern that state constitutions unfortunately are now being viewed as little more than glorified statutes, relatively easy to change" (NCRC 1997, 46). Its recommendations included a two-vote system over two electoral periods in order to slow the rush to amendment. When that was presented to voters in 2000, they roundly rejected it. Other proposals, such as having signatures collected at county courthouses, were intended to avoid the hustling of signatures on the streets by transient circulators. None of those proposals have come to fruition.

One seemingly innocuous change to the initiative process was proposed by the 1997 Constitutional Revision Commission, forwarded to voters and adopted in 1998: a requirement that required initiative measures to "contain only one subject." This proposal followed on the heels of a 1996 general election ballot that included at least three very large, initiated measures dealing with property taxes, education, and term limits (the last of which passed and occupies Article XVIII of the constitution). With this sort of logrolling danger afoot, the people passed a measure that at least initially was thought to put the people's legislation on par with the legislature's, which had always required the separation of subjects. In 2020, however, the Nebraska Supreme Court concluded that a medical-marijuana provision comprised multiple subjects and withheld it from the ballot (Wagner v. Evnen, 307 Neb. 142, 2020). Today it appears that the Nebraska Supreme Court is a significant gatekeeper to the people's power.

In any event, the real question about constitutional change, regardless of the source of the proposal or the checks on it, is whether amendments are passed too often. If the constitution has been changed on an average of 2.5 times per year since 1962, how can one regard it as the fundamental law of the state? Perhaps one needs to look beyond the numbers to determine whether Nebraskans are too cavalier in their attitude toward their constitution. The question is quality and not quantity.

The largest number of amendments, about seventy-five by our rough count, deal with the three branches, as is appropriate for a "frame of government." A number of these are technical details, but the substantial ones have moved the state in the direction generally recommended by students of government: longer terms for all officials, a reformed judiciary, greater gubernatorial control, a more professional legislature. Others are more debatable, including term limits on members of the legislature. In policy areas, by far the most contested has been state and local revenue, and it is highly unlikely that citizens are going to surrender their sovereignty in this critical area. Education has also been a major issue, as Nebraskans have struggled with the operation of this important and expensive function of the state. A perennial issue, at least since 1884, concerns the salaries and other compensation for state officers. Thirty-two efforts have been made to improve the benefits of public service, but only nine have been approved. While the voters have permitted the pay of executive and judicial officials to be determined by statute, they have resolutely refused to grant the legislature the same privilege.

For those who still believe that Nebraskans are too quick to change their basic law, a strong argument to the contrary could be found in the stability of Article I's rights provisions, the heart of constitutional democracy. Until the 2000s only two 1920 amendments arising from nativist sentiments following World War I could be reasonably classified as contracting rights and privileges of citizens. Since then, however, we have seen fit to prohibit the recognition of same-sex marriage (a provision that is currently unconstitutional under federal law) and outlaw affirmative action. Whether this significantly undermines the argument that our basic law is adequately stable is a subject upon which there is significant disagreement. In any event, Nebraskans seem to appreciate that their constitution is a very important document dealing with serious matters.

## CONCLUSION

The Nebraska Constitution will never serve as a model for other states, but overall, it appears to be a quite serviceable document. That it has been modified so often should be taken as a sign of great vitality, not instability. The several "teams" identified above have used it, not as the mere rules of the game but as the game itself. The current struggle is clearly between the elitists and the populists. Those angry citizens carrying petitions to cut back on taxing and spending and impose term limits make the elite uncomfortable. And their tenacity with casino gaming and medical marijuana suggests that popular will and representative democracy are not well aligned. The game continues, which provides assurance to those familiar with other options.

## AUTHORS' NOTE

The authors would like to acknowledge the work of the late Robert D. Miewald, professor of political science at the University of Nebraska–Lincoln and editor of the first edition of this volume. His personal and scholarly contributions to the study of Nebraska politics and government are held in high regard. In 1971 he joined the faculty of the University of Nebraska, Lincoln as an associate professor. He was promoted to full professor in 1978. At Nebraska, Bob served as chair of the department from 1974 to 1977 and 1988–90. From 1978 he served as the director of the graduate specialization in policy analysis and program evaluation. In addition to a textbook in public administration, Bob authored two other books: *The Bureaucratic State: An Annotated Bibliography* and *The Nebraska State Constitution: A Reference Guide*. He edited and coedited three others. Peter Longo was one of his admiring students. Miewald lives on with contributions from law professor Anthony Schutz. Professor Miewald died in 1993.

## REFERENCES

Bowman, Ann O'M., and Richard C. Kearney. 2022. *State and Local Government*. 11th ed. Boston: Cengage.

Cather, Willa. 1923. "Nebraska: The End of the First Cycle." *The Nation* 117 (September).

Elazar, Daniel J. 1984. *American Federalism: A View from the States*. 3rd ed. New York: Harper and Row.

NCRC (Nebraska Constitutional Revision Commission). 1997. *Report of the Nebraska Constitutional Revision Commission*. Lincoln: Nebraska Constitutional Revision Commission. Note: "The rights granted to people in this Constitution are not to be construed as limited by the interpretation placed on similar provisions in the Constitution of the United States."

Olson, James C. 1966. *History of Nebraska*. 2nd ed. Lincoln: University of Nebraska Press.

*Omaha World-Herald*. 1996. "Federal, State Courts Nibble away at Once-Noble Grassroots Right." *Omaha World-Herald*, August 16, 1996.

Peterson, Betty. 1943. "Procedures of Amending the Nebraska Constitution." *Nebraska Law Review* 22:39–44.

Pew Research Center. 2022. "Levels of Government: Federal, State, and Local." In *Americans' Views of Government: Decades of Mistrust, Enduring Support for Its Role*. Washington DC: Pew Research Center. https://www.pewresearch.org/politics /2022/06/06/levels-of-government-federal-state-local/.

Senning, John P. 1920. "The Nebraska Constitutional Convention." *National Municipal Review* 9:421–26.

Sheldon, Addison E. 1931. *Nebraska: The Land and the People*. Vol. 1. Chicago: Lewis Publishing.

# CHAPTER FOUR

# Political Parties and Voting

## NONPARTISANSHIP AND DIRECT DEMOCRACY

*Diane L. Duffin*

## INTRODUCTION

The legacies of William Jennings Bryan and George W. Norris not only shaped Nebraska's contemporary political institutions and culture; they also affected partisanship and the practice of politics in the state. In general, Bryan's grassroots, rugged individualistic, prairie populism of the late nineteenth century evolved into the rational, efficiency-based, good government politics of Norris in the early twentieth century. Together, these two strands formed the political ethos of the state. The impact of individualism on Nebraska's political DNA is probably best demonstrated in the widely read early novels of Willa Cather, Nebraska's most famous author. She provided "tender recollections of the Nebraska prairies; human fortitude and courage triumph over the harsh environment" (Federal Writers' Project [1939] 1979, 140). The other strand, sharing many characteristics with progressivism, is well exemplified in the purpose of "creating a more open and honest governmental structure that relies upon an engaged and participatory citizenry" (Center for American Progress n.d.).

Political scientist Daniel Elazar (1966) has translated these general ideas into a more penetrating understanding of political systems, arguing that politics in Nebraska carry many characteristics of a moralistic political culture, even if the more dominant subculture is individualistic in the state. The primary attributes of the moralistic culture include the following beliefs: (1) politics exist to serve the public good; (2) political engagement is the responsibility of all citizens, not just professional politicians; (3) political parties are not particularly necessary to politics; (4) corruption in government should not be tolerated; and (5) local people are well-equipped to address their own problems themselves and neither want nor need the assistance of outsiders, especially distant governments. When applied to political parties and voting, two of these characteristics seem especially apt to Nebraska: citizen engagement and nonpartisanship.

Moralistic political culture, according to Elazar, "embraces the notion that politics is ideally a matter of concern for every citizen, not just those who are professionally committed to political careers" (1966, 91). In the case of Nebraska, the Federal Writers' Project's *A Guide to the Cornhusker State* notes, "People take a personal and peculiarly close interest in government" (Federal Writers' Project [1939] 1979, 4). Citizens in a moralistic culture rely less on the good will of political elites, embracing the notion that citizens should make more of these decisions themselves. In places where the moralistic culture dominates, citizen participation is strong and direct democracy is more prominent, as often exercised through initiatives and referenda. The moralistic culture also de-emphasizes party regularity. Elazar writes that "regular party ties can be abandoned with relative impunity for third parties, special local parties, or nonpartisan systems if such changes are believed helpful in gaining larger political goals. Men can even shift from party to party without sanctions if the change is justified by political belief" (1966, 91).

This chapter provides compelling evidence that the traits of citizen engagement and nonpartisanship apply to Nebraska in the areas of voting behavior and political parties.

ELECTION LAW

Generally speaking, Nebraska law encourages participation in elections by not erecting many barriers to voting. Citizens may register in person at state offices, online, or by mail. Although Nebraska, unlike neighboring Iowa, does not allow for election-day registration, the requirements and process for registering to vote are not particularly burdensome. In-person registration must be completed by the second Friday before an election. Online or mailed registration forms must be submitted by the third Friday before an election. There is no legal minimum residency requirement to register in Nebraska—new arrivals to the state may register to vote on the day they establish residence—although there may be a practical minimum requirement. Citizens registering to vote by mail must provide some proof of residence, such as a utility bill or bank statement verifying the registrant's address, as well as a copy of a valid photo identification.

Nebraska law permits early voting (formerly known as absentee voting) beginning thirty-five days prior to a primary or general election. Citizens are not required to state a reason for requesting early voting and may request ballots in person at a county clerk or election commissioner office or by mail. Although many state governments adopted policies limiting voter access in the 2010s and 2020s, Nebraska has largely resisted this tendency. In 2022, however, Nebraska voters approved a constitutional amendment requiring voters to present a photo ID at polling places.

Nebraska election law also de-emphasizes, but does not ignore, political parties. Parties are certainly prevalent in choosing executive branch leaders in the state, with candidates for governor, lieutenant governor, attorney general, state treasurer, auditor of public accounts all running under party labels. This executive-branch partisanship is offset, though, by the nonpartisan legislature. Candidates for the Public Service Commission, however, run under party labels. This pattern of partisan executive offices and nonpartisan legislative offices continues elsewhere at the state level and in special district governments. Nonpartisan elections are held for the University of Nebraska Board of Regents, the State Board of Education, the Community College Board of Governors, educational service unit boards, and public power district, public power and irrigation district, natural resources district, and reclamation district boards (Nebraska Legislature 2015). But most offices in the counties are partisan. County clerks, registers of deeds, assessors, treasurers, sheriffs, attorneys, public defenders, clerks of the district court, surveyors, and engineers are all elected under partisan labels, as are county boards of commissioners and county boards of supervisors. Municipal and township offices, however, tend to be nonpartisan.

Political parties matter most in primary elections, which may be characterized as open (any registered voter may vote any party's ballot) or closed (only voters registered with a political party may vote that party's ballot). Nebraska enacted its first closed primary law in 1911. Currently, the state's system may be more fairly characterized as modified closed. Voters must be registered with a party in order to vote for nominees for state offices and president of the United States, but registered independents may vote in primaries to nominate candidates for seats in the U.S. House of Representatives and the U.S. Senate.

In other election-related matters, state law seeks to counterbalance the influence of parties. For example, any registered voter may apply to become a deputy registrar and conduct voter registration efforts. But all deputy registrars work in teams of two or more, and at least one team member must be registered with a different political party from the others. The same balance is sought in election judges who run polling places. Finally, state law prohibits the use of straight-ticket ballots, a provision that encourages voters to consider and select candidates on their merits, of which partisan label may be but one.

It is evident that election laws in Nebraska have not neutralized political parties, but, consistent with a moralistic political culture, parties do not play as prominent a role in government and politics as they might. The extent to which election laws encourage (or rather, fail to discourage) voting also supports the moralistic political culture of the state.

### TURNOUT

Moralistic political culture "embraces the notion that politics is ideally a matter of concern for every citizen, not just those who are professionally committed to political careers" (Elazar 1966, 91). The idea that politics is a matter of concern for every citizen comes across in Nebraskans' participation in elections.

Voter turnout, defined in this chapter as the percentage of the voting age population that cast votes in an election, provides a good indicator of citizens' commitment to civic engagement. Nebraskans, when compared with the United States as a whole, turn out in higher numbers. In the presidential elections from 1972 to 2020, Nebraskans participated at higher rates than the nation as a whole. The average turnout for the nation over these elections was 54.1 percent. Among Nebraska voters for the same time period, the average turnout was 57.9 percent, an average difference of 3.8 percentage points. Standard deviations provide an indication of how much the turnout rate in any election varies from the average. There is slightly less deviation from the mean among Nebraska voters (2.4 percent) than was the case with voters across the United States (2.6 percent), indicating that Nebraskans' average turnout numbers are both higher, and more consistently so, than the national average over time.

It is well established that presidential elections draw higher levels of participation than any other type of election, so perhaps a better indication of Nebraskans' notion that politics should be the concern of every citizen is voting in non-presidential elections. Again, as was the case with presidential elections, Nebraskan voters turn out in higher numbers than American voters as a whole. Moreover, the gap between Nebraska voters and the nation is appreciably larger in midterm elections than it is in presidential elections. Whereas the average difference between Nebraska and the nation in presidential elections is 4.1 percentage points, in midterm elections, the average difference is almost doubled, to 7.6 percentage points, from 1974 to 2018. (Nebraska's turnout averaged 43.8 percent while the national turnout averaged only 36.1 percent.)

Examining midterm election turnout data over time reveals an interesting phenomenon. The standard deviation reported for the United States is smaller, at 4.4 percent. (Without the exceptionally large turnout in 2018, the standard deviation would be less than half as large.) The temporal pattern for Nebraska tells a somewhat different story, however. The standard deviation of 4.8 percent for the Nebraska midterm elections indicates wider swings from one election to the next. This is evident from an individual examination of the data as well. In most midterm election years, turnout in Nebraska holds steady, with rates in the mid-forties. But some years, such as 1990 on the high end, at 50.9 percent, and 2002 and 2010 on the low ends, at 36.9 percent and 35.5 percent, respectively, stand out and invite further investigation.

To explain the wider variation in midterm election turnout in Nebraska, it is important to know whether anything in particular was drawing citizens to the polls or giving them reason to stay away. One important indicator is that the cycle for electing governors in Nebraska during this time period coincides with midterm congressional elections, such that in every one of the elections, Nebraskans were also choosing a governor. In addition, in two out of every three of those elections, Nebraskans also chose a U.S. senator. Having gubernatorial and Senate candidates at the top of the ticket in a midterm election does not, in and of itself, explain the wide variation in turnout, much less high turnout (Merrifield 1993). But something in the nature of the races, such as particularly high or low level of electoral competition, may influence turnout. Prior research identifies "a small but persistent positive relationship between closeness and turnout" (Berch 1993, 423). That this relationship is small suggests many exceptions to the rule, which appears to be true for voter turnout in Nebraska midterm elections.

Table 2 presents the margin of victory enjoyed by the winner in each of the gubernatorial and Senate races during those midterm elections. It demonstrates that any relationship between electoral competition and voter turnout is a sometime thing and appears to be focused on the gubernatorial races, since none of the Senate races held since 1974 were even close. The governor's races, though, show a relatively wide variation, in both turnout and competition. Some, such as Dave Heinemann's elections in 2006 and 2010, were nothing less than blowouts, with the spread between the winner's and loser's share of the two-way vote approaching fifty percentage points. Yet both elections were not consistently high-turnout events. Turnout in the 2006 race was close to average, at 45.3 percent, while in 2010, it dropped to the modern record low, 35.5 percent.

On the other end of the spectrum were the closest of all, the gubernatorial elections. The 1982 race, between Republican incumbent Charles Thone and Democratic candidate Bob Kerrey, was decided by two-tenths of one percentage point yet saw a typical level of voter turnout. On the other hand, the second-closest governor's race, in which Ben Nelson challenged Governor Kay Orr, set a turnout record for a Nebraska midterm election in the modern era. The exceptionally high turnout in this case, combined with the close electoral competition, makes it noteworthy because of two issues: a change in the state income tax system and an unpopular interstate compact that required Nebraska to serve as a low-level nuclear waste site.

Whether elections are decided by close or wide margins, the broader, persistent pattern demonstrates that voters in Nebraska participate in elections at higher levels than is true for the nation at large. This pattern conforms well within a political culture that stresses citizen engagement.

## DIRECT DEMOCRACY

Nebraska's progressive-populist tradition of open government and citizen engagement provides the foundation for the generous use of tools of direct democracy: initiative, referendum, and recall. Although all three tools are available under Nebraska law, citizens have made the greatest use of the initiative power to shape public policy according to their view of the public good.

Initiative is the power of the people to propose, by petition, and approve, through election, laws and amendments to the state constitution (Smith 2019). The constitution spells out procedures for initiatives, which vary slightly according to the initiative's purpose. Petitions for proposed amendments to the constitution require the valid signatures of 10 percent of the registered voters in the state, while petitions for proposed laws require the valid signatures of 7 percent of the registered voters. Whether an initiative's intent is to amend the constitution or write new law, the constitution requires that initiative measures contain only one subject.

It is possible to challenge the language of ballot initiatives. In 2020 the language in the marijuana legalization initiative was challenged by the Lancaster County sheriff on the grounds that it included multiple subjects. The Nebraska Supreme Court agreed and ordered it to be removed from the ballot, even after it was approved by the secretary of state.

A valid petition must include signatures from at least 5 percent of the registered voters in each of two-fifths (thirty-eight of ninety-three) of the counties of the state. Once the requisite number and distribution of signatures have been gathered, initiative sponsors must submit petitions to the secretary of state. Petitions must be filed four months before the date of a general election to be included on the ballot. Once an initiative is placed on a ballot, a simple majority vote is required to approve it, provided at least 35 percent of the voters casting ballots that day vote on the initiative measure.

Nebraska's initiative petition process can be described as open. The fact that relatively few signatures are needed to place issues on the ballot carries two important implications: (1) the initiative process has been used with increasing frequency in recent decades, and (2) national organizations have used the process to highlight controversial issues in Nebraska. Table 3 summarizes the historical patterns of initiative use in Nebraska. The state constitution was first amended to allow direct initiatives in 1912, and the first attempts to use the process came in 1914. The first initiative on the ballot in Nebraska was a women's suffrage amendment to the state constitution, which failed. The first successful use of direct initiative came two years later, when voters approved a prohibition amendment to the Nebraska Constitution in

**Table 2. Margin of victory in midterm gubernatorial and Senate elections, Nebraska, 1974–2022**

GOVERNOR RACE

| YEAR | VOTER TURNOUT (%) | WINNER | OPPONENT | MARGIN OF VICTORY (%) |
|------|------|------|------|------|
| 1974 | 42.4 | Exon* (D) | Marvel (R) | 25.2 |
| 1978 | 44.7 | Thone (R) | Whelan (D) | 12.0 |
| 1982 | 45.1 | Kerrey (D) | Thone (R) | 0.2 |
| 1986 | 47.7 | Orr (R) | Boosalis (D) | 2.8 |
| 1990 | 50.9 | Nelson (D) | Orr (R) | 0.7 |
| 1994 | 47.9 | Nelson* (D) | Spence (R) | 48.0 |
| 1998 | 44.1 | Johanns (R) | Hoppner (D) | 8.0 |
| 2002 | 36.9 | Johanns* (R) | Dean (D) | 42.0 |
| 2006 | 45.3 | Heinemann* (R) | Hahn (D) | 50.0 |
| 2010 | 35.5 | Heinemann*† (R) | Meister (D) | 47.8 |
| 2014 | 37.9 | Ricketts (R) | Hassebrook (D) | 18.0 |
| 2018 | 47.3 | Ricketts* (R) | Krist (D) | 18.0 |
| 2022 | 44.3 | Pillen (R) | Blood (D) | 24.9 |
| Mean | 43.8 | | | |
| S.D. | 4.41 | | | |

* Incumbent

† Heinemann was lieutenant governor and became governor in 2005 following Johanns's resignation.

Note: Voter turnout is percent of voting age population casting votes. At the time of this writing, 2022 national voter turnout was unavailable.

Sources: Official reports of the Nebraska Board of State Canvassers. Compiled by the Nebraska secretary of state.

SENATE RACE

| YEAR | VOTER TURNOUT (%) | WINNER | OPPONENT | MARGIN OF VICTORY (%) |
|------|-------------------|--------|----------|------------------------|
| 1978 | 44.7 | Exon (D) | Shasteen (R) | 36.0 |
| 1982 | 45.1 | Zorinsky* (D) | Keck (R) | 40.0 |
| 1990 | 50.9 | Exon* (D) | Daub (R) | 18.0 |
| 1994 | 47.9 | Kerrey* (D) | Stoney (R) | 9.8 |
| 2002 | 36.9 | Hagel* (R) | Matulka (D) | 70.0 |
| 2006 | 45.3 | Nelson* (D) | Ricketts (R) | 27.8 |
| 2014 | 37.9 | Sasse (R) | Domina (D) | 32.8 |
| 2018 | 47.3 | Fischer* (R) | Raybould (D) | 19.1 |

1916, more than two years before the Eighteenth Amendment to the U.S. Constitution was ratified.

As table 3 shows, for most of the initiative process's history, it was used sparingly. Through the 1980s initiatives were placed before the voters an average of three times per decade. Noteworthy among these were the constitutional amendment creating the unicameral legislature in 1934, the amendment abolishing the state property tax in 1966, and the 1982 amendment that prohibited outside corporate ownership of Nebraska farmland. The voters' choices in all three of these measures reflect some characteristics of the moralistic political culture. The unicameral initiative demonstrates the relative unimportance of political parties, as well as the responsibility of citizens to be politically engaged. As George W. Norris often said in his campaign for the unicameral amendment, the people should serve as the second house of the legislature. The amendment abolishing state property taxes supports the view that local people can address their own problems without the assistance or interference of distant governments. The family farm amendment, for its part, was motivated by a belief that politics exist to serve the public good. In this case, the public good meant preserving family owned and operated farms and the traditional way of life these institutions represent.

**Table 3. Historical patterns of initiative use in Nebraska, 1910–2010**

| DECADE | NUMBER ON BALLOT | NUMBER APPROVED | PERCENT APPROVED |
|---|---|---|---|
| 1910 | 3 | 1 | 33 |
| 1920 | 1 | 0 | 0 |
| 1930 | 4 | 1 | 25 |
| 1940 | 4 | 1 | 25 |
| 1950 | 3 | 1 | 33 |
| 1960 | 4 | 1 | 25 |
| 1970 | 2 | 1 | 0 |
| 1980 | 3 | 2 | 67 |
| 1990 | 10 | 3 | 30 |
| 2000 | 9 | 5 | 56 |
| 2010 | 1 | 1 | 1 |
| Total | 44 | 17 | 39 |

Source: Nebraska Legislature, *2018–2019 Nebraska Blue Book* (Lincoln: State of Nebraska, 2018).

The decades of the 1990s and 2000s saw a sharp increase in the use of initiatives. It should be noted that despite the increase, Nebraska makes comparatively less use of the process than many other states (National Conference 2023). In a study measuring the frequency of initiative use among states that allow it, Frederick Boehmke (2005) finds that between 1976 and 2000, the average number of initiatives per decade was thirteen. Nebraska only begins to approach this average in the 1990s, when a handful of initiatives were passed to set term limits for members of the state legislature, as well as for Nebraska's delegation to the U.S. Senate and the U.S. House of Representatives. Because states do not have the power to determine eligibility for members of Congress, these were struck down as unconstitutional (U.S. Term Limits v. Thorton. 514 U.S. 779, 1995). Other important proposals in the 1990s concerned setting limits on state spending and local property taxes and constraining the growth of state government revenue and spending. These measures limiting government's taxing and spending powers failed at the ballot box, as did a measure to relax further the required number of signatures necessary to qualify a petition to be placed on a ballot. In the end, the increased initiative activity during the 1990s had little direct impact on public policy. That would change in the next decade, when social issues came to dominate initiative politics in Nebraska.

In the first decade of the twenty-first century, nine initiatives were placed before Nebraska voters. It was a list in which hot-button social issues overshadowed the governmental housekeeping that to date had characterized most initiative politics. It was also a time in which organized interests, both inside and outside the state, made increased use of the initiative power to influence public policy in Nebraska. The rationale for this behavior stems from a basic institutional feature of government and politics in the United States: policymaking power is fragmented. While some have seen this fragmentation as an obstacle to policy change (Robertson and Judd 1989), fragmented power also creates multiple venues through which citizens and organized interests can seek beneficial policies (Baumgartner and Jones 1993). The initiative process in the states is one such venue, and organized interests view mechanisms of direct democracy as a way "to bypass state legislatures and governors and write the group's policy preferences directly into law" (Rozell 2012, 132). The 2010s witnessed a sharp decline in the initiative process as only one was brought before the voters.

The use of the initiative process to bypass the legislature was typified in 2000 by organizers of Initiative 416, which stated, "Only marriage between a man and a woman shall be valid or recognized in Nebraska. The uniting of two persons of the same sex in a civil union, domestic partnership or other similar same-sex relationship shall not be valid or recognized in Nebraska." Considered one of the most restrictive defense of marriage laws in the nation (Rizzo 2002), this measure was sponsored by a loose coalition of evangelical Christian and Mormon churches, which organized the petition drive after the legislature repeatedly considered, but failed to pass, bans on gay marriage in the late 1990s (Belluck 2000). After qualifying the initiative for the ballot, sponsors combined forces with the Nebraska Catholic Conference and Family First to create the Nebraska Coalition for the Protection of Marriage. Over its short lifespan, between its formal organization on September 28 and Election Day on November 7, 2000, the group spent about $740,000 in support of the initiative, about $500,000 of it from out-of-state contributors affiliated with the Church of Jesus Christ of Latter-day Saints (Hicks 2000). In the end, Initiative 416 passed with 70 percent of the vote, carrying every county in the state by lopsided margins.

A combination of in-state and out-of-state interests were also involved in direct democracy in 2004, when the legislature placed on the ballot legislation that would expand the forms of legalized gambling in the state, allow cities to permit the establishment of casinos, and provide for the taxation and distribution of gaming revenues between cities and the state general fund. Interestingly, the initiatives to authorize expanded gambling failed, while voters approved the tax provisions, a result that appears nonsensical. However, there may be a logic to this result, as Miewald, Longo, and Schutz explain: "A rational voter could have voted for the tax but against the authorizing provision. Such a voter would have in mind something like 'I am against expanded gaming, but if the majority is for it, I want to be sure the activity is taxed, and the revenue distributed in the manner presented on this ballot.' Similarly, those in favor of expanded gaming may not have supported the tax" (2009, 113). (In 2020, a revised initiative on legalized gambling was approved by a wide margin, where racetracks were authorized to establish casinos.)

In 2008 voters approved what backers called the Nebraska Civil Rights Initiative to guarantee "the state shall not discriminate against, or grant preferential treatment to, any individual or group on the basis of race, sex, color, ethnicity, or national origin in the operation of public employment, public education, or public contracting." This measure, Initiative 424, highlights the role of interest groups outside the state in generating an issue. In March 2007 Ward Connerly, a California businessman and vocal opponent of affirmative action, delivered an address at the conservative Heritage Foundation, where he announced the creation of a Super Tuesday effort to coordinate anti-affirmative-action petition drives in several states. As with other recent initiatives, the financing of Initiative 424 also represented a partnership between local and outside sources, with sources outside the state playing a dominant role.

While Nebraska law does not require interest groups that organize petition drives to be based in the state, LB 39, sponsored by Senator DiAnna

Schimek, adopted in 2008, requires that only Nebraska residents over the age of eighteen (eligible voters) be permitted to circulate petitions. The law further makes it illegal to pay petition circulators based on the number of signatures they collect, although it remains legal for initiative organizers to pay a salary or wages to petition circulators. Schimek's intent in proposing LB 39 was to limit the power of out-of-state interests to use Nebraskans' initiative power for their own purposes, saying: "We are trying to return the process to the people, instead of having big money from California, Texas, New York or wherever come in and take over the petition process" (Reed 2008).

Direct democracy in Nebraska has reflected a tension between in-state and out-of-state interests. On one hand, outside groups have partnered with local interests to change public policy, as in the case of the defense of marriage and civil rights initiatives. On other occasions, local citizens have pushed back against outsiders. This was certainly true in the case of Gambling with the Good Life and the new restrictions on outside petition organizing codified in LB 39. Whether Nebraskans welcome or spurn outside groups with respect to the initiative process, the power itself represents a commitment to citizen engagement and the belief that politics is the business of ordinary citizens, not the sole province of professional politicians. This reflects the state's moralistic political subculture.

## POLITICAL PARTIES

The long-standing nonpartisan structure of the state legislature suggests that Nebraska has done more than most states to weaken political parties. This certainly contributes to Nebraska's storied independence, as noted by the authors of *A Guide to the Cornhusker State*: "That Nebraskans are practical in temper—a trait growing out of their continual struggle for life—has been shown frequently by their choice of leaders regardless of caste or political label. The man and his actions are what count" (Federal Writers' Project [1939] 1979, 405). This attention to actions, rather than label, has been exemplified in two principal ways. Candidates of both major parties are regularly elected governor, and political mavericks make popular politicians.

This is not to suggest that political parties are irrelevant to electoral politics in Nebraska, arguably in a state historically dominated by Republicans. Voter registration in Nebraska is a partisan undertaking, and most Nebraskans register as Republican. When Nebraskans go to vote, however, it becomes evident their relationship to political parties is subtle and conditional. Party ties are very important when Nebraskans vote for president of the United States but less so for down-ballot offices. The fact that the GOP has not dominated Nebraska politics and government over the long term testifies further to the independent nature of most citizens.

During Nebraska's territorial history, both the Democratic and newly formed Republican parties were competitive in winning election to the territorial legislature, where majority-party control changed hands with some regularity. By the 1860s three factors contributed to the Republican Party's new dominance: (1) the preponderance of settlers in Nebraska came from northern states, in a time when the free-soil movement divided both the nation and the Democratic party (Olsen and Naugle 1997); (2) Democratic president James J. Buchanan manipulated homestead legislation, to the consternation of Nebraska's settlers (Pedersen and Wald 1973); and (3) strong support for the union (although not necessarily abolition) during the Civil War (Olsen and Naugle).

The end of the Civil War marked a change in fortunes for the Democratic Party in Nebraska: "Not until the area began filling up with Union veterans did the Democrats become a minority party in Nebraska" (Olsen and Naugle 1997, 136). Consequently, Republicans dominated the territorial legislature at the time statehood was proposed. Democrats at the local level attempted to postpone approval for statehood until the party could regain majority status in the territorial legislature. Having failed in the effort to delay statehood, territorial Democrats relied on President Andrew Johnson to veto the Nebraska bill approved in Congress. Certain in the knowledge that the territorial government, under Republican control, would send two more Republicans to the U.S. Senate, Johnson did indeed veto the bill that would have admitted Nebraska to the union. Nevertheless, the House of Representatives and Senate held successful override votes on February 9, 1867, and on March 1, Johnson relented, signing the proclamation that decreed Nebraska the thirty-seventh state.

From its first presidential election in 1868, Nebraska has distinguished itself as reliably Republican, choosing the Democratic candidate for president only five times out of thirty-five. The first deviation, in 1896, was a vote for favorite-son William Jennings Bryan, who lost that year to William McKinley. Bryan carried twenty-two states to McKinley's twenty-three, but Bryan's base of support in the less-populated southern, Great Plains, and mountain states produced a deficit of electoral votes. This loyalty to Bryan on the part of Nebraskans would not last, though. Of the three times Bryan won the Democratic Party's nomination for president (in 1896, 1900, and 1904), 1896 was the only time he earned the electoral votes from his home state. On the four other occasions Nebraska voted Democratic in presidential elections and was swept up in Democratic landslides: 1912 (Woodrow Wilson); 1932 and 1936 (Franklin D. Roosevelt); and 1964 (Lyndon B. Johnson).

The tendency to award the state's Electoral College votes to the Republican candidate persisted after the state, in 1994, began allocating its Electoral College votes according to the popular vote in each congressional district. Only twice, though, has a Democratic presidential candidate won an Electoral College vote under this method. In 2008 Barack Obama and in 2020 Joe Biden won a majority of the popular vote in Nebraska's Second Congressional District, consisting mainly of Omaha and part of suburban Sarpy County. None of these elections—the Democratic landslides of the twentieth century and the two Electoral College votes—indicate any enduring commitment on the part of Nebraskans to the national Democratic Party or its presidential candidates. Where presidential politics are concerned, Nebraska rightly can be characterized as a red state.

In addition to the state's record in presidential elections, some measure of the Nebraska's red hue comes from the Republican Party's advantage among registered voters there. The state began its system of permitting voters to register with one of the political parties (or not) in 1968, and in that time, registered Republicans have always outnumbered registered Democrats. Figure 7 depicts the trends in voter registration from 1968 through 2020. Throughout this time, the proportion of registered voters identifying as Republican has remained fairly stable, ranging from a high of 52.0 percent in 1968, to a low of 48.1 percent in 2010. Proportions of voters identifying with the Democratic Party have fallen steadily from a peak of 46.2 percent in 1976.

The Democrats' losses have not spelled gains for the Republicans, however, as Republican registration has changed very little. Departing Democrats have not gone to the Republican Party but to some third party (in a few cases) or more commonly to no party. When large numbers of voters discontinue their identification with a political party, political scientists call it a dealignment. Nebraska has produced a dealignment in miniature, with almost all the

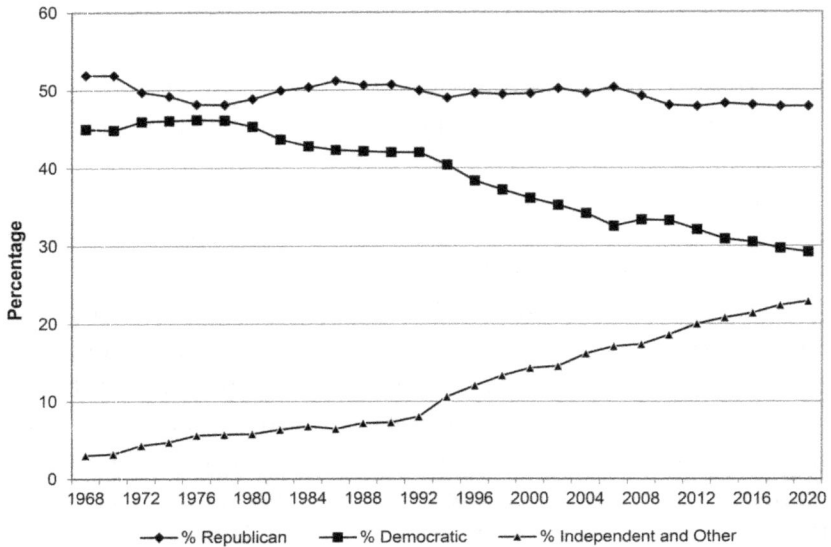

Fig. 7. Trends in voter registration, Nebraska, 1968–2020. Sources of data are the official reports of the Nebraska Board of State Canvassers. Compiled by the Nebraska secretary of state. Created by author.

dealigning coming from the Democratic Party. The increase in independent registration covaries directly with the decrease in Democratic registration. The statistical correlation (Pearson's $r$) between the two is $-.987$ ($p = .01$). Performing the same statistical test for relationships between Republican and independent registration and between Democratic and Republican registration produces a correlation not statistically different from zero, making it safe to conclude that almost all the increase in independent voter registration has come at the expense of Democratic registration.

This detachment from the Democratic Party in Nebraska fits a larger regional trend in party identification. While it is well understood that a majority of voters in southern American states changed their party loyalty from primarily Democratic to primarily Republican since 1968, less widely documented is the shift in party allegiance that took place in the mountain and Great Plains states after the 1980s. Political scientists Earl Black and Merle Black credit Ronald Reagan with inspiring "the most important shift in white partisanship since the New Deal" (2007, 38) in which "a huge Republican plurality emerged in the 1980s, and this lead continued to widen during the 1990s and early 2000s" (41). Black and Black explain that Reagan's message of conservatism—reducing the size and power of the federal government, cutting taxes, establishing a more muscular foreign policy, and taking positions on race and abortion consistent with those of social conservatives—resonated among college-educated whites, who increasingly found the national Democratic Party inconsistent with their values. The Republican Revolution of the 1990s and the presidency of George W. Bush both served to extend this piece of Reagan's political legacy. Voter registration trends in Nebraska mirror the regional pattern. The erosion in Democratic loyalty (expressed through voter registration) began in the 1980s, slid most precipitously in the mid-1990s, and continued to the 2020s level, when just about 30 percent of the state's registered voters identify themselves as Democrats.

Despite the strong preference for the Republican Party in presidential elections and voter registration, Nebraska voters historically have shown a willingness to vote for candidates from both parties. The phenomenon, known as ticket splitting, has been dissected and explained in a number of ways, but the research findings of one team of political scientists seems particularly appropriate to the Nebraska case: when ticket-splitters do identify with one of the political parties, they tend to stick with their party in voting for president and defect from their party on the down-ballot candidates (Lewis-Beck and Nadeau 2004). Nebraskans' willingness to vote for candidates of either party in down-ballot races reinforces the Federal Writers' Project's view that "the man and his actions are what count" (Federal Writers' Project [1939] 1979, 405).

Nebraskans certainly have judged their governors by their actions, rather than their party label. During the early years of statehood, Republicans were elected governor on a consistent basis, in line with the pro-union sentiments of the state's first settlers. That Republican dominance began to crack during the populist-progressive period around the turn of the twentieth century, and by the 1930s, neither party could claim ownership of the governor's office. Between 1955 and 2006, every time Nebraska voters changed governors, they also changed political parties. Not until 2007, when Republican Dave Heinemann was elected as governor, did Nebraska voters retain the same party in that office. From 1955 to 2021 Democrats have controlled the governor's office for twenty-eight years, the Republicans, forty.

Just as Nebraskans have willingly elected governors from both parties in recent decades, so has been the case with the other officers elected statewide, United States senators. Nebraska sent its first U.S. senators to the Fortieth Congress in 1867. Consistent with the partisan composition of the state government that selected them, both were Republicans. This pattern held, even though the state began holding popular preference votes for U.S. senators in 1894. For the first three cycles following 1894, the Republican candidates did not win the popular vote but were nonetheless seated by the legislature. In 1909 the state legislature mandated that the lead vote-getter in the popular preference vote be appointed to the U.S. Senate by the state legislature. Thus, even though the Seventeenth Amendment to the United States Constitution, requiring direct, popular election of U.S. senators, went into effect in 1914, 1910 serves as the starting date for popular election of senators from Nebraska.

From 1867 until 1906, when the legislature chose senators, all save one (Populist William V. Allen) were Republican. Once the voters began choosing senators in 1910, Nebraskans began to see meaningful party competition. In fact, of the individuals elected to the Senate since 1910, seven have been Democrats, while eleven have been Republicans. The fact that over the past hundred years the Republican Party has dominated neither Senate nor gubernatorial elections supports the view of Olsen and Naugle that "Nebraska voters have never slavishly followed party lines" (1997, 314). However, in the twenty-first century, it is possible that the accuracy of that statement may be challenged.

Further evidence that Nebraska voters are more attracted to individuals than to party regulars is their willingness to embrace maverick politicians. Conventional wisdom defines a maverick as "one who is unorthodox in his political views and disdainful of party loyalty" (Safire 2008, 417). Certainly, not all of Nebraska's prominent elected officials have been mavericks, but the state's political history has been littered with enough maverick politicians to suggest that acting against the positions or interests of one's party is, if not admirable, at least not damning enough to merit removal from office.

The figurative grandfather of all Nebraska mavericks must be Senator George W. Norris, whom John F. Kennedy called "one of the most courageous figures in American political life" ([1956] 2000, 173). Over his forty-year career representing Nebraska, first in the U.S. House of Representatives for ten years then in the U.S. Senate for another thirty years, Norris cultivated a history of placing principle ahead of loyalty to the Republican Party. An early, and institutionally significant, example of Norris's maverick behavior came in his leadership of the revolt against House speaker Joseph G. Cannon in 1910.

Elected speaker of the House in 1903, Cannon, a Republican from Illinois, used his authority to monopolize control over the House's agenda and the policymaking authority of all its committees. On March 17, 1910, Norris took a leading part in the revolt against Cannon's rule, introducing a resolution to change the rules by which the House of Representatives operated. After twenty-six hours of round-the-clock debate, followed by a day of recess, the House approved an amended version of Norris's proposal, 193–153, with forty-three insurgent Republicans joining the Democratic minority (Jones 1968).

Norris repeatedly exemplified his own belief that "the man and his actions are what count" (Federal Writers' Project [1939] 1979, 405). Throughout his political career, Norris advocated on behalf of rural economic development, especially as regarded the provision of electric power to farms and agricultural communities. Norris's pursuit of rural electrification led him to endorse the Democratic presidential candidate for president, Al Smith, over Republican Herbert Hoover, in 1928. Writing in his memoir, Norris explained: "In the personal sense, I had not known Governor Smith. There had been only the most casual contact between us. But I had followed with special interest his position on the development of waterpower in New York State while he was governor. I had been attracted to him by his liberal and farsighted position on that issue" (1972, 287).

Although Norris's defiance of party loyalty infuriated Republican Party regulars in the state, it did not keep him from later endorsing Democrat Franklin Roosevelt for president in 1932 and 1936 nor from being elected to the Senate again in 1930 and yet again in 1936. Both parties, in Norris's mind, were equally corrupt. Instead of retiring in 1936, however, Norris acquiesced to a petition drive, ran, and won as an independent candidate. In a show of reciprocity, President Franklin D. Roosevelt campaigned in Nebraska on Norris's behalf. Both men carried the state on Election Day, but it would be the last time for each.

George W. Norris's experience exemplifies the view that political parties are not particularly necessary to a long and distinguished career in public service, and that Nebraska voters value independence in their elected leaders. The maverick spirit that moved George W. Norris has hardly been unique among Nebraska politicians. Senators Chuck Hagel and Ben Sasse provide additional examples of a well-respected Nebraska politician who regularly put principle ahead of party.

Hagel represented Nebraska as a Republican in the U.S. Senate from 1997 to 2008. In that time, he developed a reputation among senators and reporters as a straight shooter who supported his party when the GOP position matched his ideals and showed little hesitation in disagreeing with his partisan colleagues when he thought the party was deviating from its own conservative principles. In his farewell address to the Senate in 2008, Hagel summed up his independent stance: "[While serving in the Senate] I have also learned this lesson: Bipartisan consensus is the only way a democracy will work. No party has a corner on all the virtues, nor all the answers" (U.S. Congress 2010, xi).

As a senator, Hagel found ample reason to part with the Republican Party and, by 2001, with its leader, President George W. Bush, on two of the Bush administration's signature domestic issues. Hagel opposed the president and the party, on the grounds that the social policies they pursued were steering the GOP away from its conservative roots. One such example was the No Child Left Behind (NCLB) law, which reauthorized and increased federal aid to public schools, attaching the conditions that schools use annual, standardized testing to measure student progress in reading and math. He was one of only three Senate Republicans to vote against the bill on final passage.

In addition to opposing NCLB, Hagel voted against the Medicare Prescription Drug, Improvement and Modernization Act (MMA, popularly known as Medicare Part D), enacted in 2003. This bill was also a priority of the Bush administration, as the president sought to introduce new market competition into Medicare and create a new entitlement program for seniors. Hagel was one of nine Republicans in the Senate to break with the president and the congressional majority and vote against the act.

None of Hagel's departures from the Bush administration were as public, and controversial, as the senator's deepening disenchantment with the administration's handling of the war in Iraq. It was not that Hagel doubted the threat that Iraqi dictator Saddam Hussein posed, but he urged, and even expected, the Bush administration to pursue a multilateral approach to confronting Hussein.

As the war ground on with no end in sight, Hagel began to express publicly his disappointment with the administration's handling of the war. In a Senate Foreign Relations Committee hearing at which Secretary of State Condoleezza Rice sought support for the troop surge, Hagel laid down his marker: "I have to say, Madam Secretary, that I think this speech given last night by this president represents the most dangerous foreign-policy blunder in this country since Vietnam. If it's carried out, I will resist it" (Pierce 2007, 143).

Since leaving the Senate in 2009, Hagel continued to write and speak on international affairs from a nonpartisan perspective. From 2013 to 2015 he served as the secretary of defense for President Obama, a Democrat.

Republican senator Ben Sasse, like Chuck Hagel, demonstrated the periodic independent nature of Nebraska's "renegade" politicians. He was first elected in 2014 and reelected by a wide margin in 2020. During the tumultuous presidency of Donald Trump, Sasse was an early and especially vocal critic of the president. While he was among the most consistent supporters of Republican policies, he was still willing to vigorously criticize the president for his actions on many occasions. Following the January 6, 2021, storming of the U.S. Capitol by Trump supporters during the counting of the electoral votes by a joint session of Congress, he supported the removal of Trump from office. Senator Sasse was among the few Republicans who voted unsuccessfully to convict the president at the second impeachment trial in 2021.

Hagel's and Sasse's resistance to policies and actions with which they disagreed often placed them at odds with the Republican Party. But their willingness to break ranks on high-profile, profoundly important issues places Hagel and Sasse among the likes of George W. Norris in Nebraska's political development. The senators demonstrated the limits of party loyalty in the state. Although they lived, worked, and dissented one hundred years apart in time, Norris, Hagel, and Sasse demonstrate the ongoing value of independence that lies at the heart of politics in Nebraska. Ben Nelson, a former governor and U.S. senator, a Democrat, also did not strictly follow party lines. At the state level, Earnie Chambers, the longest lasting state senator, best exemplifies the often "renegade" and fiercely nonpartisan nature of Nebraska politicians.

## CONCLUSION

The story of electoral behavior in Nebraska politics reflects the competing strands of thought that have run through the state's political culture from its beginning. Without doubt, Nebraskans value the individualism and independence articulated by William Jennings Bryan. This ethos manifests on several fronts in the state's political landscape, from its rejection of blind partisan loyalty to its expressed desire to minimize the influence of outsiders, be they governments or organized interests. But Nebraskans also have been known to set aside their devotion to individualism and act collectively, using their commitment to widespread political participation in pursuit of the public good. This strand is evident in the state's comparatively high levels of voter turnout and use of direct democracy to shape public policy. It would be understandable to label these contrasts as symptoms of a quirkiness in the state's politics, but both harken back to the progressive-populist tradition: the people are in charge, and they willingly bear the responsibility to govern themselves. As the twenty-first century unfolds, with its emphasis on strong partisan divisions, the ability of Nebraskans to hold onto their nonpartisan values is yet to be seen.

### REFERENCES

Baumgartner, Frank R., and Bryan D. Jones. 1993. *Agendas and Instability in American Politics*. Chicago: University of Chicago Press.

Belluck, Pam. 2000. "Nebraskans to Vote on Most Sweeping Ban on Gay Unions." *New York Times*, October 21, 2000.

Berch, Neil. 1993. "Another Look at Closeness and Turnout: The Case of the 1979 and 1980 Canadian National Elections." *Political Research Quarterly* 46 (2): 421–32.

Black, Earl, and Merle Black. 2007. *Divided America: The Ferocious Power Struggle in American Politics*. New York: Simon and Schuster.

Boehmke, Frederick J. 2005. "Sources of Variation in the Frequency of Statewide Initiatives: The Role of Interest Group Populations." *Political Research Quarterly* 58 (4): 576–75.

Center for American Progress. n.d. *Common Good Progressivism*. Washington DC: Center for American Progress.

Elazar, Daniel J. 1966. *American Federalism: A View from the States*. New York: Thomas Y. Crowell.

Federal Writers' Project. (1939) 1979. *Nebraska: A Guide to the Cornhusker State.* Lincoln: University of Nebraska Press.

Hicks, Nancy. 2000. "416 Foes May Not Get Refund in Time." *Lincoln Journal-Star,* October 31, 2000.

Jones, Charles O. 1968. "Joseph G. Cannon and Howard W. Smith: An Essay on the Limits of Leadership in the House of Representatives." *Journal of Politics* 3 (August): 617–46.

Kennedy, John F. (1956) 2000. *Profiles in Courage.* New York: HarperCollins.

Lewis-Beck, Michael, and Richard Nadeau. 2004. "Split-Ticket Voting: The Effects of Cognitive Madisonianism." *Journal of Politics* 66 (1): 97–112.

Merrifield, John. 1993. "The Institutional and Political Factors that Influence Voter Turnout." *Public Choice* 77 (3): 657–67.

Miewald, Robert D., Peter J. Longo, and Anthony B. Schutz. 2009. *The Nebraska State Constitution: A Reference Guide.* 2nd ed. Lincoln: University of Nebraska Press.

National Conference of State Legislatures. 2023. Statewide Ballot Measures Database. https://www.ncsl.org/elections-and-campaigns/statewide-ballot-measures-database.

Nebraska State Legislature. 2015. "The Lines of Government: A Guide to Nebraska State Government Election Boundaries." https://www.nebraskalegislature.gov/pdf/about/linesofgovt.pdf.

Norris, George W. 1972. *Fighting Liberal: The Autobiography of George W. Norris.* Lincoln: Bison Books.

Olsen, James, and Ronald C. Naugle. 1997. *History of Nebraska.* 3rd ed. Lincoln: University of Nebraska Press.

Pedersen, James F., and Kenneth D. Wald. 1973. *Shall the People Rule? A History of the Democratic Party in Nebraska Politics 1854–1972.* Lincoln: Jacob North.

Pierce, Charles P. 2007. "Before This Is Over, You Might See Calls for His Impeachment." *Esquire,* March. https://www.esquire.com/news-politics/politics/a2568/chuckhagel0407/.

Reed, Leslie. 2008. "Governor Vetoes Petition Bill." *Omaha World-Herald,* February 13, 2008.

Rizzo, Christopher. 2002. "Banning State Recognition of Same-Sex Relationships: Constitutional Implications of Nebraska's Initiative 416." *Journal of Law and Policy* 11 (1): 1–66.

Robertson, David B., and Dennis R. Judd. 1989. *The Development of American Public Policy: The Structure of Policy Restraint.* Boston: Scott, Foresman.

Rozell, Mark J., Clyde Wilcox, and Michael W. Franz. 2012. *Interest Groups in American Campaigns: The New Face of Electioneering.* 3rd ed. New York: Oxford University Press.

Safire, William. 2008. *Safire's Political Dictionary*. New York: Oxford University Press.
Smith, Kevin B., ed. 2019. *State and Local Government: 2018–2019 Edition*. Washington DC: CQ Press.
U.S. Congress. 2010. *Chuck Hagel, U.S. Senator from Nebraska, Tributes in the Congress of the United States*. Washington DC: U.S. Government Printing Office.

## PART 2

# Government and Administration

# CHAPTER FIVE

# The Nebraska State Budget

## PROCESS, POLITICS, PRIORITIES

*James Harrold and Carol Ebdon*

### INTRODUCTION

A budget is a plan that establishes government priorities and determines how public services will be financed. Nebraska provides a wide variety of programs and services, such as building and maintaining highways, housing prisoners, providing public assistance and health programs for low-income individuals, child protection, parks, and education. There are continual demands from stakeholders for new or expanded services, yet the public does not like to pay the taxes that fund most of these services. This leads to significant conflicts and the need for elected officials to balance many competing interests as they develop the budget. This important process is completed in an open and transparent manner, with the opportunity for citizens and special interest groups to express their preferences and needs.

### THE BUDGET AND THE LEGISLATURE

The most unique aspect of budgeting in Nebraska is the one-house (unicameral) legislature, an important dimension of the state's political culture. For instance, the budget does not have to be approved by two different chambers, which in some ways makes the process simpler than in other states (Koven and Mausolff 2002). In addition, due to the use of nonpartisan elections, another dimension of Nebraska's political culture, party discipline generally is not available as a tool to win budget votes. Each of the forty-nine senators, then, is important, and they each have different agendas. Leadership is key to budget adoption. As Gerald Olgimueller, budget director for the State of Nebraska, explains, "The chair of the Appropriations Committee must discuss budget priorities with other members outside the committee, trying to build a budget that reflects priorities of the whole legislature, not just the committee. The speaker plays a big role in making sure the process is understandable, and in scheduling enough time to deal with budget issues and realizing the impacts on other committees" (Gerald Oligmueller, interview by authors, July 14, 2014).

There are several contextual factors in Nebraska, because of its political culture, that distinguish it from other states. The unicameral legislature, in operation since 1937, is the most unique aspect of Nebraska government and political culture (Olson and Naugle 2015). The number of senators has been set at forty-nine since 1965, and they are elected on a nonpartisan basis (Nebraska Legislature 2012). The notion of a unicameral legislature was championed during the Progressive Era by Nebraska's nationally renowned U.S. senator George W. Norris and was seen as a way to improve legislative efficiency (Nebraska Legislature 2012). Where all other states must receive approval from two legislative chambers to adopt a budget, Nebraska has only one, but with forty-nine individual and independent senators who are not elected as members of a political party (Bowman and Kearney 2015). (See chapter 6 for more information on the operation of Nebraska's legislature.)

The state's size and population patterns also present budgetary challenges. With a large land area of 76,824 square miles and a population of nearly two million, the state ranks as the sixth least dense state, with approximately twenty-five persons per square mile (U.S. Census Bureau 2022). However, the population is concentrated in its large cities. About 65 percent live in the four metropolitan areas, with approximately 56 percent of the total population located in the three counties surrounding Omaha and Lincoln (U.S. Census Bureau 2022). Urban interests are therefore an important consideration in budget decisions, but since agriculture plays a crucial role in the state economy, representation of rural interests is also vital. In addition, providing necessary services to a small population spread across a large land area can be costly. For example, many highway lane miles are required because of the size, but with only a small number of people paying for them.

Finally, voters approved a constitutional amendment in 2000 that established a limit of two consecutive four-year terms for state legislators. Senators may be elected again after four years of being out of office (Article III, Section 12). Term limits were enacted in twenty-one states between 1990 and 2000, although later repealed in six of these (Mooney 2009). Initial national studies have found that term limits increase the influence of the governor relative to the legislature and decrease the influence of party leaders and committee chairs. In addition, term-limited legislators have been found to support statewide interests over those of their districts more than in states without term limits (Carey et al. 2006). Term limits might, then, influence budget decisions over time.

The next section provides an overview of the state budget process. Trends in revenue sources and spending priorities are then highlighted, followed by a summary of budget appropriations by type. Major challenges will be discussed in the concluding section.

BUDGET PREPARATION AND ADOPTION

Nebraska follows a standard executive budget process in which the governor submits a proposed budget to the legislature for review and adoption. The state's fiscal year is July 1 to June 30, as is the case for most other states. "As early as 1914, a joint committee of the Nebraska Senate and House recommended 'the adoption of a scientific budget system for state expenditures' with an executive centered process. This was a common reform recommendation of the Progressive Era. Since that time, the state budget process has evolved into a system initiated at the executive level but strongly influenced by legislative decision-making" (Bartle 2013).

Nebraska is one of seventeen states using a biennial, rather than an annual, budget cycle (NASBO 2022a). The budget for the next two years is adopted in the odd-numbered years. The former, long-time state budget director likes the longer-term planning opportunities of biennial budgeting (Oligmueller interview), and the legislature's former Appropriations Committee chair and state senator Heath Mello notes that it allows legislators to "dig in a little deeper to evaluate existing appropriations and be more thoughtful about new appropriations, with fewer knee-jerk reactions" (Heath Mello, interview by authors, January 9, 2014). Research studies have not found

**Fig. 8.** Nebraska biennial budget process timeline. Source: OpenSky Policy Institute, *Looking for Clarity: An Overview of Nebraska Budget and Tax Policy* (Lincoln: OpenSky Policy Institute, March 2013), 8.

conclusive empirical evidence, though, of differences in outcomes in states with biennial budgeting (Snell 2011).

Figure 8 summarizes the budget process phases and timing. The executive budget preparation is primarily done in the second half of the even-numbered years, while the legislative review and adoption occurs in the first half of the odd-numbered years. Budget decisions are driven to a great extent by estimates of the amount of revenue available to be appropriated. Because of its key role, a discussion of the revenue forecasting process follows.

## Revenue Forecasting

If income is insufficient to meet spending needs, spending must be reduced and/or taxes or other revenues must be increased. Citizens value state services but want to pay as little as possible for them, so these choices are difficult.

For this reason, the estimates of the amount of revenue that will be available for the budget are extremely important.

Nebraska's general fund revenue forecasts are determined by the nine-member Nebraska Economic Forecasting Advisory Board (NEFAB), which was created in 1984. Terms are four years, and appointments are split between the governor (four members) and the legislature (five members). Board members must possess "demonstrated expertise in the field of tax policy, economics, or economic forecasting" (Neb. Rev. Statutes, chap. 77 § 27,196.01). NEFAB meets every February and October and in April in odd-numbered years (when the budget is adopted).

NEFAB develops a consensus forecast. The Legislative Fiscal Office (LFO) and the Department of Revenue (an executive branch agency) each present econometric forecasts to the board, based on time series data and information from economic firms. Board members then discuss the economic climate and trends in their communities before making their decisions. Each member submits a written forecast, and a motion is made, typically for an amount close to the average. One board member, Jerome Deichert, stated that "about 90 percent of the time, that motion is approved, although sometimes we may need another round of discussion and voting" (Jerome Deichert, interview by authors, October 3, 2022).

In many states, revenue forecasts are highly political, with disagreements between branches and political parties and attempts to use the forecast for budget strategies to either increase or decrease spending (Mikesell 2007). These arguments do not occur in Nebraska because of the use of the independent board. Interestingly, although the NEFAB forecasts are advisory only, their numbers have always been used in the budget, without argument by either branch.

The NEFAB board has by all appearances not been politicized. The board is typically balanced between members from different geographic areas, and the current chair has been appointed by five governors of different parties. Board members try to develop the most accurate forecast possible with limited knowledge of the future economy: "It's not to anyone's advantage to try to manipulate the forecast. The board recognizes that our job is to come up with the best estimate of receipts without regard to what that will mean to increasing or decreasing taxes or spending" (Deichert interview).

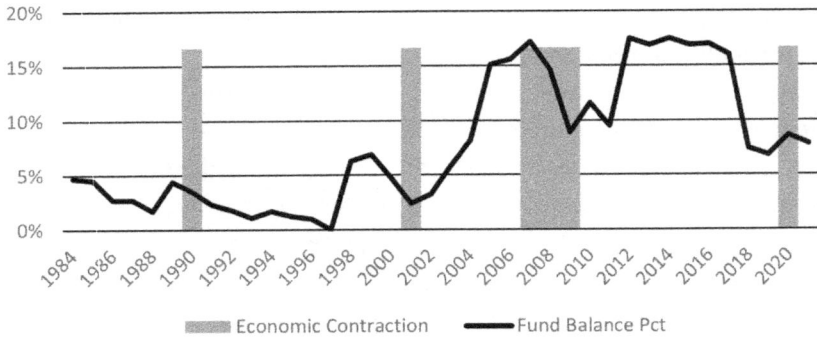

Fig. 9. Nebraska cash reserve fund balance as a percentage of revenue versus recession period, 1983–2021. Sources: Nebraska Biennial Budget (2022 Session) and U.S. National Bureau of Economic Research. Created by author.

One study found that actual tax revenue between 1988 and 2008 exceeded the board forecast by 3.74 percent, a good track record (Dearmont 2007).

## Cash Reserve Fund

Part of the reason the politics is mitigated in the forecasting process may relate to the state's rainy-day fund policies. The cash reserve fund was established in fiscal year 1983 to cover fluctuations in the balance between revenues and expenditures. By 2021 all fifty states had established some form of budget stabilization fund (rainy-day fund) (NASB 2022b), with variations in specific rules (Urban Institute 2020). In Nebraska the revenue forecast is certified at the last NEFAB meeting before the budget is adopted. If actual general fund receipts are greater than the forecast, the excess funds are transferred to the cash reserve fund. If revenues are lower than forecasted, the difference is made up from the cash reserve fund. This fund is used as a balancing mechanism for the general fund budget, which reduces pressure to manipulate revenue forecasts. The legislature has used the fund over time to resolve temporary budget shortfalls and to fund special initiatives, such as capital construction projects (Nebraska DAS 2013).

Nebraska's cash reserve fund ranks as one of the healthiest rainy-day funds across the states. According to the National Association of State Budget

Officers, Nebraska has historically maintained a balance of nearly 10 percent of general fund expenditures and is one of only five states that do so (NASBO 2022b). Figure 9 shows the fund growth and utilization. Balances have declined following economic recessions, when the fund was used to balance the budget without having to cut spending or increase taxes to the extent required in other states. During periods of economic expansion and strong state revenue growth, the fund balances have increased.

## Budget Preparation

The executive branch develops the proposed budget. Budget preparation begins one year prior to the beginning of the biennium (in July of even-numbered years). The state budget administrator works with the governor to develop instructions for state agencies to use in developing their requests. The instructions are based on the NEFAB revenue forecast, estimated expenditures, and any relevant changes adopted during the previous legislative session. Agencies submit their requests to the Budget Division by September 15. These requests are also released to the Legislative Fiscal Office and are publicly available (Oligmueller 2012).

One challenge of biennial budgeting is the difficulty of predicting what will happen three years in the future. For example, in July 2018 the state began work on the biennial budget for the period ending June 30, 2021. At that point, the upcoming pandemic that had a dramatic effect on the economy (and therefore on the state budget) beginning in spring 2020 was completely unanticipated. Unpredictable policy changes at the federal level also can have major impacts on the state budget.

The budget administrator and budget staff work with the governor and the agencies to refine and develop a balanced budget proposal. The budget provides the opportunity for the governor to focus on his or her priorities. Although these priorities change over time, there have been consistent values. According to the former budget administrator, "In Nebraska, we have significant discipline with fiscal policy and are very conservative, so each governor tends to be similar in that respect" (Oligmueller interview). While the legislature can make changes to the recommended budget, the executive establishes the framework. "To the extent that the governor is articulate about their policy and programmatic priorities, the legislature often finds itself explaining why it is not adopting the appropriation recommended by the governor. The governor can use the bully pulpit to communicate effectively with the public" (Oligmueller interview).

While agencies are expected to propose budgets that are in line with the governor's preferences, this may not always be the case. Nebraska has a considerable number of independent boards and commissions (for example, the elected State Board of Education oversees K-12 education). Budget requests from these entities may reflect the perspective of the board members rather than those of the governor (Oligmueller interview). It is then left to the legislature to resolve differences between the governor and these agencies.

The former budget administrator served in this position for more than twenty years. He noted that budget preparation has been consistent over time, but the use and availability of technology has seen significant change:

Technology is having a huge impact on both fiscal and programmatic policy processes. This is positive in that technology can enhance productivity in analysis, discussion, and decisions. The state has had about the same number of people working on the budget for 20–30 years, but the amount and accessibility of data has improved dramatically in assisting with the increasing complexity of government and the budget. There is an incredible amount of information that is readily available. However, information is not always well understood. So, a lot of rapid communication takes place—some accurate, some not as accurate. And every question must be responded to. (Oligmueller interview)

The governor submits the budget to the legislature by January 15 of the odd-numbered year. When there is a newly elected governor, the date is February 1. As is the case in forty-two other states, the governor must submit, and the legislature must approve, a balanced budget (National Conference of State Legislatures 2019). According to state statute, the submitted budget must include agency budgets as well as proposed revenue sources and tax expenditures (Neb. Rev. Statutes, chap. 81 § 125).

## Legislative Adoption

The LFO serves as the legislature's budget staff. Its work begins prior to submission of the governor's proposal when the office requests budgets from all agencies. This allows the legislative staff time to review the requests and prepare briefing documents while the governor is preparing his or her proposal. The LFO publishes a summary of each agency's submission that is used in reviewing the governor's proposed budget (Nebraska Legislative Fiscal Office 2014).

The governor's budget is introduced by the speaker of the legislature and typically referred to the Appropriations Committee. Supporting bills are referred to the standing committee with jurisdiction over that subject matter. Other bills introduced by legislators may also affect the budget. The LFO prepares a fiscal note for each bill with budgetary implications, which summarizes the estimated financial effect.

The committee's nine members, working with the LFO, develop their own spending recommendation within thirty days of the governor's submission (Nebraska Legislative Fiscal Office 2014) and file a report to the legislature in February. This report serves as the basis for the public hearings on the budget. The Revenue Committee concurrently considers bills that may affect available revenues (e.g., changes in tax bases or tax rates). Meeting together, these two committees then discuss the effects of long-term revenue projections on potential revenues and spending.

The Appropriations Committee holds budget hearings to consider each agency's budget and additional relevant bills. Hearings are open to the public, and anyone can speak. According to a former committee chair, hearings influence budget decisions: "There is a propensity for new information at hearings—from agencies and from the public at large and interest groups. They provide alternative perspectives, with data-driven analysis and suggestions" (Mello interview). While the committee plays a lead role, the budget must be passed by a majority of the legislature, so extensive informal communications take place. "Legislators may be at loggerheads; we try to find compromise between them to build consensus as a committee to get the legislature to support the Appropriations Committee budget" (Mello interview).

By law, this part of the process must be completed, and all additional budget bills submitted to the legislature by the seventieth day of the ninety-day session. Otherwise, the numbers contained in the governor's budget are introduced as bills. The state constitution requires at least three budget bills: for legislator salaries, for constitutional officers' salaries (e.g., other elected officials and judges), and all other spending. In practice, the latter is typically split into at least three bills: state operations and state aid, capital construction projects, and deficit appropriations (adjustments to the current year's budget). Other bills may be included for specific items, such as salary increases or implementation of a new program and fees.

Budget bills, like other bills, must go into the general file and be introduced on the floor. For budget bills, twenty-five votes (of forty-nine) must be obtained to introduce amendments. Bills then move to the select file and are subject to more debate and amendment, after which they receive a final reading and require a majority vote for approval. However, an emergency clause is required if a law is to take effect within ninety days after passage, and this needs a two-thirds (or thirty-three of forty-nine) majority for passage. Since appropriations bills are adopted in May and the fiscal year begins on July 1, the emergency clause is common for budget bills.

The adopted appropriations bills are forwarded to the governor, who has five days to either approve all bills as adopted, not sign (in which case the bill takes effect), veto one or more bills, or issue line-item vetoes (veto of individual elements of funding bills). Governors in most states have line-item veto power, with variations in specific rules (National Association of State Budget Officers n.d.). In Nebraska, a governor using a line-item veto has an option to decrease, but not increase, the appropriation amount (Nebraska Legislature 2013). The use of vetoes has changed over time. According to the former state budget administrator, a couple of decades ago, "the governor had to veto regularly in order to ensure that the final package of bills at the end of the legislative session comported with the resources available" (Oligmueller interview). More recently, the legislature has worked to better size their enacted appropriations and other bills with fiscal consequences to match the revenue forecasts. This has reduced the number of budget vetoes (Oligmueller interview).

The Appropriations Committee has only one day to recommend to the full legislature whether to override part or all of any vetoes. Veto overrides require thirty of forty-nine votes for passage. According to a past committee chair, "Overriding vetoes is hit or miss—over the last three years, the legislature has usually chosen not to override vetoes" (Mello interview). (Chapter 10 includes information on the history of overrides by the legislature.)

This section provided a summary of the budget process used in Nebraska and the role of the executive and legislative branches. The next section provides an overview of the Nebraska state budget for the 2020–21 biennium.

While revenue and spending will vary from year to year, at the same time, there is a great deal of overall consistency in the state's revenue and spending patterns and trends.

### REVENUE AND EXPENDITURE TRENDS

We look first at where the money comes from and where it goes for the state government overall. Data provided by the state to the U.S. Census Bureau (n.d.) are shown for three sample years over the period from 2007 to 2017 for general revenues and expenditures. This source uses consistent categories over time and allows comparisons between states. General revenues and expenditures include everything except for insurance trust funds (unemployment compensation, pension systems, and workers' compensation) (U.S. Census Bureau n.d.).

Table 4 includes general revenues by source. Total revenues grew from $9.8 billion in 2007 to $12.2 billion in 2017, an increase of 24 percent. Inflation during this same period grew at a rate of approximately 18 percent (U.S. Bureau of Labor Statistics n.d.). Taxes in total are the largest source, and the mix of sales, income, and other taxes has remained fairly constant at around 43 percent. Sales taxes and income taxes are the major workhorses of taxation, at around 20 percent of total revenue for each. The final major category of revenue is intergovernmental revenue, averaging around 27 percent of all general revenue. Most intergovernmental revenue is federal in source. (Chapter 9 on tax and fiscal policy provides further details regarding tax revenues.)

The other major revenue source is intergovernmental revenue, mostly from the federal government, which increased from 20 percent of total state revenue in 2007 to 25 percent in 2013 (U.S. Census Bureau 2017). These revenues include purposes typically expended by the state Department of Health and Human Services (HHS), primarily Medicaid, as well as education and highways. The other two revenue sources are current charges (10 percent of the total in 2013), which include direct fees for state services (e.g., park entrance fees) and other miscellaneous sources, and all other miscellaneous revenues, which constituted 9 percent of the total in 2013.

Table 5 shows selected general expenditures by function over the same time period. Expenditures increased from $7.8 billion in 2007 to $10.9 billion in 2017, an increase of 40 percent. The largest category is social services and income maintenance, at 59 percent of all expenditures in 2007 and 54

### Table 4. General revenue, Nebraska, 2007, 2012, 2017

| SOURCE | AMOUNT ($MIL) | PERCENT OF TOTAL GENERAL | AMOUNT CHANGE FROM 2007 ($MIL) | PERCENT CHANGE FROM 2007 |
|---|---|---|---|---|
| *2007* | | | | |
| Sales taxes | 2,004 | 20 | — | — |
| Income taxes | 1,864 | 19 | — | — |
| Other taxes* | 255 | 3 | — | — |
| Total taxes | 4,122 | 42 | — | — |
| Miscellaneous* | 3,138 | 32 | — | — |
| Intergovernmental | 2,533 | 26 | — | — |
| Total general | 9,793 | 100 | — | — |
| *2012* | | | | |
| Sales taxes | 2,094 | 21 | 90 | 5 |
| Income taxes | 2,073 | 21 | 209 | 11 |
| Other taxes* | 200 | 2 | (55) | (22) |
| Total taxes | 4,367 | 44 | 245 | 6 |
| Miscellaneous* | 2,309 | 24 | (829) | (26) |
| Intergovernmental | 3,148 | 32 | 615 | (24) |
| Total general | 9,824 | 100 | 31 | 0 |

percent in 2017. This category includes HHS activities such as welfare, hospitals, and health. The second largest category is education services, which made up 18 percent of the total in 2007 and increased to 20 percent by 2017. The third largest substantive function is transportation at around 12 percent to 13 percent during this period. Highways are the major transportation subcategory at about 60 percent of transportation funding.

Other functions are substantially smaller than these three areas and their shares have remained relatively consistent. Public safety, including

| SOURCE | AMOUNT ($MIL) | PERCENT OF TOTAL GENERAL | AMOUNT CHANGE FROM 2007 ($MIL) | PERCENT CHANGE FROM 2007 |
|---|---|---|---|---|
| *2017* | | | | |
| Sales taxes | 2,408 | 20 | 404 | 20 |
| Income taxes | 2,493 | 20 | 629 | 34 |
| Other taxes* | 203 | 2 | (52) | (21) |
| Total taxes | 5,103 | 42 | 981 | 24 |
| Miscellaneous* | 3,891 | 32 | 753 | 24 |
| Intergovernmental | 3,180 | 26 | 647 | 26 |
| Total general | 12,174 | 100 | 6,107 | 24 |

* Other taxes includes motor vehicle license taxes. Miscellaneous includes charges and miscellaneous general revenue.
Source: U.S. Census Bureau, government finance statistics. Compiled and calculated by author.

expenditures on police, fire, and corrections, was around 4.5 percent of all expenditures. Corrections is the major expenditure in this category. The category of environment and housing hovered around 2.5 percent to 3 percent. Finally, government administration also stayed around 3.5 percent of total expenditures.

How does spending in Nebraska compare with other states? A common method for comparison is to use expenditures per capita. Table 6 shows per capita spending by function for Nebraska and the United States during the same reference period cited above. Total general expenditures in Nebraska, not including intergovernmental expenditures, were $3,362 in 2007 and $4,289 in 2017, lower than the national average of $3,892 in 2007 and $5,355 in 2017. Spending patterns across functions are similar, except for social services and income maintenance. The national average for this category was nearly the same as Nebraska's in 2007; however, the per capita average in the United States was $4,178 in 2017, about 22 percent higher than Nebraska's $3,038. This is about 26 percent higher. Nebraska spends comparatively less

**Table 5. General expenditures by function, Nebraska and United States, 2007, 2012, 2017**

| TYPE OF EXPENDITURE | AMOUNT ($MIL) | | |
|---|---|---|---|
| | 2007 | 2012 | 2017 |
| *United States* | | | |
| Total | 1,637,964 | 2,005,873 | 2,316,037 |
| Intergovernmental | 459,742 | 502,239 | 549,867 |
| Total direct* | 1,178,222 | 1,503,633 | 1,766,170 |
| Education services | 213,527 | 272,983 | 314,551 |
| Social services* | 766,902 | 988,951 | 1,377,971 |
| Transportation | 153,143 | 165,373 | 188,193 |
|   Highways | 88,630 | 96,638 | 108,987 |
| Public safety | 66,017 | 69,123 | 74,079 |
|   Police protection | 11,387 | 12,925 | 14,952 |
|   Corrections | 44,008 | 45,612 | 49,278 |
| Environment and housing | 43,438 | 39,699 | 42,205 |
| Administration | 91,032 | 101,813 | 106,319 |
| *Nebraska* | | | |
| Total | 7,835 | 9,457 | 10,971 |
| Intergovernmental | 1,794 | 2,357 | 2,549 |
| Total direct* | 6,041 | 7,100 | 8,422 |
| Education services | 1,413 | 1,765 | 2,204 |
| Social services* | 4,618 | 4,726 | 5,965 |
| Transportation | 1,022 | 1,096 | 1,331 |
|   Highways | 558 | 680 | 809 |
| Public safety | 341 | 374 | 498 |

| | AMOUNT ($MIL) | | |
|---|---|---|---|
| TYPE OF EXPENDITURE | 2007 | 2012 | 2017 |
| *Nebraska* | | | |
| Police protection | 63 | 79 | 83 |
| Corrections | 213 | 249 | 370 |
| Environment and housing | 231 | 288 | 267 |
| Administration | 279 | 373 | 373 |

* Total direct are total direct expenditures for selected functions. Social services includes income maintenance.

Note: Numbers do not add due to rounding.

Source: U.S. Census Bureau, government finance statistics. Compiled by author.

**Table 6. General expenditures per capita, Nebraska and United States, 2007, 2012, 2017**

| | AMOUNT ($) | | |
|---|---|---|---|
| TYPE OF EXPENDITURE | 2007 | 2012 | 2017 |
| *United States* | | | |
| Total | 5,410 | 6,335 | 7,023 |
| Intergovernmental | 1,519 | 1,586 | 1,667 |
| Total direct* | 3,892 | 4,749 | 5,355 |
| Education services | 705 | 862 | 954 |
| Social services* | 2,533 | 3,123 | 4,178 |
| Transportation | 506 | 522 | 571 |
| Highways | 293 | 305 | 330 |
| Public safety | 218 | 218 | 225 |
| Police protection | 38 | 41 | 45 |

**Table 6. Continued**

| | AMOUNT ($) | | |
|---|---|---|---|
| TYPE OF EXPENDITURE | 2007 | 2012 | 2017 |
| *United States* | | | |
| Corrections | 145 | 144 | 149 |
| Environment and housing | 144 | 125 | 128 |
| Administration | 301 | 322 | 322 |
| *Nebraska* | | | |
| Total | 4,361 | 4,936 | 5,587 |
| Intergovernmental | 998 | 1,230 | 1,298 |
| Total direct* | 3,362 | 3,706 | 4,289 |
| Education services | 789 | 921 | 1,122 |
| Social services* | 2,570 | 2,467 | 3,038 |
| Transportation | 569 | 572 | 678 |
| Highways | 310 | 355 | 412 |
| Public safety | 190 | 195 | 254 |
| Police protection | 35 | 41 | 42 |
| Corrections | 118 | 129 | 188 |
| Environment and housing | 128 | 151 | 136 |
| Administration | 155 | 195 | 190 |

* Total direct are total direct expenditures for selected functions. Social services includes income maintenance.

Note: Numbers do not add due to rounding.

Source: U.S. Census Bureau, government finance statistics. Compiled by author.

on government administration. The national averages were $301, $322, and $322 in 2017, 2012, and 2017, respectively. During the same period, Nebraska spent $155, $195, and $190 per capita.

Interest on debt is low in Nebraska because the state constitution limits debt to $100,000 unless needed for purposes of defending the state against insurrection or invasion. There are three exceptions to this: highway construction, for which bonds may be repaid with fees or taxes related to highway use; revenue bonds for water construction and management structures; and revenue bonds for facilities related to education to be repaid from revenues related to their use (e.g., university dorms paid by student rental fees) (Nebraska State Constitution, Article XIII, Section 1). This restricts the use of general obligation bonds, repaid from general state taxes, which are widely used in other states.

### BUDGET APPROPRIATIONS

The previous section discussed all actual state revenues and expenditures except for insurance trusts. The focus now is on budget appropriations, the monies approved in the adopted budget for spending. Appropriations are categorized in three different ways: by agency, by major type of expenditure, and by fund type. In the current biennium, seventy-eight agencies received appropriations, ranging from large ones, such as HHS and the University of Nebraska, to small licensing and advisory boards. Appropriations are also categorized according to three major types of expenditures: agency operations (including items such as salaries and benefits, supplies and contracts), state aid (aid to individuals such as Medicaid and welfare, as well as aid to local governments such as funding for local school districts), and capital construction (for large, non-recurring expenditures such as buildings).

Finally, funds are used to segregate activities for specific purposes based on legal or other restrictions. Nebraska appropriates by four major fund types: general, cash, federal, and revolving/other. The general fund is the largest fund, and includes all revenues and expenditures related to activities for the general benefit of the public. Cash funds track activities funded by dedicated fees and charges, such as university tuition, gas taxes and other highway revenues, and fishing permits. Federal funds account for monies obtained from the federal government (except highways), such as Medicaid, while revolving funds record transfers between state agencies (e.g.,

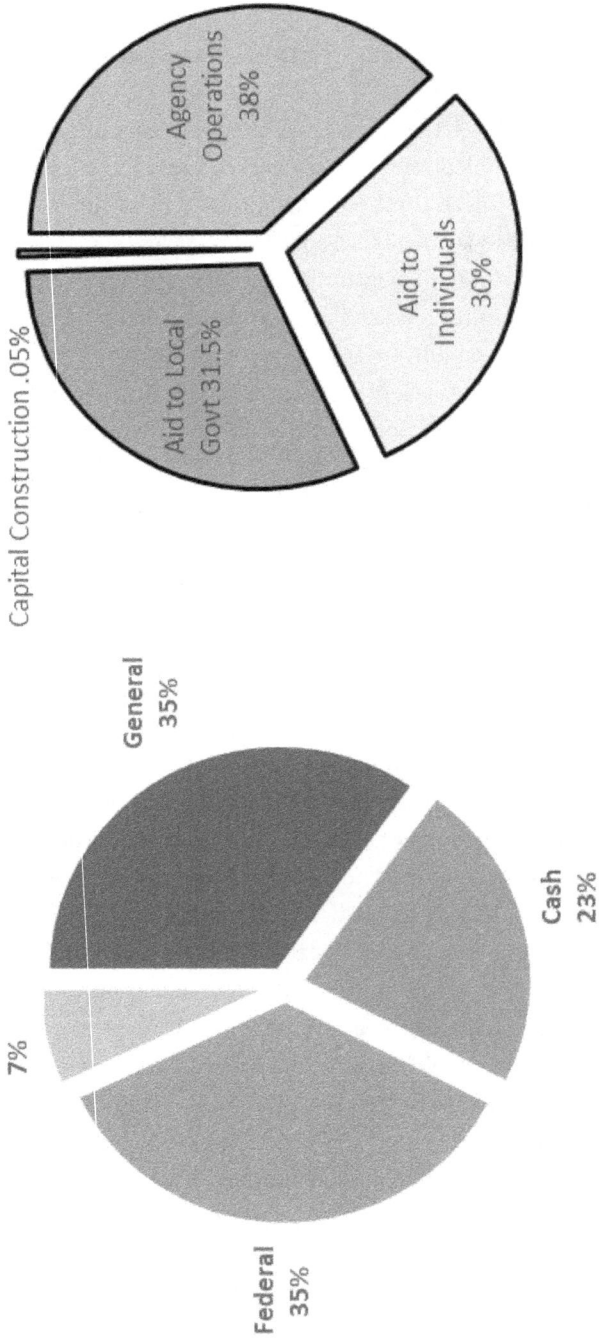

**Fig. 10.** Budget appropriations by supported expenditure category and fund type. Source: State of Nebraska, 2021–22 Biennium Budget, 2022 Session. Created by author.

the Department of Education leases office space from the Department of Administrative Services). The Nebraska capital construction fund (NCCF), included in other funds, is used for specific capital purposes.

Figure 10 depicts the adopted budget appropriations for the 2021–22 fiscal year broken down by expenditure and fund type. Total appropriations for this fiscal year were $12.6 billion. The largest appropriation by expenditure type is agency operations, at 38 percent of total appropriations, followed by aid to local governments (31.5 percent) and then aid to individuals at 30 percent. By fund type, the general fund and the federal fund are identical percentages at 35 percent each, with cash funds at 23 percent and other funds at around 7 percent.

## General Fund

Another perspective from which to consider a state's budget is by looking at the major funds. Funds serve as the accounting placeholder to track the flow of revenues and expenditures. Funds are not, in themselves, appropriations, but are the device used to fund the work of state government. This section discusses four types of funds: the general, federal, cash, and revolving funds. The general fund is the workhorse of the state budget since most expenditure items that the state legislature appropriates are part of this fund. For the 2021–22 fiscal year, this fund was about $4.8 billion, or about 38 percent of total appropriation, and is used to account for activities with broad general benefits. Forty-seven state agencies receive appropriations from this fund, which typically receives the most focus during the budget process. Table 7 shows the proportion of general funds appropriations by expenditure type for the 2022–23 fiscal year.

Agency operations cover the costs of operating state agencies, for items such as employee salaries and benefits and utilities. For the 2022–23 fiscal year, $1.9 billion, or about 36.5 percent of all general fund appropriations were for agency operations. Four major agencies consume the bulk, or about 79 percent, of this expenditure. Operations for the university system and state colleges account for about 38 percent of general fund agency operations appropriations. HHS accounts for 16 percent of agency operations, correctional services account for 15 percent, and the courts account for about 10 percent.

**Table 7. General fund appropriations by expenditure type, FY 2022–23**

| | | |
|---|---|---|
| Agency operations | $1,873,192,160 | 36.55% |
| State aid to individuals | $1,676,849,756 | 32.71% |
| State aid to local governments | $1,551,708,727 | 30.27% |
| Capital construction | 423,921,610 | 0.47% |
| Totals | $5,125,672,253 | 100.00% |

Source: State of Nebraska, 2022–23 Biennium Budget, 2022 Session. Compiled by author.

State aid, in total, is the largest portion of the general fund, and it is typically broken into aid to individuals and aid to local governments. Aid to individuals accounts for about $1.7 billion, or 33 percent of the overall general fund, and is primarily for the state portion of Medicaid and other direct welfare programs. The Medicaid program accounts for 59 percent of aid to individuals. Child welfare aid, public assistance, developmental disabilities aid, and the Children's Health Insurance program account for another 32 percent of the entire state aid to individuals category.

Aid to local governments accounts for about 30 percent of the general fund budget. Most of this category, about 83 percent, is for those local governments defined as public school entities. State aid to schools (formula aid to districts under the Nebraska Tax Equity and Educational Opportunities Act, or TEEOSA, of 1990) accounts for about 67 percent of this category. Other aid to schools including special education and other areas such as support to educational service units, high learner programs, and early childhood programs accounts for another 16 percent of the category. Aid to community colleges stands at about 7 percent, and a small percentage (about 6 percent), which has declined over time, is for aid to cities and counties, which includes refunds for homestead property tax exemptions.

Capital construction accounts for less than 1 percent of the general fund, but it is an important element in the repair and renovation of state facilities. A special category of capital construction is the Nebraska capital construction fund. This fund receives earmarked appropriations from the federal fund, the cash reserve fund, or cash funds for specific projects (Nebraska Legislature 2021, 61).

Table 8 gives a broader perspective by showing twenty-year average general fund appropriations patterns (2001–23). The last seven rows of table 8 provide the important takeaway regarding general fund appropriations. Over this period the average annual growth rate has hovered around 3.1 percent, but some areas have grown more than others. The aid to individuals appropriation has grown at a rate higher than any other appropriation categories. This means that both agency operations and aid to local government have grown at rates smaller than the overall rate of growth, and construction has grown at very low rates and for some periods grew at negative rates. The reason this situation exists has to do primarily with Medicaid expenditures, which are based on formulaic grants. The state is required to provide funding as required by the Medicaid formula. This necessarily means, for example, that agency operations, which includes the university system, and aid to local governments, which includes formulaic aid to schools, are funded at lower growth percentages.

This section focused primarily on the spending side of the general fund budget because taxes will be discussed in chapter 9. However, the revenue side of the budget is critical, since the state must pass a balanced budget, so the sources are important to mention here. Over two decades, sales and use taxes averaged 38 percent of general fund revenues. Individual income taxes were the workhorse of revenue, averaging nearly 50 percent of general fund revenues. Corporate income tax accounted for 6 percent, with miscellaneous taxes and fees averaging 6 percent (Nebraska Legislature 2021, 61).

The heavy reliance on sales and income taxes makes the general fund budget especially sensitive to economic cycles, as illustrated in figure 11. The vertical gray bars represent recession periods since the early 1980s. General fund revenue growth tends to decrease during or immediately following economic recessions, which presents a challenge for budget balancing. However, it is interesting that during the two pandemic years of 2020 to 2021, individual income tax revenues increased (Nebraska Legislature 2021, 61).

## Cash Funds

Cash funds represent about 21 percent of the overall budget and are used to account for revenues and expenditures related to dedicated fees and charges, usually originally generated from outside the state government (Nebraska

**Table 8. Historical general fund appropriations and average annual growth through select biennium years, Nebraska, FY2001–2 through FY2022–23**

| BUDGET YEAR | AGENCY OPERATIONS | AID TO INDIVIDUALS AND OTHERS | AID TO LOCAL GOVERNMENTS | CONSTRUCTION | TOTAL | PERCENT CHANGE |
|---|---|---|---|---|---|---|
| | $(mil) | | | | | |
| FY2001–2 | 989 | 646 | 9 | 27 | 2,607 | 6.0 |
| FY2002–3 | 1,004 | 648 | 952 | 18 | 2,621 | 0.6 |
| FY2003–4 | 1,000 | 706 | 930 | 21 | 2,655 | 1.3 |
| FY2004–5 | 1,018 | 786 | 935 | 19 | 2,578 | 3.9 |
| FY2005–6 | 1,080 | 851 | 1,018 | 23 | 2,972 | 7.8 |
| FY2006–7 | 1,151 | 939 | 1,059 | 31 | 3,181 | 7.0 |
| FY2007–8 | 1,173 | 978 | 1,147 | 8 | 3,306 | 3.9 |
| FY2008–9 | 1,222 | 1,016 | 1,236 | 8 | 3,482 | 5.3 |
| FY2009–10 | 1,211 | 880 | 1,220 | 14 | 3,325 | (4.5) |
| FY2010–11 | 1,254 | 947 | 1,191 | 14 | 3,405 | 2.4 |

| FY | | | | | |
|---|---|---|---|---|---|
| FY2011–12 | 1,225 | 1,057 | 1,174 | 14 | 3,471 | 1.9 |
| FY2012–13 | 1,260 | 1,136 | 1,216 | 14 | 3,632 | 4.7 |
| FY2013–14 | 1,315 | 1,213 | 1,284 | 20 | 3,838 | 5.7 |
| FY2014–15 | 1,429 | 1,305 | 1,345 | 26 | 4,106 | 7.0 |
| FY2015–16 | 1,522 | 1,349 | 1,375 | 26 | 4,272 | 4.0 |
| FY2016–17 | 1,581 | 1,399 | 1,410 | 22 | 4,412 | 3.3 |
| FY2017–18 | 1,570 | 1,379 | 1,427 | 21 | 4,398 | (0.3) |
| FY2018–19 | 1,583 | 1,416 | 1,436 | 21 | 4,456 | 1.3 |
| FY2019–20 | 1,639 | 1,437 | 1,510 | 38 | 4,625 | 3.8 |
| FY2020–21 | 1,700 | 1,491 | 1,554 | 39 | 4,784 | 3.4 |
| FY2021–22 | 1,742 | 1,526 | 1,505 | 42 | 4,815 | 0.7 |
| FY2022–23 | 1,873 | 1,677 | 1,552 | 24 | 5,126 | 6.4 |

**Table 8. Continued**

| BUDGET YEAR | AGENCY OPERATIONS | AID TO INDIVIDUALS AND OTHERS | AID TO LOCAL GOVERNMENTS | CONSTRUCTION | TOTAL PERCENT CHANGE |
|---|---|---|---|---|---|
| | | *Average annual percent growth through selected biennium years* | | | |
| FY16/FY17 | 2.8 | 3.7 | 2.6 | 1.0 | 3.0 |
| FY18/FY19 | 2.6 | 4.3 | 2.3 | (1.3) | 2.9 |
| FY20/FY21 | 2.4 | 2.6 | 1.9 | (2.4) | 2.1 |
| FY22/FY23 | 3.0 | 4.4 | 2.3 | (0.6) | 3.1 |
| Avg. FY03–FY13 (10 year) | 2.3 | 4.9 | 2.7 | 0.1 | 3.2 |
| Avg. FY13–FY23 (10 year) | 3.6 | 3.3 | 1.9 | (0.8) | 2.9 |
| Avg. FY03–FY23 (20 year) | 3.2 | 4.4 | 2.6 | 0.8 | 3.3 |

Source: Nebraska Legislature, State of Nebraska FY2021–22/FY2022–23 Biennial Budget. Compiled by author.

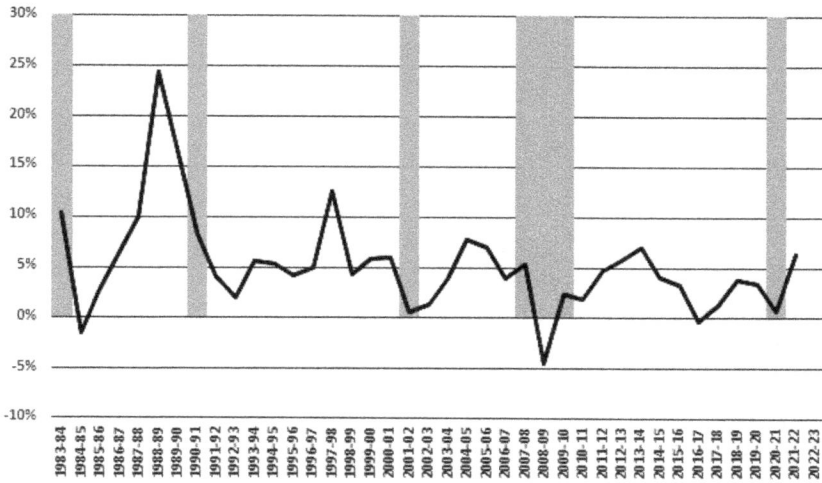

Fig. 11. Nebraska general fund revenue change with recession periods indicated, 1983–2023. Source: State of Nebraska, 2022–23 Biennium Budget, 2022 Session. Created by author.

Legislative Fiscal Office 2019). Cash funds are not necessarily an indication of original revenues or expenditures but represent a bookkeeping device. There are over two hundred cash funds, used across seventy agencies of the state government (Nebraska Legislative Fiscal Office 2019, 447–61). In effect, cash funds accounting is a way of keeping track of both revenues and expenditures that flow through these various agencies. According to the most recent report of the Legislative Fiscal Office, in 2019, three agencies or programs accounted for 67 percent of all cash fund appropriations (Nebraska Legislative Fiscal Office 2019). These are the Department of Transportation (40 percent), the University of Nebraska system (19 percent), and the Department of Health and Human Services (8 percent).

The primary fund for the Department of Transportation is the roads operations cash fund, which is used to account for the actual construction and maintenance of state-owned roads and highways, along with agency operations. Total spending was about $745 million in 2016–17 (Nebraska Legislative Fiscal Office 2019, 190). Funding for the roads operations cash fund comes from three sources. First is the highway cash fund, which is funded by state gasoline taxes as well as licensing and other vehicle-related fees. The gasoline tax provides support for this fund, but state gasoline taxes are variable. As of 2019 the fixed portion was 9.5 cents per gallon. There is a wholesale portion, which is based on the wholesale cost of fuel, and finally a variable portion. In all, the gasoline tax in 2019 stood at 29 cents per gallon, as opposed to 26.4 cents per gallon in 2015. The second source is the highway capital improvement fund, created in 2013 and funded by 0.25 percent of the state sales tax revenues (which partially accounts for the declining share of sales tax in the general fund), adding about 13 percent to the total (Nebraska Legislature 2013, 68–69). The third source for the operations cash fund is the federal highway trust fund, which is awarded to the state on a formula basis, and accounts for about 40 percent of the total funding for the operations cash fund.

Another large cash fund is the health care cash fund (about 8 percent of total), funded by the tobacco settlement trust fund (pursuant to a national agreement with tobacco companies) and the Medicaid intergovernmental trust fund (essentially excess Medicare reimbursements). This fund supports around eighteen separate healthcare programs, including biomedical research, Children's Health Insurance Program, behavioral health, substance abuse, and tobacco prevention programs (Nebraska Legislative Fiscal Office 2014).

Revolving funds support transactions from one agency to other agencies, and to account for revenue from non-tax sources. For example, the University of Nebraska system tuition and fees process through revolving funds. Overall, the university budget is funded about 22 percent from the general fund, around 20 percent from federal sources, and around 25 percent from revolving funds such as tuition and fees (Board of Regents 2022).

## Federal Funds

When total appropriations from all funds (general, cash, federal, and revolving) are totaled, federal funds account for a significant portion (about 30 percent) of all appropriations. This group of funds experienced the most growth from 1992 to 2022, expanding at a rate of 5.4 percent per year, compared with 4.4 percent for the overall budget (Board of Regents 2022). This is the second largest fund type, at about 30 percent of total appropriations in the 2014–15 biennium. Federal funds primarily are committed to three agencies: HHS, the University of Nebraska and state college systems, and the Department of Education (Board of Regents 2022).

By a wide margin, programs within HHS receive the largest share (about 59 percent) of federal funds. Of this total, 80–85 percent is appropriated for state aid to individuals for the federal portion of Medicaid and the Children's Health Insurance Program, along with several other aid programs. The second largest recipient of federal funds is the university system, accounting for about 19 percent of all federal funds. The K–12 school program receives about 12 percent of all federal funding channeled to the state. For the most part, federal funding supports programs mandated by federal law, and funded either exclusively by the federal government, or on a cost-share basis with the state.

## Revolving Funds

Revolving funds are about 8 percent of the overall budget and are established for various government departments to charge other departments for services rendered. For example, the Department of Education leases building space from the Department of Administrative Services (Board of Regents 2022). Most revolving funds appropriations are found within the university and state college systems (66 percent), which use revolving funds to account for student fees other than tuition, such as the fees charged for dormitory space, student unions, and agricultural experimental stations. This enables the university and state colleges to keep these funds distinct and separate from tuition and other fees that are handled through cash funds. Other users of revolving funds include the Department of Administrative Services (24 percent of the total), and the Department of Corrections (2 percent of the total). The NCCF, mentioned previously, uses funds from specific agencies or from the cash reserve fund to pay for construction costs of approved projects; this fund represents around 6 percent of revolving funds (Board of Regents 2022).

This section provided a summary of the major funds and types of appropriations in the Nebraska state budget. While clearly there will be changes over time due to a range of issues, in general, the pattern of where the money comes from and where it goes in the state remains fairly stable. The next section discusses significant and ongoing challenges in developing the biennial budget in Nebraska.

### MAJOR BUDGET ISSUES AND CHALLENGES

The state budget includes funding for a wide range of activities, but most of the attention tends to be on a few specific areas. According to the former

Appropriations Committee chair, "The three largest areas are the focal point: aid to education, human services, and higher education. These constitute the majority of the state budget and are the big drivers. They are always changing, especially because of the interconnectedness with other funding sources. Aid to education is tied to local funding, and federal funding affects HHS funding" (Mello interview). This does not mean that other areas are not discussed, though. The former budget administrator noted that "in Nebraska, every bill gets a legislative hearing and there's a hearing on every agency budget request, so at some point there's attention to even the smallest request" (Oligmueller interview). A current member of the Appropriations Committee, state senator Mike McDonnell, mentioned the time commitment for this responsibility: "The Appropriations Committee is the only committee out of the fourteen standing committees that meets every day" (Mike McDonnell, interview by authors, December 5, 2022).

Balancing the budget is one of the primary challenges in this process. This is due partly to volatility in major revenue sources; income and sales tax revenues are highly dependent on fluctuations in the economy, and federal aid is uncertain from year to year. In addition, there are competing priorities on the spending side, with the governor and the forty-nine legislators having different ideas on how best to allocate the available budget dollars. Decisions must be made that have far-reaching impacts on individuals and special interest groups. For example, the decision to dedicate a portion of sales tax to highways has had an offsetting negative effect on the general fund. The amount of budgeted state aid for K–12 education directly affects local property taxes, while the level of state funding for higher education impacts tuition rates.

Budget decisions require balancing not only between revenues and expenditures but also between short-term and long-term needs. For example, it is a source of pride that Nebraska has had a healthy cash reserve fund. This was one reason that the state was able to weather the Great Recession of 2008 better than many others. However, taking too much out of this fund at any given time reduces flexibility and level of comfort in future years. The use of this source typically is taken very seriously by the governor and legislature because of this trade-off.

Time is also seen as a considerable challenge in developing and adopting a budget. The former Appropriations Committee chair noted the difficulties related to "trying to balance the considerable time requirements needed to get a budget with the need to develop your own agenda" (Mello interview). The former budget administrator also views time constraints as a major budget challenge, particularly in years with a new governor who is elected in November, inaugurated in January, and must present a budget by February 1: "There is little time for the new governor to wrap their head around all that needs to be done and decided. The legislature convenes in early January and has ninety days to adopt a budget. This is quite an abbreviated period of time to develop knowledge and understanding and make decisions to adopt a budget" (Oligmueller interview).

Political differences arise between the mostly rural areas of the state and the urban areas, largely Omaha and Lincoln. Interviewees noted that this urban/rural divide is a challenge in the legislative standing committees, where decisions such as how to allocate school aid and water funding are made. It is less of an issue for the Appropriations Committee, which is fairly evenly split between rural and urban representatives, and sees a major issue as being "how to invest our commonwealth to grow our state. We're at 1.9 million people, with a population shift from the west to the east. We have to sustain and hopefully grow the west and the east and spread our tax base" (McDonnell interview). Overall, "the legislature as a whole tends to be conservative regarding expanding taxation and has discipline—so there's not as much an issue of how much money, but how to allocate it—these are policy debates that have implications for the budget" (McDonnell interview).

Legislative term limits are seen as having influenced the budget process and decisions. The Appropriations Committee has had substantial turnover because of term limits, which have "had a significant impact in the loss of institutional knowledge of past appropriations, legislation, and fiscal account-ability issues" (Mello interview). Some see this as favoring lobbyists: "There are a number of subject matter experts throughout the building but as a new senator you don't know who they are. You learn, and hopefully have an experienced staff, but term limits make the lobby stronger" (McDonnell interview). Term limits have also added to the workload of the governor's budget staff and the Legislative Fiscal Office. "There are more senators who need to be provided more information and who need to be educated and develop an understanding of laws and rules that exist and have implications for budget issues and budget decisions" (Oligmueller interview).

There are significant challenges to budgeting in the state, and serious debates about budget priorities. Overall, though, the budget has been consistent over time in terms of both outcomes and process. Elected officials use a conservative approach, as demonstrated by the healthy reserve fund that is used sparingly and the use of the independent revenue forecasting board. Finally, in line with the populist history of the state, the budget process is designed to allow all voices to be heard during the discussions over tax policy and appropriations.

## REFERENCES

Bartle, John. 2013. "Fiscal Policy in Nebraska." Lincoln: Nebraska Legislature, Report to Planning Committee.

Board of Regents, University of Nebraska System. 2022. University of Nebraska Budget Summary for 2022. Lincoln: University of Nebraska System Board of Regents.

Bowman, Ann O'M., and Richard C. Kearney. 2015. *State and Local Government: The Essentials*. 6th ed. Independence KY: Cengage.

Carey, John M., Richard G. Niemi, Lynda W. Powell, and Gary F. Moncrief. 2006. "The Effects of Term Limits on State Legislatures: A New Survey of the 50 States." *Legislative Studies Quarterly* 31 (1): 105–34.

Dearmont, David. 2007. "Forecast Accuracy by Tax Category: Do Perceptual Forecasts Increase Accuracy?" Presentation, Revenue Estimation and Tax Research Conference, Raleigh, North Carolina, September 17, 2007. http://www.taxadmin.org/assets/docs/Meetings/07rev_est/dearmont.pdf.

Koven, Steven G., and Christopher Mausolff. 2002. "The Influence of Political Culture on State Budgets: Another Look at Elazar's Formulation." *American Review of Public Administration* 32 (1): 66–77.

Mikesell, John L. 2007. *Fiscal Administration*. 7th ed. Belmont CA: Thomson Wadsworth.

Mooney, Christopher Z. 2009. "Term Limits as a Boon to Legislative Scholarship: A Review." *State Politics and Policy Quarterly* 9 (2): 204–28.

NASBO (National Association of State Budget Officers). 2022a. "Budget Processes in the States." Washington DC: National Association of State Budget Officers. https://www.nasbo.org/reports-data/budget-processes-in-the-states. Editions of this report have been published since 1975.

———. 2022b. "Fiscal Survey of States." Washington, DC: National Association of State Budget Officers. https://www.nasbo.org/reports-data/budget-processes-in-the-states.

National Conference of State Legislatures. 2019. "NCSL Fiscal Brief: State Balanced Budget Provisions." http://www.ncsl.org/documents/fiscal /statebalancedbudgetprovisions2010.pdf.

Nebraska DAS State Budget Division. 2013. "Cash Reserve Fund Status for 2012–213." Lincoln: Nebraska Department of Administrative Services, brief. http://budget .nebraska.gov/das_budget/budget13/cfstatus.pdf.

Nebraska Legislative Fiscal Office. 2014. "A Legislator's Guide to Nebraska State Agencies Prepared for the Members of the 104th Nebraska Legislature." Lincoln: Nebraska Legislative Fiscal Office. A guide is published prior to the start of odd-year sessions. See the 2013–15 guide at http://nebraskalegislature.gov/pdf/reports /fiscal/2014legguide.pdf.

———. 2019. "State Government Cash and Revolving Funds." Lincoln: Nebraska Legislative Fiscal Office. http://nebraskalegislature.gov/pdf/reports/fiscal /funddescriptions_2019.pdf.

Nebraska Legislature. 2012. *2012–2013 Nebraska Blue Book*. Lincoln: Nebraska Legislature. http://nebraskalegislature.gov/pdf/bluebook/bluebook_2012.pdf.

———. 2013. State of Nebraska FY2013–14/FY2014–15 Biennial Budget. Lincoln: Nebraska Legislature. http://nebraskalegislature.gov/pdf/reports/fiscal/2013budget.pdf.

———. 2021. State of Nebraska FY2021–22/FY2022–23 Biennial Budget. Lincoln: Nebraska Legislature. https://nebraskalegislature.gov/pdf/reports/fiscal/2021budget.pdf.

Oligmueller, Gerald. 2012. "Budget Preparation Instructions for the 2013–2015 Biennium." Memorandum to All State Agencies, Boards, and Commissions State Financial Officers, June 27, 2012. Lincoln: Nebraska Administrative Services. http://govdocs.nebraska.gov/epubs/A2200/H003-201315.pdf. The website also contains archived budget instructions to agencies and executive budget documents from several fiscal years.

Olson, James C., and Ronald C. Naugle. 2015. *History of Nebraska*. 3rd ed. Lincoln: University of Nebraska Press.

Snell, Ronald K. 2011. *State Experiences with Annual and Biennial Budgeting*. Washington DC: National Conference of State Legislatures.

Urban Institute & Brookings Institution Tax Policy Center. 2020. "What Are State Rainy Day Funds, and How Do They Work?" Tax Policy Center. https://www.taxpolicycenter .org/briefing-book/what-are-state-rainy-day-funds-and-how-do-they-work.

U.S. Bureau of Labor Statistics. n.d. "Consumer Price Index for All Urban Consumers." Washington DC: U.S. Bureau of Labor Statistics. Accessed February 13, 2023. https:// www.bls.gov/cpi/data.htm.

U.S. Census Bureau. n.d. State Government Finances. https://www.census.gov/govs /state/. Numbers may vary slightly from Nebraska state sources. Census data also excludes utility and liquor store revenues and expenditures, but Nebraska does not have these at the state level.

———. 2017. "Census of Governments, State and Local Finances by Level of Government." Washington DC: U.S. Census Bureau.

———. 2022. "Nebraska Population Neared 2 Million in 2020." Washington DC: U.S. Census Bureau. https://www.census.gov/library/stories/state-by-state/nebraska -population-change-between-census-decade.html.

# CHAPTER SIX

# The Unicameral Legislature

## UNIQUELY NEBRASKA

*Christian L. Janousek, Jerome Deichert, and Robert Blair*

### INTRODUCTION

Nebraskans can truly claim the title of the most unique state legislature in the United States. When basic texts on state and local government outline the legislative process, they include descriptions of the institutional characteristics of specific state legislatures and with explanations of the variations from the traditional two-chamber legislative body fashioned by the founders for the national government as contained in the U.S. Constitution. However, they often remind the reader that Nebraska's approach differs (see Bowman and Kearney 2008; Safell and Basehart 2005). Nebraska boasts a unicameral, one-house, legislature.

This chapter describes the conception and cultural and political underpinnings of Nebraska's state legislative system, explores the organizational and institutional structures of the legislature, and addresses the characteristics and challenges of the lawmaking process within Nebraska's exclusive unicameral design.

### NEBRASKA'S EMBRACE OF A POPULIST LEGISLATURE

As noted in earlier chapters, in the spirit of their political culture and progressive and populist foundations, Nebraskans created a legislative body with two special features: a single chamber and a nonpartisan composition. Only Nebraska operates a unicameral legislative system, and only Nebraska elects its representatives on a nonpartisan ballot. The creation of this legislative arrangement in Nebraska was not contrived in reaction to political, economic, or social situations; rather, the Unicameral, as it is popularly known by Nebraskans, resulted from years of careful deliberation and debate led by the state's political leaders. What is clear is that Nebraskans voted for these dramatic structural changes in the legislature because "they were responding to arguments grounded in the populist/progressive ideal" (Berens 2005, 1).

The one-chamber structure of Nebraska's legislature provides one of the defining features of the governance of the state. The Unicameral in many ways reflects the complex historical foundations and cultural roots of the state (Nebraska Legislature 2018). In general, too, Nebraskans seem satisfied with their atypical lawmaking body, as outcries for major changes rarely arise. Only the implementation of term limits in 2007 impacted the system since its adoption.

Prior to the twentieth century, the one-house legislature format had been utilized in a few other states: Georgia in 1777, Pennsylvania until 1790, and Vermont until 1836 (Breckenridge 1978). However, unicameralism, in addition to other government reforms such as the short ballot and the council-manager form of government, constituted an important component of the progressive movement in the late 1800s and early 1900s in the United States. Especially dominant on the reform agenda from 1912 to the 1930s, the unicameral proposition for state legislatures was considered by as many as fifteen states (Berens 2005). While various levels of interest were demonstrated, only Nebraska adopted the system and embraced its philosophy. The one-house order epitomized the business focus for government heralded by progressivism, attempting to infuse expertise, efficiency, and economics into the legislative process (Berens 2005).

Approved by the voters of Nebraska in 1934, interest in a unicameral legislature began more than twenty years earlier by political reformers during the progressive movement; in the sixty-eight years prior as a state, Nebraska possessed a senate and house of representatives. Despite four previous unsuccessful attempts, Senator George Norris, a leader of the progressive wing of the Republican Party, who served Nebraska in the U.S. House and Senate from 1903 to 1943, kept the idea alive in his home state. Norris and other unicameral advocates claimed that the checks and balances of the two-house structure failed when secret conference committees met to bargain differences between legislation passed by each house. In addition, proponents claimed unicameralism promoted transparent and open government, with a smaller legislative assembly that would reduce the influence of committees, encourage more debate, and lessen the potential for corruption. A one-house legislature with fewer elected officials, budget-minded Nebraskans concluded, also would likely be more economical to administer. One researcher of the origins of the Nebraska legislature provides a concise summary of the reasons for the adoption of the unicameral system:

> The campaign that culminated in the adoption of the unicameral in Nebraska is closely identified with the progressive movement. One of the progressives' goals was to make legislatures more democratic. They promoted sunshine reforms, to open the state's business to public scrutiny, and open committee hearings. They attacked elaborate rules that concentrated legislative power in the hands of a few individuals or interests. The reforms they suggested added up to a systematic, coherent vision of democratic participation: minimize the role of intermediaries like parties, legislators, private interests—even politics itself. The progressives' vision was of a single, united, consensual people, beyond competition and politics, and was mobilized in opposition to the concentration of private power. It was a vision the unicameral's promoters said could be a reality in Nebraska. (Berens 2004, 8–9)

Nebraska's unicameral legislature began operation in 1937. An immediate effect was a decrease in cost; the single-house forum provided for a 70 percent reduction in legislative membership, down to 43 state senators from the 133 in the bicameral (Clerk of the Legislature 2009). This number was subsequently increased to forty-nine state senators by a voter-approved constitutional amendment in 1965, arising from a growing demand for enhanced urban representation (Sittig 1987).

   Consistent with populist values, ingrained in Nebraska's political culture, and confirming independence from political alignments, the nonpartisan ballot was also introduced in the 1934 unicameral amendment. This movement likewise was championed by Norris, who argued that nonpartisanship would allow state senators "to concentrate on local interests without being influenced by national party directives" (Nebraska Legislature n.d.a.). In addition, signifying a vigilant accountability measure, Nebraska claims the smallest legislative body among the fifty U.S. states. In fact, over the main entrance to the state capitol, the motto "The salvation of the state is watchfulness in the citizen" enshrines this political ideology. Only Delaware's sixty-two-member general assembly, Alaska's sixty-member legislature, and Nevada's sixty-two legislators come close to Nebraska's forty-nine-member unicameral legislature (National Conference n.d., 2023).

## THE STRUCTURE OF THE UNICAMERAL

### Elected Officials

The forty-nine state senators of the Nebraska Unicameral are elected to four-year terms and allowed to serve two consecutive terms, because of term limits passed in 2007, with 56 percent of the vote (National Conference n.d.). After four years, term-limited senators are eligible to run for election again. Elections are held every two years (in even years) with half of the districts up for election.

State senators represent approximately forty thousand people per voting district as of the 2020 U.S. Census. The Nebraska State Constitution requires that state senators, to be eligible for election, must be registered voters, at least twenty-one years of age, and have lived in their representative district for a period of one year prior to general election (Nebraska State Constitution, Article III, Section 8). The officers of the Unicameral include the lieutenant governor (who also serves as the president of the legislature), the speaker, the clerk and assistant clerk, and the sergeant at arms. The senators elect the speaker, who is a member of the legislature. The clerk, assistant clerk, and the sergeant at arms, who are not senators, are appointed by recommendation of the Executive Board of the Legislative Council (Neb. Rev. Stat. § 50-111).

### Legislative Council

As of 1949 all state senators are technically members of the Legislative Council, placing all services and personnel under the council. Consisting of the personal staff of each senator and committee staff, the support offices of the council include the clerk of the legislature, revisor of statutes, Legislative Fiscal Office, Legislative Audit Division, Legislative Research Division, and ombudsman. The Executive Board of the Legislative Council oversees the management of legislative services and staff and represents the council in legislative affairs (Nebraska Legislature 2020).

The clerk of the legislature, elected to a two-year term, maintains records of the legislature, aids legislative activities, ensures legal procedures are followed, and provides legislative information to the public. The Office of the Clerk operates the Legislative Bill Room, Transcribers' Office, and Technology Center. The Unicameral Information Office produces publications, such as the *Nebraska Blue Book*, manages the legislature website, and distributes other informational brochures (Nebraska Legislature 2020).

The revisor of statutes, placed under the Legislative Council in 1967 (Neb. Rev. Stat. § 49-701), drafts bills, resolutions, and amendments and reports legal defects of statutes. The Legislative Fiscal Office provides financial and budgetary information to the legislature and prepares fiscal notes on bills. The Legislative Audit and Research Divisions conduct legal and policy research for the legislature and audits of state programs. The ombudsman, referred to as the Office of Public Counsel, mainly receives and addresses complaints by citizens against state agencies.

The Executive Board of the Legislative Council consists of nine senators: a chairperson, vice chairperson, speaker, and six other state senators. Board members are selected at the beginning of legislative sessions in odd-numbered years to serve two-year terms. State law requires that board members be representative of all congressional districts. The executive board also includes representatives from two offices: Accounting and Budget Office and the Coordinator of Legislative Services (Neb. Rev. Stat. § 50-401.01).

## Standing Committees

The committee structure of the Nebraska legislature exemplifies the foundation of the lawmaking process and is critical to the functioning of the Unicameral. Fourteen standing committees, shown in table 9, manage the legislative process and hold public hearings on bills after they are introduced. Two standing committees deal with the budget (revenue and appropriations), with the remainder handling an array of broad policy issues. All state senators, with the exception of those on the Appropriations Committee, serve on more than one standing committee.

There are also four select committees that make committee assignments, refer bills to appropriate committees, consider legislative procedural rules, and review the technical aspects of legislation. Select committees are impor-

**Table 9. Standing committees of the Nebraska legislature**

Agriculture

Appropriations

Banking, Commerce, and Insurance

Business and Labor

Education

General Affairs

Government, Military, and Veterans Affairs

Health and Human Services

Judiciary

Natural Resources

Nebraska Retirement Systems

Revenue

Transportation and Telecommunications

Urban Affairs

Source: Nebraska Legislature, *2014–2015 Nebraska Blue Book* (Lincoln: Nebraska Legislature, 2014).

tant committees within a nonpartisan and unicameral system. The four select committees are the Committee on Committees, which makes committee assignments; the Enrollment and Review Committee, which considers technical aspects of bills and amendments; the Reference Committee, made up of executive board members and which refers bills and appointments to committees; and the Rules Committee, which recommends legislative procedural rules (Nebraska Legislature 2020).

In addition to standing and select committees, special committees may be created to address specific issues and provide legislative oversight in policy areas. Examples of special committees in the Nebraska Legislature include the Legislative Performance Audit Committee, Legislature's Planning Committee, State-Tribal Relations Committee, and the Department of

Correctional Services Special Investigative Committee (Nebraska Legislature n.d.b.). Compact commissions administer various interstate compacts and agreements in which Nebraska is involved, such as the Midwestern Higher Education Commission and Midwest Interstate Passenger Rail Compact.

## LEGISLATIVE SESSIONS AND DISTRICTS

The legislature meets for ninety days on odd-numbered years (first session) and sixty days on even-numbered years (second session). The first session is thirty days longer because it is during this session that the legislature creates a budget for the next two fiscal years. Prior to a constitutional amendment in 1970 that authorized annual assemblies, the legislature met only on odd-numbered years. A four-fifths vote of the legislature extends sessions beyond the standard meeting period. During these regular sessions, all legislative operations pertaining to state government may be considered, as opposed to special sessions that only deal with particular topics. The governor can call special sessions between regular sessions for specific purposes, or two-thirds of the legislature may appeal upon the governor to call a special session. This is rarely done. From 1935 to 2018 there have been only thirty-six special sessions of the legislature, and only four legislatures have convened for more than one special session during their tenure (Nebraska Legislature 2020). In general, special sessions address revisions or provisions to existing legislation, budgetary or fiscal adjustments, or changes in statutes due to judicial rulings.

Only members of the legislature, or committees, may introduce new bills. From 1973, when revenue bills were no longer counted in the total number of bills, to 2016, there has been an average of 731 bills introduced in first sessions (ninety days) and 463 bills introduced in second sessions (sixty days). Over that same time, the average number of bills passed as laws was 283 in first sessions and 204 in second sessions (Nebraska Legislature 2020). Although the number of bills introduced per session has moderately increased since the 1980s, the number of laws passed per session has correspondingly decreased.

A common supposition espoused by proponents of a unicameral legislature was improved representation of the citizenry in state affairs, indicating another reflection of Nebraska's political culture and populist orientation toward its governmental structure. Certainly, rural and urban distinctions played a part in the reapportionment of state legislative districts in the conversion to a one-house configuration. The ongoing clash of representation between the eastern and western sections of the state remains a sensitive issue.

The 1935 legislature assigned the responsibility of district alignment for the new Unicameral and designated forty-three legislative districts, with special attention to rural representation (Berens 2004). This number was eventually increased to forty-nine districts in 1965 in response to arguments of urban underrepresentation, again exhibiting the enduring rural versus urban contentiousness.

In the 2021 Unicameral, the three most populous counties in the state (Douglas, Lancaster, and Sarpy) contained twenty-five legislative districts fully within their borders and parts of three additional legislative districts. As situated, each state legislative district in Nebraska will represent approximately forty thousand constituents because of the 2020 Census. After redistricting, in 2021, it is expected that these three counties will pick up an additional one or two districts. In 2020, when compared with other states, only eight states have fewer people represented per senate district: Alaska, Maine, Montana, North Dakota, Rhode Island, South Dakota, Vermont, and Wyoming (National Conference n.d.).

### THE LAWMAKING PROCESS

A criticism of a one-house legislature may be the tendency to produce hastily approved legislation. Critics contend that this type of legislation results from the absence of judicious consideration by two chambers, with different institutional practices and constituencies. One of the foundations of bicameral theory is that the two chambers must ultimately agree on the final language of the bill. Nebraska addresses this concern by developing rules and procedures that mandate lengthy and multiple considerations of the bills during full debate on the floor of the legislature, resulting in a process described as "unusually full, exacting and methodical" (Todd 1998, 155).

Senators or committees introduce most bills during the first ten days of the legislative session by filing the bill with the clerk of the legislature. Bills may contain only one topic, and the Legislative Fiscal Office prepares a fiscal note that estimates the bill's economic impact. Bills referred to standing committees must receive a public hearing before the committee can act, allowing for citizen input on the bill. Following the hearing, committees determine if the bill is sent to General File, postponed, or if no action will be taken. Each bill must receive three separate votes by the full chamber before it is sent to the governor for consideration.

First, in General File, the bill is debated among the full legislature, a decisive stage in the legislative process. It is here that amendments and compromises are deliberated, and a majority vote (twenty-five members) must be reached to move the bill to the next phase. Second, the bill is sent to another round of debate in Select File. If the bill again receives a majority vote, it goes through a process of enrollment and review for amendment additions and technical/grammatical assessment. According to Sue Crawford, former Nebraska state senator, "The select file is also an important step for amendments and compromise. Bills often get passed on general file onto select with a promise that the senators will work on the bill together before it comes back for select. Select also acts as a higher level of scrutiny and bills that got through the first round get caught there. This matches the intent that the second round provides added scrutiny" (interview by authors, June 5, 2024). Third, the bill reaches Final Reading, in which the bill is read aloud by the clerk of the legislature, unless a three-fifths vote waives this requirement. In the Final Reading, the bill may not be amended or debated; the legislature may vote on final passage or return the bill to Select File.

Upon final passage, the bill is referred to the governor for signing, veto, or no action. The governor has line-item veto authority, and the legislature needs a three-fifths vote to override vetoes. (See chapter 10 for information on the number of overrides in Nebraska compared to other states.) Bills then become law three months after the legislature adjourns, unless an emergency clause is attached by a two-thirds vote (Clerk of the Legislature 2009) (figure 12).

Several institutional factors affect the policymaking process in the Nebraska legislature. These factors include a unicameral structure, nonpartisan environment, the relationship with the governor, and the part-time status of senators. The unicameral structure understandably gives the committees more power to shape policy since there is no need to balance the interests of the other legislative chamber. In this way, a small group of senators may decide the fate of many bills prior to full legislative debate

# UNICAMERAL PROCESS

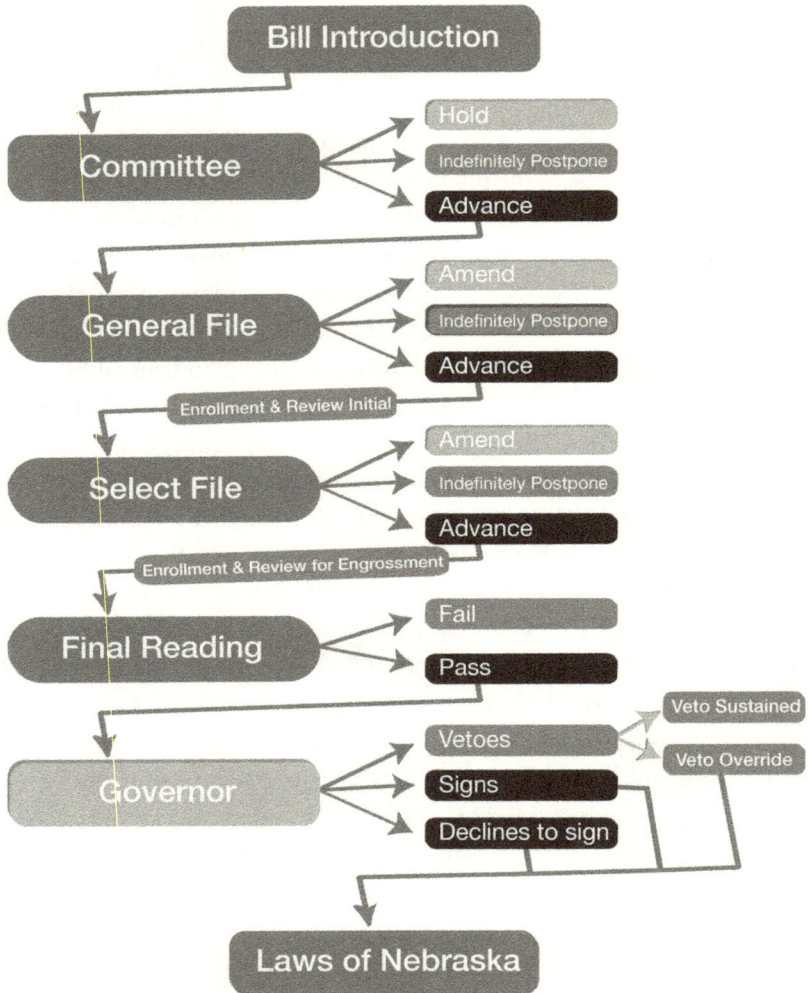

Bill Introduction

Committee
- Hold
- Indefinitely Postpone
- Advance

General File
- Amend
- Indefinitely Postpone
- Advance

Enrollment & Review Initial

Select File
- Amend
- Indefinitely Postpone
- Advance

Enrollment & Review for Engrossment

Final Reading
- Fail
- Pass

Governor
- Vetoes
  - Veto Sustained
  - Veto Override
- Signs
- Declines to sign

Laws of Nebraska

Fig. 12. How a bill becomes a law. Source: Unicameral Information Office, *The Nebraska Legislature: The Nation's Only Unicameral* (Lincoln: Unicameral Information Office, 2013), 10.

(Sittig 1987). The leadership role of committees in the legislative process escalates the importance of committee assignments (Bowman and Kearney 2008). As such, senators hotly contest the chairmanship of key committees.

In the nonpartisan tradition of Nebraska's political culture, a formal political party system is eliminated within the legislature, which may strengthen the influence of interest groups and various lobbies. Within this setting, voting alliances often change for each policy area, displaying very little consistency or cohesion (Welch and Carlson 1973). For example, the urban senators may form loose agreements on urban-related policy issues, but conflict between the two major cities, Omaha, and Lincoln, often dilutes long-term effectiveness. This unpredictability in voting behaviors and coalitions seems to contradict the intent of greater citizen control through nonpartisanship. Lacking a formal party structure in the legislature, interest groups may fill the gap in the lawmaking process through spurring the initiation of policy and providing critical research on debates. For instance, one of the primary functions of the League of Nebraska Municipalities, a service organization to cities, is monitoring legislation.

As the chief executive, the governor plays a seminal role in state policy, proposing policy and influencing debate through the bully pulpit. Yet the nature of the relationship between the governor and the Unicameral is complex. The nonpartisanship of the Unicameral will often limits the governor's political influence on the legislative process and in fact, governors who maintain intransigent party adherence may experience difficulties in accomplishing legislative goals. In general, Nebraska governors who have had legislative success are willing to reach compromise and embrace nonpartisan practicality.

The part-time status of the senators also affects the policy process. Even before the implementation of term limits, in 2006 Nebraska had the second highest turnover rates among legislatures (Hove and Hovey 2007). In addition, senatorial and committee staff can wield considerable policy influence, and the nonpartisan character of the Unicameral may complicate leadership. All these institutional factors affecting policymaking in the Nebraska legislature likewise contribute to a range of challenges and critical issues, which will be discussed in more detail in the following sections.

POLICY CHANGES OF THE NEBRASKA LEGISLATURE

Capacity and Leadership

In the late 1960s the Citizens' Conference on State Legislatures conducted an extensive study of the legislatures in the United States, identifying aspects that influenced performance and effectiveness. This landmark study selected five criteria: functional, accountable, informed, independent, and representative (Citizens' Conference 1973). The researchers then ranked the states according to measures of these criteria. The study resulted in broad self-evaluation by the states and, in many cases, efforts by the states to improve the institutional capacity of their legislatures. Following these reforms, "states have made tremendous strides in institution building" (Bowman and Kearney 2008, 151–52).

Evaluation of the institutional capacity of state legislatures continues to this day. One measure that may signify the ability of the legislature to work effectively, or the "capacity of the legislatures to function as independent branches of government" (National Conference n.d.) according to the National Conference of State Legislatures (NCSL), is the size of their support staff. In other words, as per the NCSL, the capacity of the legislative body, or the ability to balance power with the office of the governor and gain access to independent information to make effective policy decisions, is a function of the size of legislative staff.

As of 2015 the legislative staff of the Nebraska legislature numbered 229 permanent staff and 7 session-only staff, for a total of 236 staff members during session (National Conference n.d.). This includes administrative assistants, clerks, legislative aides, legal counsels, and research analysts, as well as the staff of the Legislative Council offices of the clerk, audit, fiscal analyst, ombudsman, research, and revisor of statutes. Nebraska ranks fortieth in size of legislative staff as compared with the other U.S. state legislatures. However, looking at the ratio of legislative staff to number of legislators, Nebraska ranks eighteenth, with around five legislative staff per state legislator.

Full versus part-time status of the legislators may be another measure of legislative capacity and functionality. The NCSL classifies state legislatures by the full or part-time status of the incumbents, referring to the amount of time spent on legislative work, compensation, and number of staff (National Conference n.d.). NCSL divides the state legislatures into three main categories: full-time, high pay, large staff (ten states); part-time, low pay, small staff (fourteen states); and a hybrid category into which most states (twenty-six) fall, including Nebraska.

Nebraska state senators technically serve on a part-time basis, earning $12,000 plus benefits annually with reimbursed expenses. Legislators residing within fifty miles of the capital receive $55 per day, and legislators residing more than fifty miles from the capital receive $151 per day. With a few exceptions, they have other employment. There have been attempts to raise the salaries of state senators. A proposed measure to raise salaries to $22,500 a year was soundly defeated by Nebraska voters on November 6, 2012. The issue was placed on the ballot as a legislatively referred constitutional amendment, not as a citizen-driven initiative.

Despite the low salary and small staff, Nebraska's legislature is categorized by the National Conference of State Legislatures as a hybrid, meaning that state legislators spend more than two-thirds of a full-time job on legislative work with a medium-sized staff. According to a 2014 survey by the National Conference of State Legislatures, the average job time of hybrid state legislators is 74 percent, with an average salary of $41,110, having on the average a total staff of 479. (The Nebraska Unicameral has a staff of 236.) The border states of Colorado, Iowa, and Missouri have hybrid legislatures, while Kansas, Wyoming, and South Dakota have low-pay, small staff legislatures.

Leadership in the Unicameral, because of its nonpartisan disposition, must be facilitated by a process other than through political parties. Nonpartisanship not only affects the selection of legislative leaders but also impacts the development and promotion of policy proposals. Nebraska legislators do not caucus by political parties to develop proposals and prepare positions on specific bills. In addition, the absence of a party whip limits the extent of political party discipline exerted over state senators.

The original design of the unicameral intentionally diminished the potential for dominant leadership, effectively neutralizing the clout of political obedience (Berens 2004). However, over time, the speaker gained internal power, exacting authority over committee systems, setting the daily agenda, and serving as the presiding officer of floor deliberations, a power formally designated to the lieutenant governor (Sittig 1986). Consequently, the leadership role of the lieutenant governor has been significantly reduced, with the growth of legislative staff contributing to this as well. Select committees, most notably the executive board and the Committee on Committees, maintain a role in leadership through supervision and committee assignment (Sittig 1987).

However, according to Sue Crawford:

> The speaker power varies by person and is weaker than any other state to my knowledge. The bill agenda usually follows worksheet order, so agenda setting is in the margins. The priority bill process also puts the speaker's agenda setting power within strict parameters. The speaker is supposed to get all priority bills to the floor, so all senators are setting the agenda. This is a very unique agenda setting mechanism. All senators get one bill to the floor, all committees get two bills to the floor, the speaker gets twenty-five. This is why a bill that is never successful can continue to be on the floor over and over. If it can get out of committee, any senator can prioritize it and then it gets floor time. (Crawford interview)

Nevertheless, political party representation in the Nebraska legislature tends to reflect the conservative leanings of the state populace. For example, in the 2021 legislature, Republican senators outnumbered Democratic senators thirty-two to seventeen, a ratio of nearly two to one. All seventeen of the Democratic senators represent districts located in the large urban counties of Douglas, Lancaster, and Sarpy, accentuating the urban-rural division. Republican chairpersons headed eleven of the fourteen standing committees and three of the four select committees. In recent years, there appears to be a growing partisanship division in the body (Crawford interview).

While direct party leadership may be diluted due to the structure of the unicameral, political affiliation undoubtedly yields some influence in legislative affairs. Yet the limitations of party organization and discipline provide for a more open system of coalition building, albeit at times more unpredictable because of these characteristics. Voting coalitions may form on various other premises, such as rural-urban, geography, seniority, or technical expertise (Berens 2005). As such, the punitive actions of citizens dissatisfied with legislative actions, that is, voting out members of the culpable party, are similarly obscured by the nebulous nature of voting alliances (Rodgers, Sittig, and Welch 1984).

## The Veto, the Initiative, and the Referendum

The Unicameral's nonpartisan structure essentially removes any substantive "institutional means" for the governor to exert political party leadership in legislative processes (Rodgers, Sittig, and Welch 1984, 82). Therefore, the veto power of the governor represents a distinct method of gubernatorial influence yet also perhaps the most controversial. Nebraska governors possess slightly above average veto powers, exempted only in constitutional amendments and legislature resolutions. Yet an extremely small percentage of legislative measures elicit a veto from the governor, and due to the associated political implications and confrontational nature of such actions, Nebraska governors exercise this authority cautiously.

After the final passage of a bill, the governor has five days to act on legislation. A veto returns the bill to the legislature, and a three-fifths vote (thirty members) is needed to override the veto. The difficulty of the three-fifths coalition leads to the political sensitivity of the veto, which may be perceived as an affront to the intent of the legislature and, in turn, the citizenry. However, in the instance that the veto override is achieved, such a visible political defeat may have repercussions for the governor's policy agenda and the executive-legislature relationship during the remainder of the governor's term in office. Rather than vetoing the whole bill, Nebraska governors may utilize the line-item veto only for appropriations. While the average number of vetoes per session ranges from ten to fifteen, some governors have utilized the veto quite liberally; for instance, Governor J. James Exon executed a record 141 during his two terms from 1971 to 1979, averaging nearly 18 per session (U.S Congress 2005). (Chapter 10 includes a discussion of the trend in veto overrides.)

Consistent with the political culture of Nebraska, several methods of citizen control exist in governmental enterprise, with two, the initiative and the referendum, most prominent in the legislative process. Nebraska is one of twenty-four states with the initiative petition, which may be used to add or change a state law or amend the state constitution, and the popular referendum, which may repeal a law passed by the legislature (National Conference n.d.). The Nebraska initiative is direct, meaning that successful petitions go directly to the ballot without requiring legislature approval. An initiative must be filed with the secretary of state's office and must attain the required number of signatures from Nebraska registered voters to reach the ballot. A 1994 Nebraska Supreme Court decision decreed that signatures from seven percent of the registered voters in the state is required for an initiative proposing a law and 10 percent for a constitutional amendment, also necessitating that the signatures must represent five percent of registered voters from at least thirty-eight of the ninety-three counties (Nebraska Secretary of State n.d.).

The referendum, added to the Nebraska Constitution in 1912, represents a similar tool of public oversight of the legislature. In Nebraska the referendum may be used to repeal a law recently passed by the legislature by collecting enough signatures to demand a popular vote. The referendum process mirrors that of the initiative, requiring signatures from 5 percent of registered voters, 10 percent to suspend a law, and must meet the stipulated county representations. These instruments of citizen lawmaking in Nebraska embody the progressive state government reforms of the early twentieth century to ensure the responsiveness of state legislatures to citizen interests (Sittig 1986). The initiative and referendum demonstrate the importance placed on citizen safeguards in the state government. While occasionally used for most of Nebraska's history, they now appear to be used more frequently.

## Lobbying in the Unicameral

George Norris, in his vision of the Nebraska Unicameral, heralded the eradication of special-interest lobbying from the state legislature through a more objective, transparent, and nonpartisan process (Berens 2004). The simplicity and openness of the unicameral legislative structure did succeed, at least, in providing for enhanced regulation and scrutiny of lobbyist dealings, and the removal of lobbyists from the legislative chamber in 1965 offered a symbolic gesture of distancing lobbying pressures from lawmaking. Despite these attempted deterrents, the lobbyist constituency remains formidable in Nebraska; the 2021 listing of registered lobbyists identifies 582 lobbying principals of the state legislature (Clerk of the Legislature 2015).

Lobbying in the nonpartisan atmosphere of the Nebraska Unicameral assumes a unique quality. In theory, the lack of political parties should be detrimental to the influence of special interest, but, it may have the opposite effect. A generally accepted view is that the weakening of political party competition tends to strengthen the power of interest groups by reducing disciplinary barriers and partisan admonitions (Kolasa 1978). While most lobbyists in Nebraska maintain partisan affiliations, the political neutrality of legislators may make them more open to special interest lobbies without fear of retribution from party leadership. In addition, the party persuasion of the governor and the coveted endorsements of politically favorable lobbyist groups tend to weigh heavily in the election campaigns of state senators (Masket and Shor 2015), suggesting that partisanship and special interests may still pervade the policy decisions and alignments of legislators.

Special-interest lobbying seems inevitable, despite the viewpoint that its influence is harmful. This perception of harm exemplifies Nebraskan's general distrust of external interferences and corporate intrusions in the public realm. In surveys from 2000 and 2001, approximately 60 percent of citizens and 50 percent of lawmakers agree that the Unicameral is too heavily influenced by lobbyists. Yet the extent of this influence is debatable; 70 percent of state senators reported that citizens are the more frequent source of information on legislative actions, as opposed to only 27 percent that reported the same of lobbyists (Berens 2005).

## CRITICAL AND ENDURING ISSUES

The distinctive characteristics and structures of the Nebraska legislature, while inherently representative of the political history and cultural underpinnings of this midwestern state, also impart dutiful responsibilities of maintenance and viable governance. The unicameral system, fundamentally idiosyncratic, demonstrates populism in action, separating Nebraska from its counterparts and invoking an exclusive atmosphere of state politics and government (Comer 1980). As such, a few current and enduring issues embody both the continued functionality and progression of the unicameralism ideal into the future.

The 2007 legislative session ushered in term limits approved by voters, amending the Nebraska Constitution. Henceforth, state senators may serve only two consecutive four-year terms. As of 2023 only fifteen other states mandate term limits on state legislators, with six of these states decreeing a lifetime limit that restricts elected officials from ever seeking reelection to the legislative body (National Conference n.d.). In Nebraska the term limits are consecutive, meaning that former term-limited members may run for office again in four years after their two consecutive terms. As a distinguished example, state senator Ernie Chambers of Omaha, currently the longest-serving state legislator in Nebraska history at forty-two years, returned to office in 2012 after being term-limited in 2008 following the initial implementation of the new constitutional amendment. He again was term-limited in 2020.

The enactment of term limits undoubtedly alters the scheme of the Unicameral. Proponents contend that term limits contribute to expanded competition in elections, the removal of entrenched career politicians, the reinvigoration of responsiveness to constituents, and a timely renewal of views and leadership. Yet many legislators argue that the restrictions of term limits will inhibit the lawmaking process, reducing experience, interrupting leadership continuity, dissolving cultivated bipartisan relationships, and exacerbating lame-duck scenarios (Bend 2006). Term limits also may impact other aspects of institutional effectiveness, placing more emphasis on politically salient topics while detracting from less prominent legislative obligations such as oversight and monitoring of state agencies and administrative systems (Sarbaugh-Thompson et al. 2010). These concerns have prompted state legislators to pursue modifications to the constitutional limits, although such measures have been repeatedly defeated including a public vote in 2012 on extending the limits to three terms (Duggan 2015). The Nebraska Term Limits Amendment, also known as Amendment 3, was on the November 6, 2012, ballot as a legislatively referred constitutional amendment, not a citizen-driven initiative. It was defeated by a vote of 65 percent to 35 percent.

The debate of nonpartisanship also continues to confront the Nebraska legislature. While demonstrative of an altruistic attempt to dismantle preemptively the establishment of onerous political party controls, notable implications have surfaced within the Unicameral due to this edict, as have been discussed in length within this chapter and others in this book. Representing a testament to the progressive and populist tenets enshrined within Nebraska state government, the nonpartisanship of the legislature follows a tradition of citizen-based politics and decentralized interests, adding another layer of protection to an already simplified one-house structure (Berens 2004). It will be seen if this nonpartisan tradition continues in the Unicameral.

Nebraska nonpartisanship, one of the state's political culture foundations, generally provides for a legislative environment more amenable to compromise, cooperation, and issue-orientated voting, which does not exist in other legislature partisan settings. An example of how a nonpartisan legislature allows senators from different parties and ideologies to work together to achieve a common goal occurred in November 2021. Five Nebraska state senators, as a team, climbed Africa's Mt. Kilimanjaro. Two senators were Democrats from urban Omaha districts, and three were Republicans from rural districts in the state. Additionally, one was Native American, one was African American, and one was a woman. Together they were able to achieve a common goal, which was climbing Mt. Kilimanjaro, despite their differing characteristics and political affiliation and philosophy. While the senators may have differed on policy issues debated in the legislature, the fact that they could work together as a team demonstrates how a nonpartisan ethos can facilitate a level of collaboration. That is a hopeful sign in a combative political world.

However, as history has shown, the influences of political parties, while discrete, have found means to permeate the Unicameral's institutions. Moreover, nonpartisan elections may stifle turnout and increase the advantage of incumbents (Schaffner, Streb, and Wright 2001). Although term limits and the predominantly conservative leanings of the voting populace may additionally ameliorate some of these apprehensions, nonpartisanship, somewhat contrary to its original intent, has complicated the dynamic of the Nebraska legislature.

Both issues have implications for the operation and future effectiveness of the Unicameral. In the age of governmental reform and devolution, the adaptability of state governments, particularly in the management and decentralization of bureaucracy and administration, has become an invaluable asset. The function of state legislatures to oversee and enable such reforms depends on the makeup and nature of legislative processes. Research in this area suggests that less professional legislatures with term limits, both indicative traits of the Nebraska Unicameral, display an association with more positive influences in administrative outcomes, expressly in the efficacy of administrative systems and the utilization of performance management techniques (Bourdeaux and Chikoto 2008). The design of the Nebraska legislature has a basis in reform and efficiency, and the unicameralism philosophy espouses the performance and productivity of government. Thus, in the traditions of enhanced citizen representation and nonpartisan processes, the demonstrated capability of the Unicameral to adapt to the changing needs of state government may further help to ensure the continued longevity of this uniquely Nebraskan institution.

## REFERENCES

Bend, Doug. 2006. "Term Limits for Nebraska State Senators: A Challenge to the Future Effectiveness of the Nebraska State Legislature." *Creighton Law Review* 40:3–39.

Berens, Charlyne. 2004. *Power to the People: Social Choice and the Populist/Progressive Ideal.* Lanham MD: University Press of America.

———. 2005. *One House: The Unicameral's Progressive Vision for Nebraska.* Lincoln: University of Nebraska Press.

Bourdeaux, Carolyn, and Grace Chikoto. 2008. "Legislative Influences on Performance Management Reform." *Public Administration Review* 68 (2): 253–65.

Bowman, Ann O'M., and Richard C. Kearney. 2008. *State and Local Government: The Essentials.* 7th ed. Boston: Houghton Mifflin.

Breckenridge, Adam C. 1978. "The Origin and Development of the Nonpartisan Unicameral Legislature." In *Nonpartisanship in the Legislative Process: Essays on the Nebraska Legislature,* edited by John C. Comer and James B. Johnson, 11–27. Washington DC: University Press of America.

Citizens' Conference on State Legislatures. 1973. *The Sometimes Governments: A Critical Study of the 50 American Legislatures.* 2nd ed. Kansas City MO: Citizens' Conference on State Legislatures.

Clerk of the Legislature. 2009. *A Look at Your Unicameral.* Lincoln: Unicameral Information Office.

———. 2015. *Principals and Registered Lobbyists of the Current Session—As of July 17, 2015.* Lincoln: Nebraska Clerk of the Legislature.

Comer, John C. 1980. "The Nebraska Nonpartisan Legislature: An Evaluation." *State and Local Government Review* 12 (3): 98–102.

Duggan, Joe. 2015 "Nebraska Lawmakers Decide against Asking Voters to Extend Term Limits." *Omaha World-Herald,* April 13, 2015.

Hovey, Kendra A., and Harold A. Hovey. 2007. *Congressional Quarterly's State Fact Finder: Rankings across America.* Washington DC: CQ Press.

Kolasa, Bernard D. 1978. "Lobbying in the Legislature: The Influence of Nonpartisanship." In *Nonpartisanship in the Legislative Process: Essays on the Nebraska Legislature,* edited by John C. Comer and James B. Johnson, 91–100. Washington DC: University Press of America.

Masket, Seth, and Boris Shor. 2015. "Polarization without Parties: Term Limits and Legislative Partisanship in Nebraska's Unicameral Legislature." *State Politics and Policy Quarterly* 15 (1): 67–90.

National Conference of State Legislatures. n.d. "About State Legislatures." Accessed February 8, 2023. https://www.ncsl.org/about-state-legislatures.

———. 2023. "Legislatures at a Glance." https://www.ncsl.org/about-state-legislatures/legislatures-at-a-glance.

Nebraska Legislature. n.d.a. "History of the Nebraska Unicameral." Accessed February 8, 2023. http://nebraskalegislature.gov/about/history_unicameral.php.

———. n.d.b. "Select and Special Committees." Accessed February 8, 2023. http://nebraskalegislature.gov/committees/select-committees.php.

———. 2018. "Inside Our Nation's Only Unicameral." https://www.nebraskalegislature.gov/pdf/about/lookbook.pdf.

———. 2020. *2020–2021 Nebraska Blue Book*. Lincoln: Nebraska Legislature.

Nebraska Secretary of State. n.d. "How to Use the Initiative and Referendum Process in Nebraska." Accessed February 8, 2023. https://sos.nebraska.gov/sites/sos.nebraska.gov/files/doc/01-init_ref.pdf.

Rodgers, Jack, Robert Sittig, and Susan Welch. 1984. "The Legislature." In *Nebraska Government and Politics*, edited by Robert D. Miewald, 78–80. Lincoln: University of Nebraska Press.

Safell, David C., and Harry Basehart. 2005. *State and Local Government: Politics and Public Policies*. 8th ed. New York: McGraw Hill.

Sarbaugh-Thompson, Marjorie, John Strate, Kelly Leroux, Richard C. Elling, Lyke Thompson, and Charles D. Elder. 2010. "Legislators and Administrators: Complex Relationships Complicated by Term Limits." *Legislative Studies Quarterly* 35 (1): 57–89.

Schaffner, Brian F., Matthew Streb, and Gerald Wright. 2001. "Teams without Uniforms: The Nonpartisan Ballot in State and Local Elections." *Political Research Quarterly* 54 (1): 7–30.

Sittig, Robert. 1986. *The Nebraska Unicameral after Fifty Years*. Lincoln: University of Nebraska–Lincoln.

———. 1987. "The Nebraska Legislature: Policy Implications of its Organization and Operation." In *Nebraska Policy Choices*, edited by Russell L. Smith, 273–95. Omaha: University of Nebraska at Omaha Center for Public Affairs Research.

Todd, Tom. 1998. "Nebraska's Unicameral Legislature: A Description and Some Comparisons with Minnesota's Bicameral Legislature." *Journal of the American Society of Legislative Clerks and Secretaries* (Spring).

U.S. Congress. 2005. *J. James Exon Late a Senator from Nebraska Memorial Addresses and Other Tributes in the Congress of the United States*. S. Doc. 109-6. Washington DC: U.S. Government Printing Office.

Welch, Susan, and Eric H. Carlson. 1973. "The Impact of Party of Voting Behavior in a Nonpartisan Legislature." *American Political Science Review* 67 (3): 854–67.

# CHAPTER SEVEN

# The Executive Branch

EFFICIENCY VERSUS RESPONSIVENESS

*Robert Blair, Christian L. Janousek, and Jerome Deichert*

### INTRODUCTION

As described in chapter 1, Nebraska's political culture, a mixture of individualistic and moralistic dimensions, shapes state institutions, including the structure and operation of the office of the governor and state agencies. In particular, the dominant dimension of Nebraska's political culture, individualism, with its emphasis on efficiency, significantly impacts the organization of the governor's office and state government. Though with less impact, moralism focuses on populism and responsiveness and also influences the functioning of these arms of state government. Thus, chapter 7 discusses the conflict between efficiency and responsiveness in the executive branch of Nebraska government.

A governor, however, can impact the conflict between efficiency and responsiveness within the operation of the office. For example, Governor Pete Ricketts, in 2021, emphasized efficiency. He had on his website a page titled "Running Government like a Business," where he said that his administration is "applying commonsense management practices that are standard in private sector business" (Nebraska Office of the Governor 2021).

This chapter provides an overview of the structure and function of state government and its various agencies. It includes a discussion of the office of the governor and his or her role as chief executive, the organizational arrangements of the executive branch, and the nature and structure of Nebraska state government and administration.

## THE GOVERNOR OF NEBRASKA

The Nebraska governor, according to the state constitution, holds supreme executive power of the state to "take care that the laws be faithfully executed, and the affairs of the state efficiently and economically administered" (Article IV, Section 6). The governor serves as the chief budget officer of the state and fulfills several executive duties, including appointing state officials, acting as the commander-in-chief of national and state guards, enforcing criminal laws, and signing or vetoing bills passed by the state legislature (Nebraska Legislature 2018). Nebraskans elect governors to a four-year term, limited to two consecutive terms, and governors must be at least thirty years of age and a resident of Nebraska for at least five years prior to election (Nebraska State Constitution, Article IV, Section 2).

The governor receives assistance from the Governor's Policy Research Office, a division within the governor's office. Additionally, by law, the lieutenant governor performs duties as assigned by the governor.

In Nebraska, like most states, the governor acts as the chief administrative officer of state government. However, this was not always the case. Throughout most of U.S. history, governors, including Nebraska's, acted as weak governmental executives. Initially designated primarily as political figures, governors lacked the tools to be effective administrators of state government (Beyle 1996). Historic distrust of all political executives in the United States hampered the heads of states from acquiring significant sources of power, including gubernatorial control over the administrative structure of the state government (Wyner 1985).

Reforms in public administration, rooted in the Progressive Era taking place toward the end of the nineteenth century, however, initiated the long process of giving governors greater powers, including much stronger roles in the management of state agencies (Cooper 2008). For instance, the preparation of the executive state budget by the governor and submitted to the legislature, consistent with individualistic political culture, enhances organizational efficiency.

One of the key responsibilities of the governor today now includes growth management, serving as the chief promoter of state economic development (Gray and Eisinger 1997; National Governors Association n.d.b.). The governor's other duties include chief policymaker, chief legislator, chief of state, chief executive, and chief administrator. This is also the case for Nebraska.

Several factors contribute to the growing importance of this executive office of state government. Most significantly, changes in the relationship between the national and state governments give the states more responsibility for domestic program administration (McClure Brooks 2008). Today, governors act as important figures in state and national governmental politics and administration, and from 1976 to 2012, four presidents first served as former governors.

As the chief administrative officer, governors perform at least three specific executive duties: head of management, head of program development, and head of external relations (Abney and Lauth 1986). The management role of the governor involves directing and coordinating the agencies of state government toward a common set of general policy goals. The program development task includes the drafting and modifying of individual programs, striving to keep them consistent with statewide policy goals. The external relations job embraces interaction with the actors in the policy processes of the state, including interest groups, the state legislature, and the public. Of course, the nature and effectiveness of these gubernatorial administrative responsibilities vary from state to state.

The following section discusses the role of the Nebraska governor as the chief administrator in state government in three ways: (1) examining the perceptions of the governor's influence over state administration; (2) reviewing one of the governor's chief administrative tools, agency reorganization; and (3) evaluating and comparing Nebraska's gubernatorial power rating to other states.

### THE CHIEF ADMINISTRATIVE OFFICER
### OF STATE GOVERNMENT

Like many public institutions and large bureaucratic organizations, state government agencies often react slowly to input from governors and other actors. Frequently, governors lack formal or institutional authority over several state offices, which may "have a perspective that is independent of the governor" (Cox 1991, 62). Nonetheless, many governors still effectively direct state government actions, as many states have steadily increased the executive power of the governor (Garnett 1985).

Abney and Lauth, in a landmark 1986 study, provide a baseline for examining gubernatorial power over state government administration. They asked state agency heads to estimate the relative level of influence of their governor over the management of their departments. The study revealed that governors greatly influence administrative matters if administrators consider the governor's policy position as the most important one, indicating agency independence.

Abney and Lauth examined how much influence the governor has over state agencies in terms of administrative matters. Their research showed that only 37 percent of the agency heads in Nebraska responded that the governor had the most influence over administrative matters. When compared to other states, the Nebraska governor's perceived administrative influence rated about average. Nebraska placed in the middle of twenty states where only one-fourth to one-half of the administrators responded that the governor demonstrated the most administrative influence. In general, then, at least in 1986, U.S. governors, like Nebraska's, showed only a moderate amount of influence over the administration of state agencies. It is expected that the Nebraska governor's level of influence, in most cases, has not changed significantly since the study.

The Abney and Lauth study also measured agency dependence on the governor. Their research showed that Nebraska overall ranked low when compared to other states. Nebraska placed in the top ten states in terms of high levels of preference for agency, or internal task selection, and forty-second for percent of time spent by agencies on lobbying activities. State agencies in Nebraska, then, at least according to this study, appear to be relatively independent from the governor when compared to other states. This helps explain the historically weak governor stance portrayed by many Nebraska governors (Welch 1984).

It is important to note that more recent research suggests that the governor's role in state administration has remained relatively constant since the 1986 Abney and Lauth study. This research finds a consistency of limited direct interaction by most governors in the management and administration of agencies. Despite a general expansion of gubernatorial powers in U.S. states, agency heads continue to perceive only a modest increase in the governors' control and oversight of administrative matters (Burke, Cho, and

Wright 2008; Moynihan and Ingraham 2010). Nebraska, as shown below, generally follows this pattern.

## REORGANIZING, STREAMLINING, AND CONSOLIDATING AGENCIES

Another measure of the chief administrator role of the governor relates to state agency cooperation and partnerships. This involves efforts by governors to ensure coordination of state administrative functions. Reorganization is an administrative tool commonly employed by governors to focus accountability and improve coordination of state agencies. State government reorganization usually includes consolidation of state agencies. Governors employ departmental reorganization schemes in response to pressures to "revamp their administrative apparatus" (Garnett 1985, 11) and to improve agency synchronization and enhance efficiency.

Traditionally, state constitutional provisions and political customs limited the reorganization options available to governors. While governors may shuffle minor administrative tasks from agency to agency as part of executive restructuring, comprehensive government reorganization involves shifting significant public authorities and responsibilities among agencies, often requiring statutory or constitutional revisions. By the 1990s most of the states undertook major structural reorganizations of government agencies "in order to locate responsibilities for decisions" (Gray and Eisinger 1997, 167) through enhanced administrative accountability. Of the thirty-six states completing comprehensive reorganizations from 1965 to 1995, twenty-six occurred before 1980, mostly in the South and West. Nebraska did not successfully implement a comprehensive state reorganization during that thirty-year period (Chi and Wiley 1996).

Many governors, at that time, "spearheaded major reorganizations of the executive branch, striving for greater rationality and for reductions in the number of boards and commissions" (Gormley 1996, 163). Guided by reorganization and reinvention principles, Nebraska used this administrative tool in the mid-1990s albeit relatively conservatively. Nebraska use of the reorganization process ranked in the bottom half of all fifty states toward the end of the century (Brudney, Hebert, and Wright 1999).

In the late 1990s, however, Nebraska finally underwent a major restructuring. Under the direction of the governor, the state created the Nebraska

Health and Human Services System. After a two-year period of study and following the passage of appropriate state legislation, on January 1, 1997, four major state departments (Departments of Aging, Health, Public Institutions, and Social Services) and one office from another department (Office of Juvenile Services from the Department of Correctional Services) disappeared as independent agencies of state government. They merged to form a superagency committed to a unified health and human services network in the state. Officials claim this consolidation of state agencies resulted in "the most far-reaching government reorganization project ever undertaken in Nebraska" (Nebraska Health and Human Services 1996, 1).

Governor Ben Nelson formally initiated the agency reorganization effort in 1995 (four other governors also proposed comprehensive state reorganizations that year in their state of the state messages) (Chi and Wiley 1996). Nelson issued an executive order to "review health activities and increase the state's capacity to affect health policy through research, information transfer, advocacy, public/private partnerships, cooperation among communities, and coordination among service providers and state agencies" (Nebraska Partnership Project 1995, 4). This major departmental reorganization formed a health and human services policy cabinet, consisting of the directors of three new functional agencies: services delivery, licensure and regulation, and finance and support, plus a policy secretary.

The formation of the Nebraska health and human services superagency attempted to achieve two goals: improve agency coordination and efficiency by focusing on achieving measurable outcomes and expand partnerships with local communities for program delivery "through flexibility, joint problem-solving, decentralized decision making and shared accountability" (Nebraska Partnership Project 1994, 2). Reorganization successes generally are measured by the realization of agency goals. Despite some achievements, in the years since reorganization, in 1997, the department encountered many challenging issues and public criticisms related to oversight and accountability, resulting in numerous changes in agency heads, and calls for new waves of reform (Young 2014).

Nevertheless, by reducing the number of executive agencies in this reorganization effort and creating a policy cabinet to oversee the administration of the superagency, Nebraska at last followed a national streamlining trend during the 1990s reflecting expanded state responsibilities and resources

(Herbert, Wright, and Brudney 1992). Many states, like Nebraska, developed a cabinet type of organizational structure, similar to the national government, where a limited number of department heads report to the governor and meet periodically to advise on policy development and agency coordination (Chi 1992). By 1995 forty states had adopted a cabinet form of executive government, up from fourteen states in 1965 (Chi and Wiley 1996).

One approach to concentrating the administrative and management power of the governor includes limiting the number of state agencies reporting to the governor. As described above, Nebraska took this step toward improving its cabinet structure in 1997. This resulted in some positive results. The Pew Center on the States, in their 2008 state government performance indicators grading, noted that "Nebraska is a responsible fiscal steward and uses a long-term perspective when making tax and expenditure decisions" (1). Nebraska received a grade of B, with only eight states receiving higher grades, with a national average of B− (Pew Center 2008). In addition, in 2017 the Nebraska legislature further reduced the number of agencies directly controlled by the governor when it created the Nebraska Department of Transportation, merging the Department of Roads with the Department of Aeronautics.

### MEASURING ADMINISTRATIVE POWER

A final assessment of the administrative role of the governor includes an evaluation of the overall power of the office. A benchmark measure of gubernatorial power (the Beyle index) includes several dimensions of formal executive authority: number of separately elected executive branch officials, tenure potential of office, appointing power over executive leadership positions, budget power, veto power, and party control governor's party have in legislature (Beyle 2008). Since the Nebraska legislature is nonpartisan, the dimension of party control contributes less to the Nebraska governor's index of power.

Beyle's estimate of the formal power of the governor's office appears to be largely associated with the chief administrator role: the centralization of administrative authority (for example, number of other elected state executives and the governor's appointing power), the level of policymaking influence (for example, budget authority and the type of veto power), and the amount of programmatic discretion (for example, budget-making and personnel appointing authority). Empirical evidence shows that "more powerful governors have greater impact on administrative action and decisions" (Elling 1992, 163), supporting the Beyle index focuses on the formal and administrative roles of the governor.

In 2007, according to the Beyle index, the Nebraska governor measured 3.8 in gubernatorial power. When compared to other governors in the United States, the Nebraska governor ranked as one of the more powerful, tied with five states for fifth place. The power index of U.S. governors ranged from weak (2.5 for Vermont) to strong (4.3 for Massachusetts). The median power rating for all U.S. states was 3.5 (Beyle 2007). Tracking this measure of gubernatorial power since 1960, however, Beyle noted in 2008 that overall, "there has not been a considerable increase in the institutional powers of governors" (207).

The Beyle power index explains more when used in conjunction with other measures of the office of the governor. Beyle's index, which shows the Nebraska governor moderately powerful in relation to other states, is supported by other studies. While the National Governors Association (NGA) does not employ a formal rating scale, they track gubernatorial institutional powers using information which incorporates qualifications and tenure, legislative budget and veto authority, and appointment sovereignty (National Governors Association n.d.a.). Nebraska continues to rank relatively high nationally by these standards, despite term limits and shared appointment approval (Council of State Government 2014). Thus, by most measures, the formal office of the Nebraska governor rates moderate to very powerful when compared with other states. How institutional power is exercised by Nebraska governors is examined in the following sections.

## THE EXECUTIVE BRANCH

The executive branch of state government includes the structure and organizational arrangement of state offices and agencies by function and task. States differ in their approach to government organization. Most state governments, by design, dispersed executive authority and administrative power. Organizational centralization and agency control rarely existed in state government systems, and until recently, the dispersion approach to state administrative power prevailed (Council of State Governments 2022). Nebraska's framework for state government agencies embodies that time-honored organizational model with some exceptions.

## Traditional Structuring of State Government

Nebraska's constitution provides for a traditional administrative structure for state government, consisting of several integrated executive agencies under the governor's control mixed with several independently elected top-level state executives and other agencies administratively separate from the governor (Maddox and Fuquay 1981). Traditional state governments typically utilize five classes of executive branch agencies: (1) agencies led by governor-appointed officials; (2) offices headed by elected constitutional executives; (3) public authorities and corporations; (4) agencies supervised by independent board members or commissioners; and (5) independent agencies (Chi and Wiley 1996). Nebraska employs variations of all five classes of agencies.

## Governor-Appointed Officials

Executive agencies of Nebraska state government consist of two basic types of units: code and non-code agencies. Code and non-code state agencies maintain separate staff and appear as distinct items in the state budget. Code agencies include those departments and offices directly controlled by the governor. The governor appoints the heads of code agencies. They report to the governor and serve at his or her pleasure. The governor's executive budget submitted to the legislature includes the code agency budgets.

Non-code agencies, discussed in more detail in subsequent sections, function independently, not subject to direct control by the governor. Their directors are appointed by a board or commission, not by the governor (Nebraska Legislature 2018), though the governor does have indirect influence in several ways that will be described later.

According to the 2020 *Nebraska Personnel Almanac*, Nebraska state government contained eighteen executive code agencies that employed 12,440 permanent FTEs. The thirty-nine non-code agencies employed 969 permanent FTEs. Additionally, there are constitutional agencies created by the Nebraska State Constitution. Excluding the University of Nebraska and state colleges, the remaining sixteen constitutional agencies employed 2,733 FTEs (State Personnel Division 2020). As such, the governor directly controls 77 percent of the total executive branch employees. In Nebraska the executive branch includes the eight independent constitutional agencies and all the code and non-code agencies.

Nebraska's code agencies provide a variety of services to the citizens of the state. Departments under gubernatorial control, in most states, meet public needs in several functional areas, including (1) health, safety, and environmental protection; (2) economic, community and employment development; (3) transportation improvement; and (4) human services provision. Code agencies in Nebraska also regulate portions of the state's agricultural, banking and finance, health care, and insurance industries. The remaining code agencies provide administrative and policy support. Some strategic state functions, however, operate outside direct control by the governor of Nebraska and are considered non-code agencies.

Education policy and program development, for example, an important responsibility of state government, occurs without direct influence by the governor in Nebraska. This lack of gubernatorial control may be critical since most states play a major policy, funding, and regulatory role in education (Goertz 2003, 179). The state university system, the state college system, and the state Department of Education, in this regard, function as non-code agencies, with only indirect control by the governor. Nebraska citizens directly elect the members of the University of Nebraska Board of Regents and the State Board of Education. According to government organizational charts (Chi and Wiley 1996), only six states structure their state educational systems like Nebraska's elected boards.

The Nebraska governor maintains important budgetary and veto power over state education and other non-code agency funding and programs. However, he or she shares little policy direction and development with the independently elected boards.

## Elected Constitutional Offices

The Nebraska state constitution, following the traditional state government model, disperses administrative power by providing for the election of six state officials and three boards or commissions that administer independent state executive agencies. Popularly elected state political executives in Nebraska, in addition to the governor, include the auditor of public accounts, treasurer, secretary of state, attorney general, and lieutenant governor. In contrast to the legislature, these six state executives are elected on a partisan basis. The lieutenant governor is selected by the governor and runs on the same ticket.

Independently elected are also the members of the State Board of Education and the University of Nebraska Board of Regents. Like the Nebraska legislature, the elections for the Board of Education and the Board of Regents are nonpartisan. The State Board of Education supervises and regulates the state's local school programs and districts and appoints the commissioner of education who heads the Department of Education. The Board of Regents provides policy guidance to the four-campus University of Nebraska system, with a large portion of the state government workforce.

Another independently elected body, though on a partisan basis, is the Public Service Commission. This commission regulates the rates and services of common carriers in the state.

Like many states with traditional state government structures, many of Nebraska's basic state responsibilities function beyond the direct control of the governor. This represents a challenge to the governor, the chief administrator of state government.

## Public Authorities and Quasi-government Corporations

Many states, including Nebraska, rely on public authorities and quasi-government corporations to deliver specialized public services. Authorities and government corporations significantly differ in structure from other state government agencies. Designed as self-supporting and revenue-generating entities, structured for flexible operations, and organized to function independently from direct government influence and financial support, governmental authorities and corporations pursue essentially commercial missions (Shafritz 1980). Classified as quasi-governmental agencies, they are instrumentalities of state governments: created and sometimes initially funded by the legislature to meet a pressing public need yet structured to operate much like a private corporate entity. Some states extensively use public authorities and corporations.

Public authorities and corporations contain both advantages and disadvantages in meeting the public interest, much like individualism and moralism, the two often conflicting elements of Nebraska's political culture. They can function efficiently because of their political autonomy and independent revenue-generating capacity. At the same time, authorities and corporations may lack accountability, an important aspect of moralistic political culture, to the public interest because of their autonomous structure and can act irresponsibly. Only a few statewide public authorities or government corporations exist in Nebraska, mostly operating on the local level, including housing, hospital, airport, and transit authorities.

In 1983 the Nebraska legislature established the Nebraska Investment Finance Authority (NIFA) as an independent instrumentality of the state. NIFA facilitates single-family home ownership, low-income housing tax credits, industrial development, and agricultural finance by issuing tax-exempt bonds. Proceeds from bonds support NIFA finance and technical assistance programs. Since its inception, NIFA has financed over ninety-one thousand single-family mortgage loans (n.d.). NIFA resulted from the consolidation of three quasi-governmental corporations: the Nebraska Agricultural Corporation, the Nebraska Development Finance Fund, and the Nebraska Mortgage Finance Fund. Governed by a nine-member board, six appointed by the governor, and agency directors from the Department of Economic Development, Department of Agriculture, and the Nebraska Investment Council, NIFA functions as an independent statewide government instrumentality in Nebraska.

## Independent Boards or Commissions

As described, states employing a traditional government model separate several core public service activities. In this way, many important state responsibilities in a traditional governmental structure are fulfilled beyond the direct control of the governor or the legislature.

Nebraska's thirty-nine non-code agencies, or those offices independent of the governor, exemplify the traditional model. They constitute many of the licensing and regulating boards in the state. While independent in nature and scope, the governor indirectly controls many of the non-code agencies by making appointments to the commissions and licensing boards and using the budget veto power to influence administration and policy. Non-code agencies are described in further detail in the next section.

In addition to non-code agencies, Nebraska maintains approximately 150 other special-purpose advisory committees and licensing boards, usually affiliated with larger agencies, but not including those committees or boards mandated by federal law, multi-state compacts, or ad hoc bodies (Governor's Policy 2002). Nearly one-half of these boards serve in the Department of Health and Human Services, regulating related activities, licensing occupations, or advising state programming and policy. Other departments with licensing and regulatory bodies include Agriculture and Education. In addition, many statutorily created advisory committees and boards assist the Department of Administrative Services. The governor also appoints individuals to approximately thirty other boards, committees, and commissions, not established by the legislature, that primarily advise state agencies.

### Independent and Non-code Agencies

As noted, Nebraska's governor appears to retain considerable institutional power, at least in relation to the governors of many other U.S. states, to manage the machinery of state government. However, formal constraints in the state government system and Nebraska's political culture and traditions limit this power. Non-code agencies, where the governor has little or no authority, prepare their own budget proposals, and develop their own policies. The governor retains at least indirect control over these agencies, given that he or she often appoints the members of the boards or commissions who independently administer the non-code agency.

A dimension used to measure the strength of a state's organization structure includes the number and character of independent agencies. Weak state structures (and weak governors) rely heavily on boards and commissions to handle routine administrative work (Garnett 1985). Nebraska's thirty-nine independent non-code agencies is a relatively small number compared to many states; for example, California relies on more than four hundred independent boards and commissions. Independent boards and commissions, it is often contended, should not perform duties that are purely administrative, as they should be limited to regulatory or rulemaking tasks that are quasi-judicial or quasi-legislative in nature (Maddox and Fuquay 1981).

The establishment of independent agencies in Nebraska and other state governments follows the same reasoning for their development on the national level. Formed to perform tasks requiring actions and decisions with little or no influence from political or private interests, these independent agencies, isolated from other units of government, theoretically act solely in the public interest. These tasks normally include regulation, licensing, and adjudication of selected industries and occupations.

Created in the state constitution or by statute, the thirty-nine non-code and independent executive agencies in Nebraska perform a number of functions. While many are small, specialized government offices with part-time staff, some of the non-code agencies are large and very influential political bodies that operate independently from the governor. The roles of most of the non-code agencies of Nebraska coincide with the generally accepted arguments for independent state government agencies, in part influenced by the state's complex political culture.

While the governor technically holds limited administrative authority over the non-code agencies, he or she can use the political command of the office to sway the legislature to modify the powers of the independent agencies. In addition, the governor has influence in the budget process in the state legislature, with line-item veto power.

In 1986, for example, Governor Bob Kerrey supported the passage of the Telecommunications Act that greatly reduced the power of the Public Service Commission to control telephone rates. The lessening of regulatory power of the commission was supported as an economic development move to enhance Nebraska as a location for the telecommunication industry and to increase the competitiveness of existing firms (Wilson 1993, 203).

Several of the Nebraska non-code agencies, such as those engaged in educational, cultural, and recreational, or industry promotional activities, arguably could be under administrative control by the governor to improve accountability and increase efficiency. The independent executive agencies, such as the secretary of state, the state treasurer, and the public auditor, that perform primarily administrative functions also could be coordinated and controlled by the governor.

Nebraska initially failed to embrace the national trend beginning in the 1960s in the "reductions in the number of boards and commissions" (Gormley 1996, 163), centralizing executive power in the governor. The state's political culture, with an emphasis on responsiveness, favors many independent executive offices and administrative functions independent of the governor.

Nebraska clearly supports the independent administration of several major state functional areas. The autonomy of the Department of Education and University of Nebraska system, for example, appears to counter efforts of administrative streamlining and executive centralizing in Nebraska (such as the creation of the Health and Human Services System in 1997). Attempts to centralize control of the University of Nebraska and the Department of Education in the governor's office would face many obstacles because the

Nebraska Constitution provides for independently elected policy boards for education in the state (except for the appointed members of the State College System Board of Trustees). As a result, changes in the executive structure of administrative control in Nebraska would require constitutional modifications, an inherently arduous and lengthy process and one that appears to counter elements of the state's political culture.

GROWTH AND CHANGE IN STATE GOVERNMENT EMPLOYMENT

In addition to looking at the structure and organization of state agencies, an examination of state government also includes the employment levels of the combined agencies. The number of state government employees reflects the size and nature of state government. Likewise, over time, trends in state employment illustrate shifts in the priorities and character of public service.

Considering the total number of full and part-time employees, in 2017 Nebraska state government employed 41,944 persons (31,459 FTE) (U.S. Census Bureau 2019). This number includes employees of the University of Nebraska and state colleges that were excluded from employment totals discussed earlier. By this measure, Nebraska ranks thirty-eighth among U.S. states. When making state comparisons many factors affecting the number of state employees in a particular state need to be considered. For example, the "ratio of employees to residents is lower in the larger (more populous) states, reflecting economies of scale" (Gray and Eisinger 1997, 181). On a per capita basis, Nebraska state government employment ranks twenty-third overall, with 164 full-time employees per ten thousand population in 2017 (U.S. Census Bureau 2019).

State government employment, however, does not remain static, but rather responds to shifts in public demand, policy priorities, technology, resources, or other factors. Table 10 shows FTE employment figures for Nebraska governments for 1982, 1992, 2002, 2012, and 2017 according to the U.S. Census of Governments (U.S. Census Bureau 2020a).

Labor statistics in table 10 include state government and local government. FTE employment for state government from 1982 to 2017 grew 18 percent. The table also indicates that the total state and local government workforce expanded approximately 27 percent, relatively consistent with national trends.

Direct general state expenditures exceeded $7.4 billion in 2017, placing Nebraska in the bottom one-fifth of states nationally, with two-thirds of

**Table 10. Government employment (FTE) in Nebraska, 1982–2017**

|  | 1982 | 1992 | 2002 | 2012 | 2017 |
|---|---|---|---|---|---|
| State government | 26,897 | 28,746 | 33,184 | 32,094 | 31,655 |
| Local government | 61,153 | 69,488 | 80,821 | 88,818 | 89,822 |
| Total state/local | 88,050 | 98,234 | 114,005 | 120,912 | 121,477 |

Source: U.S. Census Bureau, U.S. Census of Governments. Compiled by author.

the spending (66.6 percent) dedicated to education and public welfare. All spending for that year totaled $10.6 billion. Total revenues for that year amounted to $12.2 billion, with $10.1 billion in general revenue (U.S. Census Bureau 2020b).

However, since many state services are jointly delivered by state and local government, aggregated state and local data may provide a more accurate picture of sub-national public sector employment. According to 2017 data, Nebraska ranked fourth overall in state and local employment FTEs per ten thousand population when compared with the other states, with 633 FTEs per ten thousand population (U.S. Census Bureau 2019). The U.S. average was 511 state and local employees per ten thousand persons. (If public power employees were not included, Nebraska would have 601 FTEs per ten thousand persons and rank eighth nationally.)

The array and distribution of responsibilities between the state government and local governments varies among states, affecting public employment patterns. It is important, then, when comparing governmental employment and functions among states, to examine the structural details of state and local government. In other words, what is the nature of the state's public service delivery structure? Are there specific characteristics of the state and local government workforce that affect its public employment? Nebraska, for example, emphasizes special districts in the delivery of many public services.

In relation to state government employment, Nebraska consists of many elements of local government in part because of its public service delivery network. According to the 2017 Census of Governments, the state contains 2,538 units of local government, which ranks fifteenth among the other states (U.S. Census Bureau 2020c). Special districts (1,234) constitute a large proportion of those government units. Chapter 8 discusses special districts and other units of local government in more detail.

The historical orientations of the Nebraska governor, executive branch, and state bureaucracy reflect the enduring impact of Nebraska's political culture in shaping governmental procedures and constructs. In particular, the populist roots of the state's political cultures espouse a lingering distaste for concentrated political power, especially that which is perceived to stray from citizen accountability and responsiveness (Weinschenk and Helpap 2015). Moreover, partisan politics often are deemed inconsequential, or at least secondary, in Nebraska governmental policies and initiatives, affecting the governor in terms of policy agendas and political strategies. The administrative structure of the executive branch in Nebraska state government, following a traditional model of dispersion and agency independence, it has been shown, limits gubernatorial influence. This displays a cultural and structural institution that attempts to keep government closer to the people.

Reorganization of the state bureaucracy, however, to some extent, increased executive capacity in state government functions. Still, the governor's authority in administration remains moderate, sustained by the cultural penchant for agency and governmental independence. The locality of Nebraska state government, exemplified in the liberal usage of referendum and the unique duty of the ombudsman, likewise equates to an expectation of locality in public services. At the same time, the perception of the state legislature as a super city council detracts from these objectives, limiting the discretionary authority of local officials (Krane 2001). Given the overall growth in local government employment from 1982 to 2017 and the reliance on local and special districts in state governmental operation, the reconciliation of state government reorganization and the steadfast protection of local autonomy perseveres as a contentious and enduring issue in Nebraska. This demonstrates the conflict between efficiency and responsiveness, dimensions of the state's political culture.

Nebraska state government continues to grow in size and influence, contrasting with the argument against bigger government commonly echoed throughout the state (Steinman 1984). By most accounts, however, the state is doing quite well. The Pew Center on the States, for instance, place Nebraska above the national average in government performance, with strong showings in financial management and major gains in information technology and infrastructure (Pew Center 2008), indicating efficiency, despite growth.

Following a traditional model of executive structure, embedded in a political culture of localness and accountability, yet with an emphasis on efficiency, Nebraska governors must set forth agendas consistent with the Nebraskan design of state government. Nebraska's political culture, with its elements of individualism and moralism, creates an environment that demands both efficiency and responsiveness in the functioning of the state's administrative machinery, headed by the governor. That is no easy task.

## REFERENCES

Abney, Glenn, and Thomas P. Lauth. 1986. *The Politics of State and City Administration.* Albany: State University of New York Press.

Beyle, Thad. 1996. "Being Governor." In *The State of the States*, 3rd ed., edited by Victoria Van Son, 53–80. Washington DC: Congressional Quarterly.

———. 2007. "Governors' Institutional Power Rating, 2007." In *Congressional Quarterly's State Fact Finder: Rankings across America*, edited by Kendra Hovey and Harold Hovey, 112. Washington DC: Congressional Quarterly.

———. 2008. "The Evolution of the Gubernatorial Office: United States Governors over the Twentieth Century." In *A Legacy of Leadership: Governors and American History*, edited by Clayton McClure Brooks, 202–18. Philadelphia: University of Pennsylvania Press.

Brudney, Jeffrey L., F. Ted Hebert, and Deil S. Wright. 1999. "Reinventing Government in the American States: Measuring and Explaining Administrative Reform." *Public Administration Review* 59 (1): 19–30.

Burke, Brendan F., Chung-Lae Cho, and Deil S. Wright. 2008. "Continuity and Change in Executive Leadership: Insights from the Perspectives of State Administrators." *Public Administration Review* 68 (s1): s29–s36.

Chi, Keon S. 1992. "Trends in Executive Reorganization." *Journal of State Government* 65:33–40.

Chi, Keon S., and Catherina Wiley. 1996. *State Government Organization Charts.* Washington DC: Council of State Governments.

Cooper, John Milton, Jr. 2008. "Challenges of a New Century: Woodrow Wilson and the Progressive Era." In *A Legacy of Leadership: Governors and American History*, edited by Clayton McClure Brooks, 12–34. Philadelphia: University of Pennsylvania Press.

Council of State Governments. 2014. *Book of the States 2014*. Washington DC: Council of State Governments.

————. 2022. *Book of the States 2022*. Lexington KY.

Cox, Raymond, III. 1991. "The Management Role of the Governor." In *Gubernatorial Leadership and State Policy*, edited by Eric B. Hezik and Brent W. Brown, 55–72. New York: Greenwood Press.

Elling, Richard. 1992. *Public Management in the States: A Comparative Performance and Politics*. Westport CT: Praeger.

Garnett, James. 1985. "Organizing and Reorganizing State and Local Government." In *State and Local Government Administration*, edited by Jack Rabin and Don Dodd, 3–32. New York: Marcel Dekker.

Goertz, Margaret E. 2006. "State Education Policy in the New Millennium." In *The State of the States*, 4th ed., edited by Carl E. Van Horn, 141–66. Washington DC: CQ Press.

Gormley, William T., Jr. 1996. "Accountability Battles in State Administration." In *The State of the States*, 3rd ed., edited by Carl E. Van Horn, 101–19. Washington DC: Congressional Quarterly.

Governor's Policy Research Office. 2002. *Nebraska State Government Executive Branch Organization*. Lincoln: Governor's Policy Research Office.

Gray, Virginia, and Peter Eisinger. 1997. *American States and Cities*. 2nd ed. New York: Pearson.

Herbert, F. Ted, Deil S. Wright, and Jeffrey Brudney. 1992. "Challenges to State Governments: Policy and Administrative Leadership in the 1990s." *Public Productivity & Management Review* 16 (1): 1–21.

Krane, Dale. 2001. "Nebraska." In *Home Rule in America: A Fifty-State Handbook*, edited by Dale Krane, Platon N. Rigos, and Melvin B. Hill Jr., 236–46. Washington DC: CQ Press.

Maddox, Russell W., and Robert Fuquay. 1981. *State and Local Government*. 4th ed. New York: D. Van Nostrand.

McClure Brooks, Clayton. 2008. "Governing the 21st Century." In *A Legacy of Leadership: Governors and American History*, edited by Clayton McClure Brooks, 220–22. Philadelphia: University of Pennsylvania Press.

Moynihan, Donald P., and Patricia W. Ingraham. 2010. "The Suspect Handmaiden: The Evolution of Politics and Administration in the American State." *Public Administration Review* s70:229–37.

National Governors Association. n.d.a. "Governors' Powers and Authority." Accessed February 9, 2023. https://www.nga.org/consulting/powers-and-authority/.

————. n.d.b. "NGA Center for Best Practices." Accessed August 18, 2023. https://www.nga.org/bestpractices/.

Nebraska Health and Human Services. 1996. *Nebraska Health and Human Services Report: A Report to Governor Ben Nelson and the Nebraska Legislature.* Lincoln: Nebraska Partnership.

Nebraska Investment Finance Authority (NIFA). n.d. "About NIFA." Accessed February 9, 2023. http://nifa.org/about/index.html.

Nebraska Legislature. 2018. *2018–2019 Nebraska Blue Book.* Lincoln: State of Nebraska.

Nebraska Office of the Governor. 2021. *Running Government Business.* Lincoln: Nebraska Office of the Governor. https://governor.nebraska.gov/press/running -government-business.

Nebraska Partnership Project. 1995. *Unified Health and Human Services for Nebraska's Future: A Blueprint for Action.* Lincoln: Governor's Office.

Pew Center on the States. 2008. *Government Performance Project: Grading the States, Nebraska.* Washington DC: Pew Research Center.

Shafritz, Jay M. 1988. *The Dorsey Dictionary of American Government and Politics.* Chicago: Dorsey Press.

State Personnel Division. 2020. *State of Nebraska 2020 Personnel Almanac.* Lincoln: Nebraska Department of Administrative Services.

Steinman, Michael. 1984. "The Bureaucracy." In *Nebraska Government and Politics,* edited by Robert D. Miewald, 104–24. Lincoln: University of Nebraska Press.

U.S. Census Bureau. 2020a. 2017 Census of Governments: Employment (Revised date: June 2020). Washington DC: U.S. Census Bureau.

———. 2020b. 2017 Census of Governments: Finance (Revised date: September 2020). Washington DC: U.S. Census Bureau.

———. 2020c. 2017 Census of Governments: Organizations. Washington DC: U.S. Census Bureau.

U.S. Census Bureau Population Division. 2019. Table 1. Annual Estimate of the Population for the United States, Regions, States, and Puerto Rico: April 1, 2010 to July 1, 2019 (Release date: December 2019). Washington DC: U.S. Census Bureau.

Weinschenk, Aaron C., and David J. Helpap. 2015. "Political Trust in the American States." *State and Local Government Review* 47 (1): 26–34.

Welch, Susan. 1984. "The Governor and Other Elected Executives." In *Nebraska Government and Politics,* edited by Robert D. Miewald, 35–56. Lincoln: University of Nebraska Press.

Wilson, Robert H. 1993. *States and the Economy: Policymaking and Decentralization.* Westport CT: Praeger.

Wyner, Alan J. 1985. "The Governor as Administrator." In *State and Local Government Administration,* edited by Jack Rabin and Don Dodd, 225–44. New York: Marcel Dekker.

Young, Joanne. 2014. "Head of State Health and Human Services Department Working on Culture Change." *Lincoln Journal-Star,* January 26, 2014.

# CHAPTER EIGHT

# Nebraska Local Government

## A REFLECTION OF ITS POLITICAL CULTURE

*Christian L. Janousek, Robert Blair, and Jerome Deichert*

### INTRODUCTION

Few aspects of Nebraska government and politics better demonstrate the unique and often conflicting dimensions of the state's political culture than the organization, structure, and scope of local governments. Nebraska's political culture, a mixture of individualism, which emphasizes efficiency in government, and moralism, with its attention to populism and responsiveness, impacts many facets of local government. While individualism is the dominant element in the state culture, as this chapter demonstrates, moralism also influences the organization of local government and governance structures. For instance, Nebraska's populist traditions shaped institutions such as nonpartisan elections for most local governments (only counties have partisan elections). And as part of the populist movement that recognized the importance of responsiveness, Nebraska cities, in 1912, gained the right to govern themselves by home rule.

As legal creatures of state statutes, municipalities must petition the Nebraska legislature and be granted authority for most initiatives. Under the guise of increasing the efficiency of local governments, the state legislature and courts have reluctantly granted additional independent powers to Nebraska cities. In fact, "recent research reveals a significant upsurge of state governments preempting policy actions of local governments" (Blair and Starke 2017, 275). Nebraska has followed that national trend of preemption. The ability of Nebraska municipalities to be responsive to local needs and issues, then, has diminished over time, reducing their autonomy. Local governments in Nebraska seem to be losing power and independence.

This chapter examines the nature and composition of local government in Nebraska. Topics addressed in this chapter include an overview of general-purpose governments and special purpose governments with an emphasis on cultural contexts; the structural operation and management of local governments; and intergovernmental relations. The chapter ends with a discussion of enduring issues facing local governments in Nebraska.

## LOCAL GOVERNMENT IN NEBRASKA:
### FORMATIONS AND PATTERNS

Nebraska's settlement patterns in the mid-nineteenth century influenced the location of cities in the state and played a key role in shaping the character of state-city relationships. During this period of westward development in America, the railroads, as noted in chapter 1, provided the groundwork for growth, and the railroads routinely established cities as construction depots and service points along the routes. As a result, many Nebraska cities owe their founding and initial economic livelihood to the expansion of the railroads across the state. The railroads likewise contributed to the populating of Nebraska by attracting residents with the lure of homesteads, offering to sell to settlers a portion of the 4,846,108 acres of land deeded to them by the federal and state government to increase revenues (Federal Writers' Project [1939] 1979). Anxious to dispose of excess property, the railroads made long-term credit available to buyers (Olson and Naugle 1997), thus indebting many in the rural population and helping to build a love-hate relationship between the farmers who controlled the state legislature at that time and the railroad companies.

Omaha was one of the first cities to benefit from this burgeoning transportation industry as the starting point of the westward expansion of the transcontinental railroad by Union Pacific in the mid-1860s. Undertaking an industrial project of this magnitude required an unprecedented approach, and Omaha was the original recipient of this extraordinary effort (Ambrose 2000). This city-railroad symbiosis helped to fashion ties between localities and the state, creating an accord of shared advantage and mutual interest.

Nebraska, like most U.S. states, embraces the vital role of local governments, exemplifying American values of individualism and autonomy (Berman 2019). True to its populist roots and political culture that emphasizes government responsiveness to citizen needs, Nebraska boasts a relatively large number of units of local government. As noted by Robert Miewald (1984), a longtime observer of Nebraska government, "Nebraskans prefer quantity and variety in their local government" (165). According to the 2017 U.S. Census of Governments (U.S. Census Bureau 2021), the state includes 2,538 units of local government and ranks fifteenth in the United States for number of local governments. In terms of the number of local governments per one hundred thousand residents, Nebraska's ranks fourth (132.4). Only the Dakotas and Wyoming exceed this ratio, with Kansas close behind in fifth place. The states range from a low of 5.7 (Maryland) to 352.8 (North Dakota).

Nebraska's units of local government consist of 93 counties, 529 municipalities, and 366 towns or townships. Nebraska also has 1,281 special districts for the delivery of a variety of single-purpose public services and 269 independent school districts (U.S. Census Bureau 2021).

In total Nebraska contains 988 general purpose governments and 1,550 special purpose governments. General purpose governments, municipalities, and counties provide a comprehensive range of services to citizens. Single purpose governments, such as school districts and other specific districts, provide a specialized range of services to a selective group of citizens. Nebraska followed the trend of slowly increasing the number of special districts while decreasing the number of school districts and townships.

## Municipalities

Most Nebraska municipalities are located in the eastern portion of the state. Many of the larger and growing cities in Nebraska follow the Interstate 80 corridor, benefiting from their position along this national highway transportation system. Along the backbone of the country, Interstate 80 parallels the Platte River across the state and mirrors the Great Platte River Road, traversed by covered wagons and the transcontinental railroad in the nineteenth century. In addition to unequal geographic distribution of the state's municipalities, there is a disproportion of population across the state. The concentration of Nebraska's population continues to shift to the eastern and urban portion of the state. Located in this region are Nebraska's two largest municipalities: Omaha, with a 2022 estimated population exceeding 485,000, and Lincoln, with an estimated population over 292,000. The third largest city in the state, Bellevue, contains more than 63,000 people and belongs to the Omaha metropolitan statistical area.

Nebraska classifies municipalities into five categories according to population size: metropolitan class (300,000 or above); primary class (100,001 to 299,999); first class (5,001 to 100,000); second class (801 to 5,000); and villages (100 to 800) (U.S. Census Bureau 2021). Under state law, villages that exceed a population of eight hundred residents may choose to reorganize as a second-class city or remain a village (Neb. Rev. Stat. § 17-313). The minimum population for incorporation of a village in Nebraska is one hundred residents, although due to declining rural populations, many incorporated villages within the state are now below this number but are not required to disincorporate (Nebraska Legislature 2018).

State statutes specify municipal powers and responsibilities designated for each classification, and cities with populations greater than five thousand are permitted to develop their own charter. In 2019 Nebraska had 30 first-class cities, 117 second-class cities, and 380 villages (League 2019). The metropolitan class contains only the City of Omaha, and the primary class contains only the City of Lincoln. The two largest cities operate under strong mayor-council systems of government and maintain home rule charters allowed through the state constitution. State statutes include an extensive set of laws that apply exclusively to each class of municipality. In part resulting from their different classifications, Omaha and Lincoln often unilaterally petition the state legislature for the authority and mechanisms to undertake new initiatives, whereas other municipalities in the state lobby the legislature collectively. The League of Nebraska Municipalities (2023) serves that purpose.

Nebraska statutes recognize three basic forms of municipal government structure for first- and second-class cities: mayor-council, council-manager, and commission. The mayor-council structure is the most common form of local government among Nebraska municipalities. Unless a council-manager or commission form of government is adopted by popular election, first-class cities function under a strong mayor-council system and second-class cities under a weak mayor-council system. Both types of mayors are popularly elected. A strong mayor may appoint department heads and other city employees without council approval. A weak mayor must gain council approval for most appointments.

According to Nebraska statute, the mayor of a first-class city

> shall preside at all the meetings of the city council and shall have the right
> to vote when his or her vote will provide the additional vote required to
> create a number of votes equal to a majority of the number of members
> elected to the council. He or she shall have the superintending control
> of all the officers and affairs of the city and shall take care that the ordi-
> nances of the city and the provisions of law relating to cities of the first
> class are complied with. He or she may administer oaths and shall sign
> the commissions and appointments of all the officers appointed in the
> city. (Neb. Rev. Stat. § 16-312)

The mayors of second-class cities have less conferred authority and latitude.
They "may appoint such officers as shall be required by ordinance or otherwise required by law," but only with the consent of the council; however, "such
officers may be removed from office by the mayor" (Neb. Rev. Stat. § 17-107).

If a first- or second-class city adopts the council-manager form of government by popular vote, then the appropriate state statutes apply. The council-
manager plan represents a professional form of local government management (Valcik and Teodoro 2023). The city manager, appointed by a majority
of city council members and serving at the will of the council, acts as the
chief administrative officer of city government. Ten cities in Nebraska have
adopted this structure of local government. Alliance was the first city to adopt
the council-manager plan in 1921. The city manager appoints department
heads, submits the annual budget, and advises the city council on policy
issues and problems. State law iterates that

> the chief executive officer of the city shall be a city manager, who shall
> be responsible for the proper administration of all affairs of the city. He
> [or she] shall be chosen by the council for an indefinite period, solely
> on the basis of administrative qualifications, and need not be a resident
> of the city or state when appointed. He [or she] shall hold office at the
> pleasure of the council, and receive such salary as it shall fix by ordi-
> nance. During the absence or disability of the city manager the council
> shall designate some properly qualified person to perform the duties of
> the office. (Neb. Rev. Stat. § 19-1645)

The mayor in the council-manager plan, an elected council member, fulfills mostly a ceremonial post, elected to the office by fellow council members. The mayor cannot serve as the city manager.

First- and second-class cities with mayor-council forms may create the position of city administrator. In most cases this professional officer functions much like a city manager, as the administrative head of city government. However, local ordinance as described in city code, rather than state statute, provides the powers and responsibilities of the city administrator. Most first-class and many larger second-class Nebraska cities appoint city administrators to oversee the implementation of city programs and policies. While there are minor differences among local ordinances, city administrators generally work for both the mayor and council. Nebraska laws stipulate that if a first-class city establishes the office of city administrator, then the mayor must receive council approval for appointment and removal of the city administrator (Neb. Rev. Stat. § 16-308). For second-class cities, the mayor needs council approval for hiring officers as required by ordinance, such as a city administrator, but not for dismissal (Neb. Rev. Stat. § 17-107).

In 2021 forty-eight communities in Nebraska met professional management standards as established by the International City/County Management Association (ICMA), a government leadership and professional management organization (ICMA n.d.a.). ICMA criteria for recognition of professionally managed jurisdictions include employment based on professional qualifications; significant budget preparation; appointing and organizational authority; and policy formulation responsibilities (ICMA n.d.b.).

Congruent with the sentiment of the dominant individualistic political subculture prevalent within the state (Elazar 1994), Nebraska citizens generally accept professional management in their communities, with its emphasis on efficient government operation. Of the forty-six first- and second-class cities in the state with populations exceeding 2,500, only one does not have a city manager, city administrator, or city administrator/clerk. The Nebraska City/County Management Association (NCMA), a unit of the League of Nebraska Municipalities and a state chapter of the International City/County Management Association (ICMA), serves as the professional support organization for city managers and administrators within the state.

Evidence of professionalism in local government management in Nebraska extends to city clerks. Municipal clerks are appointed by city councils or boards. Many smaller cities have created a combined city clerk/administrator position, since clerks often perform professional administrative roles. The Nebraska Municipal Clerks Association provides for the professional development of clerks through a certification program of the Nebraska Municipal Clerks Institute and Academy, from the International Institute of Municipal Clerks (iimc), offered by the School of Public Administration at the University of Nebraska at Omaha.

The other type of municipal government is the commission form, found in only one municipality, Nebraska City. One of the state's oldest communities, the city embraces the unique status employing a rarely used form of government with roots in the Progressive Era. Elected at-large, commissioners perform both legislative and executive tasks in a specific city government area, such as public works, parks, or finance. One commissioner serves as mayor. Nebraska City also has a city administrator (City of Nebraska City n.d.).

Most municipalities in Nebraska are villages and operate under a distinct structure. Villages are governed by a board of trustees of elected members that direct various departments and act as the legislative body of the local government. A chairperson is selected from among the members of the board. The village clerk, appointed by the board of trustees, conducts most of the administrative duties of villages. As such, village clerks often assume various titles/roles in addition to their clerkship, including administrator and treasurer.

## Counties

Like many of its neighboring states in the Great Plains, Nebraska features a large number of county governments that derive their authority from state statutes. Historically, county governments were organized to support a widespread rural population. Even though their responsibilities have evolved in the more urbanized eastern portion of the state, many large-land-area counties in western Nebraska with rural orientations still perform critical roles in local governmental management and services (Nebraska Association of County Officials n.d.). Legislative attempts to consolidate county and municipal governments have been met with skepticism and resistance by residents (Stoddard 2010), and thus Nebraska continues to keep its ninety-three county governments.

There are two forms of county government in Nebraska: commissioner and township. Under the commissioner structure, a three, five, or more member board of commissioners is elected to serve four-year terms. Under the township structure, a seven-member board of supervisors is elected to four-year terms. Township counties also include appointed officers. There are sixty-seven commissioner counties and twenty-six township counties within the state. In both systems the county board oversees funds and taxation, planning and zoning, buildings and property, and various public services not reserved for the state or municipal governments (Nebraska Legislature 2018).

All counties in Nebraska must have a clerk, a sheriff, a treasurer, and an attorney. Based on the population and form of government of the county, other elected offices may include assessor, register of deeds, and surveyor; appointed office include such as highway superintendents, emergency managers, and planning and zoning directors. Counties are the only local government in Nebraska where officials are elected on a partisan basis. County boards may also appoint a county administrator, who implements policies and programs, makes legislative recommendations, and manages county operations. However, only the three most populous counties, Douglas, Lancaster, and Sarpy, have county administrators. The Nebraska Association of County Officials (naco) delivers professional development, education, research, and lobby assistance for all of the state's ninety-three member counties (Nebraska Legislature 2018).

## Special Districts

Nebraska, like many states, emphasizes local control of many government processes, a time-honored tradition in America and consistent with the state's political culture, with an emphasis on responsiveness. These locally managed functions differ from state to state. Special districts include single-purpose governments, providing services in education, economic development, health care, natural resource management, public utilities, and transportation. Although all special districts contribute to the dissemination and management of public and governmental ventures within the state, four types of special districts merit certain attention.

*School Districts*

According to the 2017 Census of Governments, Nebraska contains 269 school districts with four classifications determined by population size: class II (1,000 or fewer); class III (1,001 to 149,999); class IV (100,000 or more); class V (200,000 or more). Class IV is reserved for primary cities (Lincoln) and class V for metropolitan cities (Omaha). State legislation in 2005 consolidated class I (maintained only elementary grades) and class VI districts, which maintained only high school or only high school and grades seven and eight. School districts also include community college areas, educational service units (ESUS), and unified school systems. An elected board of officials presides over each district, and the boards have the authority to levy ad valorem taxes. The districts in unified school systems apportion resources and remain separate legal entities. The Nebraska State Board of Education oversees school districts (U.S. Census Bureau 2021).

While the overall number of special districts in Nebraska has increased, the number of school districts has diminished dramatically. In 1952 there were 6,392 school districts in Nebraska. The 269 school districts in 2017 represents a 96 percent decline (U.S. Census Bureau 2021). Contrary to Nebraskans' preference for localized control, budget restrictions and waning rural populations have encouraged district reductions, mergers, and consolidations throughout the state.

School district boundaries may cross county lines. Boundary issues and financial disparities among Nebraska school districts, specifically in Omaha, resulted in the creation of a learning community. The Learning Community of Douglas and Sarpy Counties adjoins eleven independent school districts within those two counties. The Learning Community promotes interlocal cooperation among the districts through a number of programs addressing the needs of low-income neighborhoods, and socioeconomic diversity and equity (Learning Community n.d.).

*Public Power Districts*

In 1933 the Nebraska legislature created public power districts to distribute electric power to all citizens. Public power districts function as political subdivisions in the state. Elected board members govern the districts. The state contains four large districts and many rural districts and cooperatives, utilizing coal, gas, nuclear, hydro, oil, and wind energy generation (Patent 2018).

As the only U.S. state with exclusively public electric utilities, Nebraska's commitment to public power makes it unique, a significant component of its political culture. Differing from most U.S. states that rely on private suppliers, Nebraska prohibits privately owned electric utility companies. Public power in Nebraska owes its legacy to George Norris, the U.S. senator from Nebraska who helped initiate the Tennessee Valley Authority, a public power organization, in the 1930s. The provision of electricity and energy by public power districts, municipalities, and cooperatives typifies Nebraska's populist history.

The complete reliance on public power districts and other public suppliers significantly affects Nebraska's local government employment structure in terms of the size of the local workforce. According to the 2017 U.S. Census of Governments, Nebraska employed 6,253 people in electric power (U.S. Census Bureau 2021). These public employees mostly work in local government utility departments or electric power districts serving large geographic areas in the state. Although extensive local public power organizations exist in Washington and Tennessee, most pool with U.S. government agencies like the Tennessee Valley Authority or federal hydroelectric power plants.

*Natural Resource Districts*

In 1969 the Nebraska legislature merged several special purpose entities into natural resource districts, or NRDs, to solve flood control, soil erosion, irrigation run-off, and groundwater quantity and quality issues. These districts do not necessarily align with county boundaries, but instead are organized around major river basins to formulate and deliver water and natural resource policies and conservation programs specific to watershed areas. NRDs are involved in a wide variety of projects and programs to conserve and protect the state's natural resources in a decentralized manner. These NRDs have locally elected boards of directors, a distinctive governance structure found only in Nebraska, consistent with its populist traditions. The majority of funding for NRDs comes from property taxes. There are currently twenty-three NRDs throughout the state (Nebraska Association of Resource Districts n.d.a.).

According to the Nebraska Association of Resource Districts, which coordinates the collective efforts of NRDs to improve the state's natural resources and environment, "NRDs are involved in a wide variety of projects and programs to conserve and protect the state's natural resources" (Nebraska Association of Resource Districts n.d.a.). Nebraska state law assigned twelve areas of responsibility to NRDs, including erosion and flood prevention and control; soil conservation; water supply, groundwater and surface water management and conservation; drainage improvements; solid waste disposable; fish and wildlife habitat; recreation and park facilities; and forestry and range management.

All NRDs share these duties, yet each district sets its own priorities and develops its own programs to best suit local needs. Districts often team with other agencies to carry out projects. The Natural Resources Conservation Service, through the U.S. Department of Agriculture, provides technical services and administration for many NRD programs. State funding for flood control and soil and water conservation projects is channeled through the Nebraska Department of Natural Resources. Local partners often include cities, counties, and extension offices (Nebraska Association of Resource Districts n.d.b.).

### Sanitary and Improvement Districts

Nebraska state law defines sanitary and improvement districts, or SIDs, as political subdivisions and quasi-municipal corporations with specific designated functions in the realm of public improvements (Neb. Rev. Stat. § 31-727). SIDs support housing and development by private developers and homeowners by financing infrastructure and other public improvements.

State legislation identifies the responsibilities of SIDs as installing electric service lines and conduits, sewer systems, water systems, sidewalks, public streets, and related appurtenances. SIDs may contract for: water for fire protection and for resale to residents, police protection, and access to a range of public facilities and services (Neb. Rev. Stat. § 31-727).

SIDs, a type of special district unique to Nebraska, provides a financial and developmental mechanism for urban growth (Blair 2001). Some municipalities employ SIDs because they allow private developers to assume most of the economic obligations and risks of residential and commercial expansion at the urban fringe. Municipalities have veto authority over construction within the city's zoning jurisdiction to ensure compliance with existing structures. (Neb. Rev. Stat. § 31-740). Governed by an elected board of trustees, SIDs possess the power to levy assessment taxes (Neb. Rev. Stat. § 31-755) and issue bonds (Neb. Rev. Stat. § 31-739); however, SIDs cannot create ordinances, zoning, or building codes. Most SIDs are located in the Omaha metropolitan area.

### TRIBAL GOVERNMENTS

There are four Native American tribal governments in Nebraska. Three Native American tribes, the Omahas, Santee Sioux, and Winnebagos, manage reservations in the northeastern part of the state. The Ponca tribe does not have a reservation. The tribes are governed by their own constitutions, with tribal councils comprised of elected members of the tribes. Recognized as sovereign in local affairs, with jurisdictional oversight administered by the state and federal governments, tribal governments may create local laws. Public Law 280 states that Nebraska has criminal jurisdiction over Native American tribes; however, the state has relinquished some of this authority, allowing for tribal courts and local law enforcement. The tribal governments in Nebraska work with the Nebraska Commission on Indian Affairs, a state agency with commissioners appointed by the governor, and the U.S. Bureau of Indian Affairs (Nebraska Legislature 2018).

### INTERGOVERNMENTAL RELATIONS AND COLLABORATION

Nebraska local governments continue to evolve, providing citizens with a varying and changing array of public services. State government plays a significant role in intergovernmental processes, as state legislation and mandates influence the character and scope of local autonomy and responsibility.

Intergovernmental relations (IGR) continue to present challenges to local government in Nebraska and elsewhere. As noted by one observer of IGR, "Local officials throughout the 1990s and into the 21st century commonly voiced concern about the quality of federal-local and state-local relations. They worried about the loss of local governmental authority, the lack of sufficient discretion to generate revenues, the lack of support of federal and state agencies, and perhaps, most of all, the growth of unfunded mandates" (Berman 2003, 29). Federal dictates and laws affecting local governments, including, for instance, substantial systemic modifications in health care and immigration policy, and regulatory agency directives, will undoubtedly increase the demands on localities in all states. Furthermore, the preemption of local authority by state governments (noted earlier in this chapter) and the federal government creates additional concerns to local officials in Nebraska and elsewhere.

State-local relations in Nebraska, like other states, cannot be easily described. State government exerts control over many of the affairs of localities, and the legislature continues to add and/or amend laws aimed at local governments' powers and responsibilities (Kim, McDonald, and Lee 2018). The two largest cities in Nebraska, Omaha, and Lincoln, for example, each have extensive sets of state statutes that grant them select powers and responsibilities. Consistent with the state's political culture, Nebraska local governments value autonomy and control, however, they can be challenged by the actions of the state legislature and state agencies.

The Nebraska Constitution allows for cities with more than five thousand residents to frame a charter, however, the provisions must be consistent "with and subject to the constitution and laws of the state" (Nebraska State Constitution, Article XI, Section 2). Technically, then, Nebraska provides for home rule, yet an examination of its state-municipal relationships depicts a complex picture. While home rule has been available to cities since a 1912 constitutional amendment, only Omaha and Lincoln presently maintain home rule charters. Regardless of having home rule or not, municipalities in Nebraska can only pass laws and engage in activities permitted by state law, representing a strict application of Dillon's rule (Krane 2001). The Nebraska Supreme Court has "emphasized the state legislature's primacy in decisions over what powers may be exercised by local governments" (Krane and Blair 1999, 21). Thus, when compared to practice in many other states, Nebraska does not bestow true home rule to its municipalities.

Local governments in Nebraska have long embraced interlocal cooperation. These local-local connections constitute an expanding arena of intergovernmental relations within the state. The Interlocal Cooperation Act, approved by the Nebraska legislature in 1963, decrees that "any two or more public agencies may enter into agreements with one another for joint or cooperative action," including all local governmental units, state agencies, and adjacent political subdivisions in other states (Neb. Rev. Stat. § 13-804). For cooperative agreements, the act specifies the provisions of duration, organization or nature, purpose, financing, termination, taxing, and other necessary matters. Unlike formal consolidation, interlocal cooperatives let local governments maintain independence while concurrently benefiting from joint services; economies of scale; and shared costs, personnel, equipment, and liability.

Interlocal relations in Nebraska encompass a full spectrum of governmental units and types of agreements. Collaborative enterprises among municipalities, counties, and special districts may address general short-term needs through informal pacts or more specific long-term and organized efforts through formal mechanisms. Common informal arrangements among Nebraska local governments include mutual aid in emergency situations, pledges of civil protection services such as fire and law enforcement, professional practitioner associations, and shared equipment and purchasing. Formal linkages, which tend to be more structured and of a specified duration, may involve regional and economic development districts, contracted public and technical services, joint facilities and utilities, and gaming and lottery activities.

The motivations for cooperation vary among local governments, but they typically relate to improved efficiency, enhanced effectiveness, improved quality of services, and aversion to risk (Bae and Feiock 2012). However, the bottom line is usually cost savings. Research suggests that interlocal collaboration in Nebraska has shifted toward informal varieties and away from formal mechanisms, displaying a "tendency for the more indefinite, casual, and need-based exchanges of resources" (Blair and Janousek 2013, 280). This may be attributed to a desire for more autonomy in local-local relations, notably among smaller communities (Kraus 2012).

## Councils of Government

In a state the geographic size of Nebraska, with a wide dispersion of cities, a network of regional government organizations provides a variety of essential services to communities. These regional government structures, called development districts, or councils of governments, consist of a voluntary association of local governments in a specific sub-state geographic region, which coordinates regional planning (Bowman 2008). Nebraska development districts also play a role in housing, community, and economic development. There are eight development districts within the state. The Metropolitan

Area Planning Agency in Omaha serves the counties of Douglas, Sarpy, and Washington. Dakota County is part of the Siouxland Interstate Metropolitan Planning Council of Sioux City, Iowa (Nebraska Regional Officials Council n.d.). All development districts are members of the Nebraska Regional Officials Council, a nonprofit association headed by district representatives.

In Nebraska, development districts are formed as voluntary associations of governments as provided by the Interlocal Cooperation Act, previously discussed. The act permits "local governmental units to make the most efficient use of their taxing authority and other powers by enabling them to cooperate with other localities on a basis of mutual advantage and thereby to provide services and facilities in a manner and pursuant to forms of governmental organization that will accord best with geographic, economic, population, and other factors influencing the needs and development of local communities" (Neb. Rev. Stat. § 13-802).

A principal service supplied by development districts is the guidance and management of the Community Development Block Grant (CDBG) program offered through the Nebraska Department of Economic Development and the U.S. Department of Housing and Urban Development. From 1997 to 2012, development districts in Nebraska oversaw 794 CDBG grants in nonmetropolitan communities (Nebraska DED 2013). In addition, development districts assist with financing and research and function as liaisons to state and federal agencies.

### ENDURING ISSUES

Overall, the nature, composition, and functioning of Nebraska local governments embody the political culture of this midwestern, Great Plains state. Moving forward, some challenges remain for local governments and intergovernmental relations. Urbanization patterns signify a migration of the rural population, with urban growth concentrated in the eastern portions of the state. Indicative of this repositioning, in 2013 the U.S. Office of Management and Budget defined the Grand Island area as the state's third metropolitan statistical area, in addition to Omaha and Lincoln. The Sioux City, Iowa, MSA includes two counties in Nebraska. Continued decreases in rural populations have redirected the availability of resources and raised concerns about rural sustainability, especially in the western regions of the state.

In addition to urbanization, as described in chapter 2, there are two additional changing demographics that will likely affect the financing and the mix and delivery of local services: aging and diversity. Nebraska is an aging state, especially in rural areas, and that will affect the composition of the workforce and the financing of public services. Also, Nebraska is increasingly diverse. For example, the Hispanic and Latino population continues to grow. In terms of the total Nebraska population, the percentage of Hispanic or Latino residents nearly doubled from 2000 to 2010 (5.5 percent to 9.2 percent) and was estimated at 11.4 percent in 2019 (U.S. Census Bureau 2022).

All states historically have struggled with revenue shortages and limitations. Yet Nebraska has fared relatively well during most economic recessions, including the 2020 recession related to the COVID-19 pandemic, maintaining a low unemployment rate and placing an emphasis on job creation (Gallup 2013). Accordingly, economic development and long-term financial viability persist as primary objectives of local officials. Uses of interlocal cooperation reveal that Nebraska local governments are willing to assist each other in this regard, moving toward more informal partnerships and agreements.

Traditionally, and true to the state's political culture, Nebraska localities desire greater autonomy and self-sufficiency. Increased and intensified oversight by the legislature in local affairs, however, provokes push back from local governments and citizens. Finally, the proliferation of special districts, with its diffusion and fragmentation effect, is creating challenges to local government and governance structures.

## REFERENCES

Ambrose, Stephen E. 2000. *Nothing Like It in the World: The Men Who Built the Transcontinental Railroad 1863–1869*. New York: Simon and Schuster.

Bae, Jungah, and Richard C. Feiock. 2012. "Managing Multiplexity: Coordinating Multiple Services at a Regional Level." *State and Local Government Review* 44 (2): 162–68.

Berman, David R. 2003. *Local Government and the States: Autonomy, Politics, and Policy*. Armonk NY: M. E. Sharpe.

———. 2019. *Local Government and the States*. 2nd ed. New York: Routledge.

Blair, Robert. 2001. "Managing Urban Growth: Can Policy Tools Approach Improve Effectiveness?" *Public Works Management and Policy* 6:102–13.

Blair, Robert, and Anthony M. Starke Jr. 2017. "The Emergence of Local Government Policy Leadership: A Roaring Torch or a Flickering Flame?" *State and Local Government Review* 49 (4): 275–84.

Blair, Robert, and Christian L. Janousek. 2013. "Collaborative Mechanisms in Interlocal Cooperation: A Longitudinal Examination." *State and Local Government Review* 45 (4): 268–82.

Bowman, Ann, and Richard Kearney. 2008. *State and Local Government*. 7th ed. Boston: Houghton Mifflin.

City of Nebraska City. n.d. "City Council." Accessed February 7, 2023. https://nebraskacityne.gov/city-council/city-council/.

Elazar, Daniel J. 1994. *The American Mosaic: The Impact of Space, Time, and Culture on American Politics*. Boulder CO: Westview.

Federal Writers' Project. (1939) 1979. *Nebraska: A Guide to the Cornhusker State*. Lincoln: University of Nebraska Press.

Gallup. 2013. "State of the States: Job Creation Index 2013." Omaha: Gallup.

ICMA (International City/County Management Association). n.d.a. "Directory of ICMA-Recognized Local Governments." Accessed February 7, 2023. https://members.icma.org/eWeb/DynamicPage.aspx?webcode=recognizedlocalgovresult&state=Nebraska.

———. n.d.b. "ICMA Local Government Recognition." Accessed February 27, 2023. https://icma.org/icma-local-government-recognition.

Kim, Junghack, Bruce D. McDonald III, and Jooho Lee. 2018. "The Nexus of State and Local Capacity in Vertical Policy Diffusion." *American Review of Public Administration* 48 (2): 188–200.

Krane, Dale. 2001. "Nebraska." In *Home Rule in America: A Fifty-State Handbook*, edited by Dale Krane, Platon N. Rigos, and Melvin B. Hill Jr., 258–68. Washington DC: CQ Press.

Krane, Dale, and Robert Blair. 1999. *The Practice of Home Rule*. Lincoln: Nebraska Commission on Local Government Innovation and Restructuring.

Kraus, Neil. 2012. "The Challenges and Possibilities for Regional Collaboration among Small Jurisdictions." *State and Local Government Review* 44 (1): 45–54.

League of Nebraska Municipalities. 2019. *Nebraska Directory of Municipal Officials*. Lincoln: League of Nebraska Municipalities.

———. 2023. Legislative Session Recap. July. *Nebraska Municipal Review*. https://www.lonm.org/news/publication-links/nebraska-municipal-review.html.

Learning Community of Douglas Sarpy Counties. n.d. Website. Accessed February 7, 2023. https://learningcommunityds.org/.

Miewald, Robert. 1984. "Local Government." In *Nebraska Government and Politics*, edited by Robert D. Miewald, 165–86. Lincoln: University of Nebraska Press.

Nebraska Association of County Officials. n.d. "Nebraska Counties Explorer." Accessed August 18, 2023. https://nebraskacounties.org/nebraska-counties/.

Nebraska Association of Resource Districts. n.d.a. "About NRDs." Accessed February 7, 2023. https://www.nrdnet.org/about.

———. n.d.b. "NRD Programs." Accessed February 7, 2023. https://www.nrdnet.org/programs.

Nebraska Department of Economic Development (DED). 2013. *Community and Rural Development Projects List*. Lincoln: Nebraska Department of Economic Development.

Nebraska Legislature. 2018. *2018–2019 Nebraska Blue Book*. Lincoln: State of Nebraska.

Nebraska Regional Officials Council. n.d. "Members." Accessed February 7, 2023. http://www.nrocne.com/members.

Olson, James C., and Ronald C. Naugle. 2000. *History of Nebraska*. 3rd ed. Lincoln: University of Nebraska Press.

Patent, Keisha. *Public Power in Nebraska: A Legislative Office Backgrounder*. Lincoln: Legislative Research Office.

Stoddard, Martha. 2010. "County Consolidation Bill Gets Chilly Reception." *Omaha World-Herald*, January 23, 2010.

U.S. Census Bureau. 2021. "2017 Census of Governments." https://www.census.gov/programs-surveys/cog.html.

———. 2022. "Quick Facts Nebraska." https://www.census.gov/quickfacts/fact/table/NE/PST040218.

Valcik, Nicholas A., and Teodoro J. Benavides, eds. 2023. *Local Government Management: ASPA Series in Public Administration and Public Policy*. New York: Routledge.

# CHAPTER NINE

# Tax and Fiscal Policy

## THE PRICE OF LOCAL CONTROL

*John Bartle*

### INTRODUCTION

This chapter compares Nebraska to neighboring states in four areas of government: the number of local governments; employment and payroll in state and local government; state and local government expenditures, revenue, and debt; and tax burdens on Nebraska taxpayers. National comparisons are also included in several areas. Many of the comparisons are to the west north central states of Nebraska, North Dakota, Minnesota, Iowa, Missouri, Kansas, and South Dakota. In addition, the bordering states of Colorado and Wyoming are included in the comparisons.

While Nebraska is near the national averages for most features of government spending and taxes, it differs from the nation in certain distinct ways. It has a large number of local governments in part because of its low population density and the numerous small towns but also due to a cultural preference for government that is closer to the people. Leonard White's description of frontier democracy in the early nineteenth century described a government structure consistent with "a rural rather than an urban community, of an individualistic rather than a cooperative society, of a democratic rather than a bureaucratic state" (White 1993, 143). This characterized the Nebraska government for most of its history and is indicative of its political culture.

A particularly important deviation from this characterization was the adoption of all public electric power which at its essence is socialistic. Public power is one of the key dimensions of the state's political culture, as discussed in previous chapters.

Over the last fifty years, state efforts to reduce local property taxes led to more centralized fiscal actions, and more recently, growth in the personal income tax. However, the property tax is still high, as Nebraskans have consistently been willing to pay more for education and roads. These distinctive features of Nebraska government and political culture will be discussed below.

It is important to note that the data and analyses included in this chapter are for specific time periods. However, as will be shown, the trends and patterns have generally held steady for many years.

## NUMBER OF LOCAL GOVERNMENTS

Nebraska was settled quickly between the years 1860 and 1890. Numerous local governments were created, in part because the new residents assumed that Nebraska's settlement pattern would be similar to that in the eastern and mid-western parts of the nation from which they migrated and as a result of the communities functioning as service centers for the expanding railroads. Another reason for the rapid proliferation of local governments in the state was the policy of the Homestead Act to grant land to settlers. Staking a land claim required surveying, courts to enforce these rights, and soon afterward, public services such as roads, fire protection, and law enforcement. In short, local government was a necessity of life even in pioneer times. Counties were created based on reasons that were sensible at the time, but probably do not apply in this age.

School districts proliferated rapidly because they received revenue from the sale of public lands. The only restriction on the size of school districts was that they be greater than four square miles. As a result, by the 1920s, there were approximately seven thousand school districts in the state (Molnar 1996). School consolidation was a major issue in the twentieth century. The number of school districts fell from 6,392 in 1952, 797 in 1992, and 272 in 2012 and has held steady since then (269 in 2017).

As a result of this decline in the number of school districts, the number of local governments in Nebraska has decreased significantly, but Nebraska is still high compared to other states. In 2017 Nebraska ranked fifteenth in the nation in the number of local governments in the state. For all types of local governments, the number is above the median. Nebraska ranks ninth in the number of special districts and tenth in the number of counties. Since 2007, there are sixteen fewer school districts, twenty-seven fewer special districts, and thirty-five fewer towns and townships.

Nebraska is particularly high in the number of local governments per capita, ranking fourth in 2017 behind North Dakota, South Dakota, and Wyoming. All the states in this region are above the median in this measure, in part due to their low population density. Nebraska is substantially above the national average for all types of local governments when compared to its population. For total local governments per one hundred thousand population, Nebraska has about five times more governments than the national average (132.4 compared to 27.7). Nebraska is also noteworthy in its especially high number of special districts per one hundred thousand population, with 80.8 compared to the national average of 15.8 (U.S. Census Bureau 2021a).

It is often argued that there are an excessive number of local governments given the state's relatively small population. For instance, the Nebraska Tax Research Council advocated eliminating townships and cemetery districts, unincorporating towns with populations less than two hundred and consolidating counties with fewer than five thousand residents (Molnar 1997). This package of reforms would reduce the number of governments in Nebraska by 27 percent. It argued that this will reduce the cost of government by eliminating duplication and realizing economies of scale.

Two studies on county consolidation in South Dakota and North Dakota provide evidence on the potential impact of county mergers on the cost-of-service provision. Both found that there are some economies of scale that can be realized by merging counties, but savings differ by service type. The South Dakota study noted that administrative cost savings can be realized up to about eight thousand in population, but for services where transportation costs are significant (such as public safety), the costs increase (University of South Dakota 1997). Service quality is also important. As noted by Krause, in the North Dakota research, "Quality of public safety services is largely based on the quickness of response to threats and emergencies, the prevention of problems through education and frequent patrols, and responsiveness to community preferences regarding how services are provided" (1996, 13). Therefore, the farther the residents live from the consolidated public safety offices, the higher the travel costs and the lower the perceived quality of services. Other examples of services that require quick responsiveness include snow removal and certain health and welfare services (Krause 1996). There would also be new and additional costs in forming a new government, and some residents may face cost increases while others would enjoy cost reductions.

A study of the economic impact of city-county consolidation concluded that consolidations have a limited but positive effect on the efficiency of local government operations. Efficiency can be achieved by the unification of administrative functions or achieving economies of scale in administrative expenses. Large efficiency gains can occur if "there are completely separate city and county services before the merger and all the services are merged post-consolidation" (Leland and Thurmaier 2010, 273) In contrast, small efficiency gains occur when some merged functions already exist prior to the consolidations, or there was no merger of any functions after the consolidations (Leland and Thurmaier 2010).

Therefore, there is some potential to reduce costs by reducing the number of local governments in Nebraska, but the savings would be small, and the changes would need to be made carefully. There are alternatives to mergers and consolidation that can achieve some of the same efficiencies, such as inter-local agreements that can share the costs of expensive inputs such as information technology, specialized vehicles and equipment, and specialized personnel such as legal and planning, as discussed in chapter 8 on Nebraska local government. Further, there are other important considerations besides efficiency such as local control, access to services, responsiveness, and accountability (Hanson and Zeemering 2021).

EMPLOYMENT IN STATE AND LOCAL GOVERNMENT

This section examines employment and payroll in state and local government. Nebraska's low population density, strong support for public education, and the presence of public power are three important factors that affect government employment. The low density causes the state to have a high number of local governments and consequently a high number of local government employees per capita. For many years Nebraska has provided a high degree of support for public education (primary, secondary, and higher education). Nebraska employs 32 percent more elementary and secondary school teachers than the national average and spends more on this function. Public electric utilities are another distinctive feature of Nebraska and its political culture that causes local government employment to be high. Also, electric utility employees in Nebraska earn relatively high incomes compared to other public employees.

In 2020 state government employment per capita in Nebraska was 185.53 full-time equivalent employees per ten thousand population, above the national average of 135.73 (U.S. Census Bureau 2021b). Nebraska is higher than the national average in all functional categories except public welfare and public health and utilities. Between 2017 and 2020 Nebraska state employment decreased in government administration and public works and planning and recreation and increased in public safety, transportation, public welfare, education and "other."

Despite high levels of state employment, Nebraska paid its state employees substantially less than the national average. Average payroll was less than all states in the region except for Missouri (which ranked fiftieth), and Nebraska ranks forty-third in the nation in payroll for state employees in 2020. Nebraska is lower than the national average for all functions of state government in state employees' payroll (U.S. Census Bureau 2021b).

At the local level, in 2020 government employment in Nebraska was fifth highest in the nation, substantially above the national average and higher than all states in the region with the exception of Kansas and Wyoming (U.S. Census Bureau 2021b). In 2020 Nebraska local government employment was above the national average in government administration, transportation, leisure and planning services, utilities, and education. Most of the difference from the national average can be explained by a higher level of instructional employees and electric power employees. In Nebraska public power districts are considered units of local government. Nebraska's low population density in many areas is another factor causing transportation employment to be higher. Nebraska is below the average for public safety (including both police officers and firefighters), public welfare and health services, and public works (U.S. Census Bureau 2021b).

Payroll for Nebraska local government employees in 2020 was less than the national average and ranks third among the nine states in the region. This pattern holds for all functions of government except for utilities and firefighters (U.S. Census Bureau 2021b).

Thus, government employment in Nebraska differs from the national average because of two long-standing aspects of political traditions and policy decisions: the presence of public electric power and the strong emphasis on public education. The high employment for transportation is a result of serving low-density areas in many parts of the state with roads and highways. Otherwise, Nebraska is relatively similar to the national average. Payroll for state and local employees is below the national average for public employees apart from the electric utilities.

## STATE AND LOCAL GOVERNMENT EXPENDITURES, REVENUE, AND DEBT

### Expenditure Comparisons

Total state and local government general spending in Nebraska is below the national average, as the following will show. State government spending is 83.5 percent of the national average, while local spending is slightly higher, reflecting Nebraska's preference for local control. Nebraska is lower than the national average in local spending for all functions except for education, transportation, environment and housing, and utilities, as expected. Like public employment, the support for these three functions of government reflects the state's preferences, demographics, and history, consistent with Nebraska's political culture.

State government direct general spending per capita in Nebraska in 2020 was below the national average. Nebraska per capita state spending rose only 2 percent since 2016, compared to a 17.5 percent increase in the national average. The two largest categories of state spending in Nebraska were social services and income maintenance and education. For the functions of education, transportation, public safety, and "other," state spending was higher than the national average. Education and transportation are consistently above average over time, reflecting in part the high number of teachers and the low population density. Nebraska state spending was significantly lower than the national average for social services and income maintenance (only 63 percent of the national average), government administration, environment and housing, and interest on general debt (U.S. Census Bureau 2021c).

Local government direct general spending per capita in Nebraska is slightly above the national average. Nebraska local spending increased by

10.6 percent from 2016 to 2020, compared to a 14.9 percent increase for the United States. Nebraska was lower than the national average for all functions apart from education, transportation, environment and housing, and utilities. Education constitutes more than one-half of local general government spending in Nebraska. Utility spending in Nebraska is more than three times the national average because of the presence of public power in the state. Local government spending is below the average in social services and income maintenance, public safety, government administration, and interest on the general debt (U.S. Census Bureau 2021c).

The expenditure data are consistent with the employment data and show the priorities of the state and its political culture. Education and transportation have consistently received staunch support from citizens over many years. These are also two of the more expensive functions of state and local government, requiring revenues to support them. High spending on education puts pressure on the property tax, the main tax source used to support this government function. Similarly, the main source of transportation spending is taxes on motor fuels, requiring substantial revenue from this source.

## Revenue Comparisons

Governments, of course, need revenue to support services. Nebraska does not have high pressure on taxes because spending is moderate, and income and other tax bases are close to national averages. However, transportation tends to be supported by earmarked taxes such as the motor fuels tax, so this tax is relatively high. Similarly, one of the major revenue sources for education is property tax, and here again, Nebraska has consistently been higher than the nation.

Figures 13 through 16 use U.S. Census Bureau data to compare per capita state and local revenue collections from 2004 to 2016. Updated 2020 figures are discussed although not graphed. The figures compare Nebraska to both the national average and the average for the West North Central (WNC), which includes North Dakota, South Dakota, Nebraska, Kansas, Iowa, and Minnesota. They do not include the adjacent states of Colorado, Missouri, and Wyoming.

Figure 13 shows that Nebraska is significantly above the regional average in personal income tax collections and close to the national average throughout this period. Compared to the region, South Dakota does not have an income tax and North Dakota's income tax is quite low. State income tax collections are above the national average, but there is no local income tax in Nebraska, while there are in some other states. As a result, the combined state and local total is close to the national average.

The personal income tax was adopted in 1968 as a flat 10 percent of federal liability. In 1987 the tax structure was changed to the current approach where liability is based on federal adjusted gross income. From 2003 to 2022 the top rate was 6.84 percent. Historically, personal income tax collections in Nebraska have been below the national average, but in the 2004–16 time period, Nebraska mirrored the national average and slightly exceeded it from 2011 to 2016. This was a notable change, given Nebraska's historical position. It was a policy choice to rely more heavily on the personal income tax than on other sources of revenue, as the personal income tax is not earmarked for specific expenditures. In 2022 Nebraska was 97.3 percent of the national average. In 2022 a reduction in the personal income tax was passed, reducing the top rate from in phases from 2023 to 2027 from 6.84 percent to 5.84 percent. While state coffers in 2020 could afford a revenue reduction, an important question going forward is whether there will need to be reductions in state spending or an increase in the general sales tax, the only other tax with sufficient capacity to replace the personal income tax.

Figure 14 shows the trend in corporate income tax revenue from 2004 to 2016. Nebraska has been below the national average throughout this period except in 2015 and 2016. Nebraska was also below the regional average between 2007 and 2013 then above the region from 2014 and 2016. In 2020 Nebraska was 109 percent of the U.S. average. This tax was adopted in 1968 along with the personal income tax. In per capita terms, it declined from 2006 to 2011 but increased significantly from 2011 to 2015. The corporate income tax is a volatile revenue source. Collections decreased nine times in the thirty years from 1986 to 2015. This instability is a concern and occurred despite a stable tax rate. The top rate of 7.81 percent has been in place from 1991 to 2023, indicating that the volatility is due to fluctuations in corporate profits or refunds and changes in federal income tax policy that affect taxable income. In 2022 this tax was also reduced to 6.5 percent in 2024 and 5.84 percent in 2027.

The trend in collections from the general sales tax and selective sales (excise) taxes is displayed in figure 15. Nebraska is consistently below the

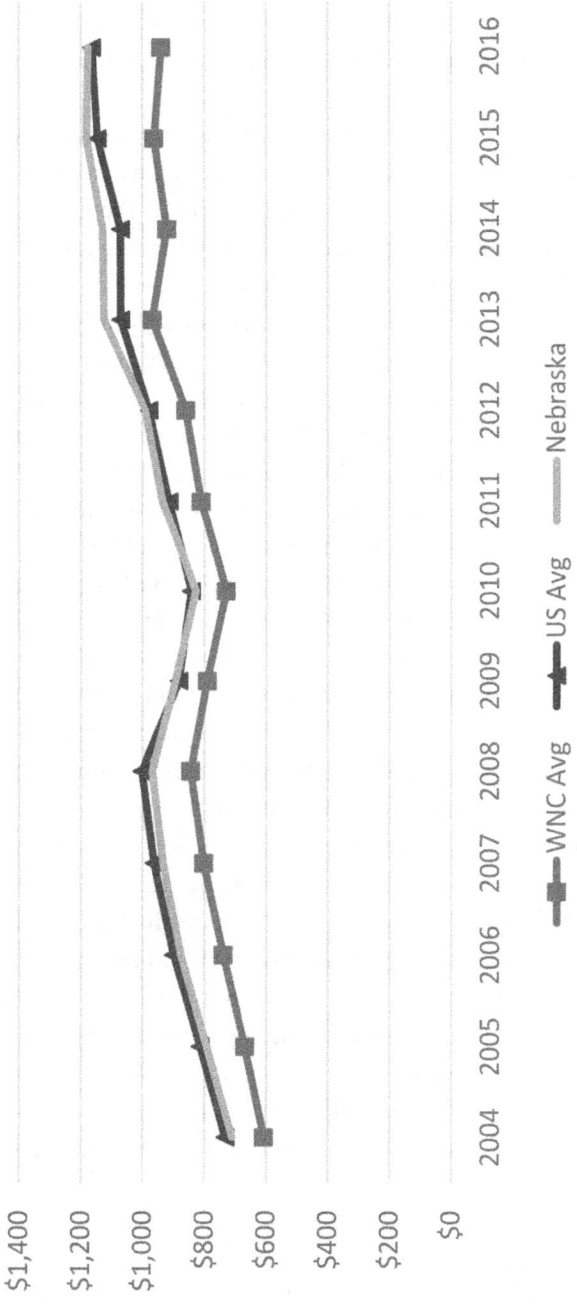

**Fig. 13.** Personal income tax revenue per capita, United States, West North Central Region, and Nebraska, 2004–16. Source: U.S. Census Bureau. Created by author.

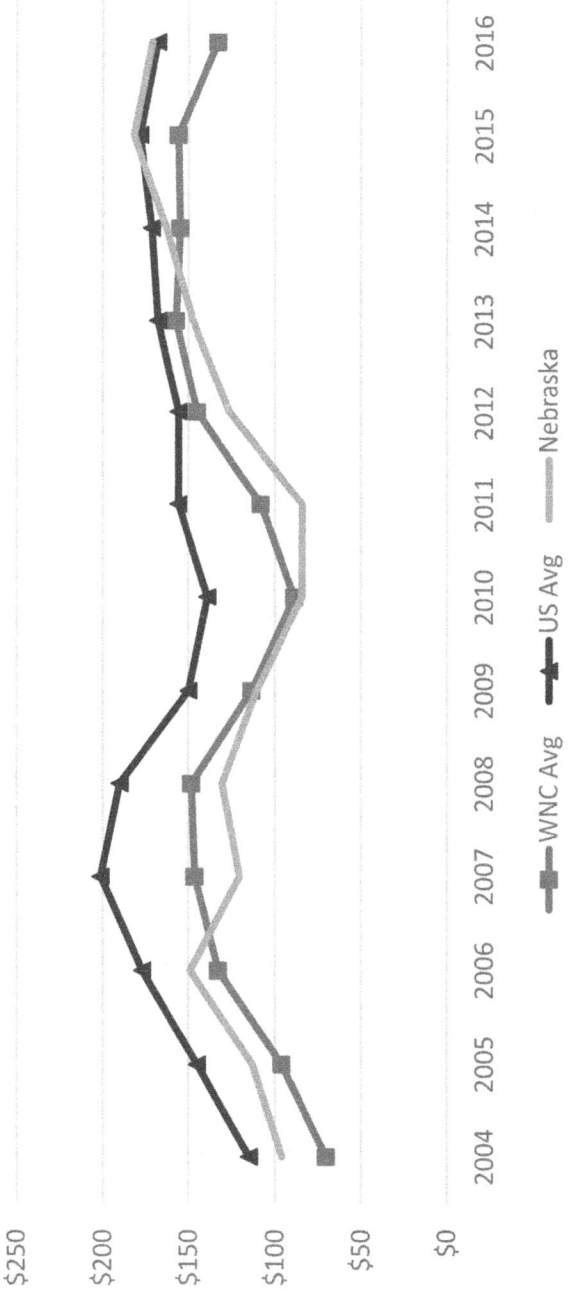

**Fig. 14.** Corporate income tax revenue per capita, United States, West North Central Region, and Nebraska, 2004–16. Source: U.S. Census Bureau. Created by author.

national and regional average since 2006, and this still is true in 2020. The trends for all three are similar, and the 2008–10 recession had a minor effect on revenues. The regional average has increased faster than Nebraska and the national average from 2010 to 2016. In 2020 Nebraska was 86.2 percent of the national average.

The state general sales tax was adopted in 1967 at a 2.5 percent rate. The local option sales tax was first allowed in 1969 at 0.5 percent. The state sales tax rate in 2022 was 5.5 percent with local rates up to 2.5 percent, for a maximum combined rate of 8.0 percent (Nebraska Department of Revenue n.d.). Compared to the states in the region, Kansas and Minnesota both have higher state rates and maximum combined rates. Missouri, South Dakota, and North Dakota have lower state rates but higher maximum local rates. Iowa has a higher state rate but a lower combined rate. In the other neighboring states; both rates are lower in Wyoming, while Colorado has a low state rate of 2.9 percent but a maximum combined rate of 11.2 percent (Tax Foundation 2022).

While tax increases are not popular, if Nebraska needs to increase taxes in the future, one logical option might be to increase the general sales tax to move closer to the national and regional averages. But as we shall see in the next section, this would shift the tax burden from higher income people to lower income people.

The major excise taxes are those on motor fuels, alcoholic beverages, and cigarettes and tobacco. The gasoline tax was adopted in 1925 and by 2020 had increased to 33.2 cents per gallon. In 2022 it was reduced to 24.8 cents per gallon. There are several components to the tax paid at the pump, including a fixed excise tax, a variable excise tax, and a wholesale rate. The fixed excise tax increased by six cents from 2016 to 2019 and has been stable since then. The variable excise tax has been significantly reduced since 2020 (Federation of Tax Administrators 2022). The combined excise tax rate in Nebraska in 2022 was higher than Colorado, Kansas, Missouri, North Dakota, and Wyoming and lower than Iowa, Minnesota, and South Dakota. Because of the relatively high spending on highways in Nebraska, this difference is understandable.

Alcoholic-beverage taxes were adopted in 1935. Currently, the tax rates on wine and beer are above the national median, while the distilled spirits tax is slightly below the median. Cigarette and tobacco taxes were adopted in 1947. The cigarette tax rate of 64 cents per pack is below the median of $1.78

per pack. The Nebraska rate has been unchanged since 2002, while some other states in the region have increased the rate by significant amounts. For example, Kansas increased its tax rate on cigarettes from fifty cents to $1.29 in 2015. An attempt by the Nebraska Unicameral to raise the cigarette tax by $1.50 per pack failed in 2016.

Figure 16 shows that the trend in the property tax has been one of steady increase in revenue over the 2004–16 period. From 2010 to 2016 Nebraska's property tax collections increased by 29.0 percent, compared to a regional increase of 9.0 percent. In 2020 Nebraska property tax collections were 15.3 percent above the national average. Nebraska is the highest in the region.

The property tax is the oldest tax in the state, having been adopted by the territorial legislature in 1857, ten years before statehood. It was originally a broad tax used by both state and local governments on property wealth (including livestock, personal property, and intangible wealth). Over time it was narrowed to a local tax on real estate land and structures. In 1965, property tax revenues were 34 percent above the national average and perceived to be too high. Tax reform in 1966–67 abolished the state tax and eliminated intangible property and household goods from the tax base. The general sales tax was adopted to replace the revenue lost to the state. Two years later the state income tax was adopted.

The burden of the tax on agricultural property has been an ongoing issue in Nebraska. It has been reduced by several reforms such as the exemption of farm machinery and inventories (1977), a constitutional amendment (1990) that provided for agricultural land to be assessed and taxed by "a method other than actual or market value" (Nebraska Legislature n.d.), and a statutory setting of the assessment for agricultural property at 75 percent of actual value (2006).

Historically, there have been efforts to reduce the property tax on agricultural property. However, any successful policy initiative that shifts the burden from agriculture would likely necessitate either a shift onto other property, to another tax, or a reduction in local spending. In 2020, the Nebraska legislature passed an act that provides a refundable income tax credit for any taxpayer who pays school district property taxes. Beginning in tax year 2020, the credit is equal to a percentage determined by the Nebraska Department of Revenue multiplied by the amount of school taxes paid during the tax year.

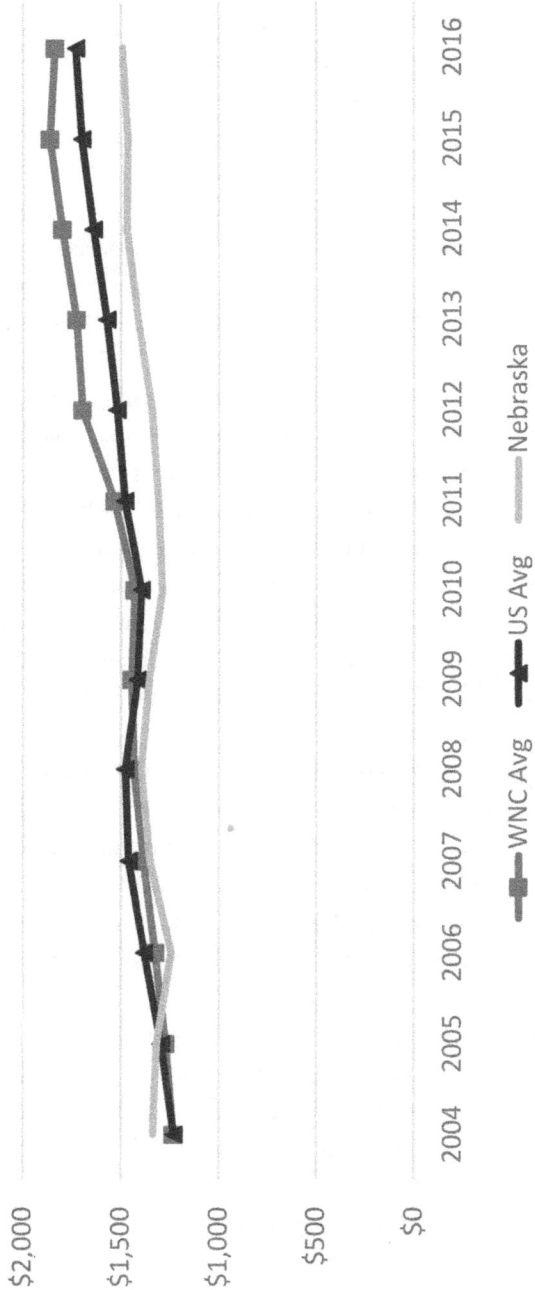

**Fig. 15.** General and selective sales tax revenue per capita, United States, West North Central Region, and Nebraska, 2004–16. Source: U.S. Census Bureau. Created by author.

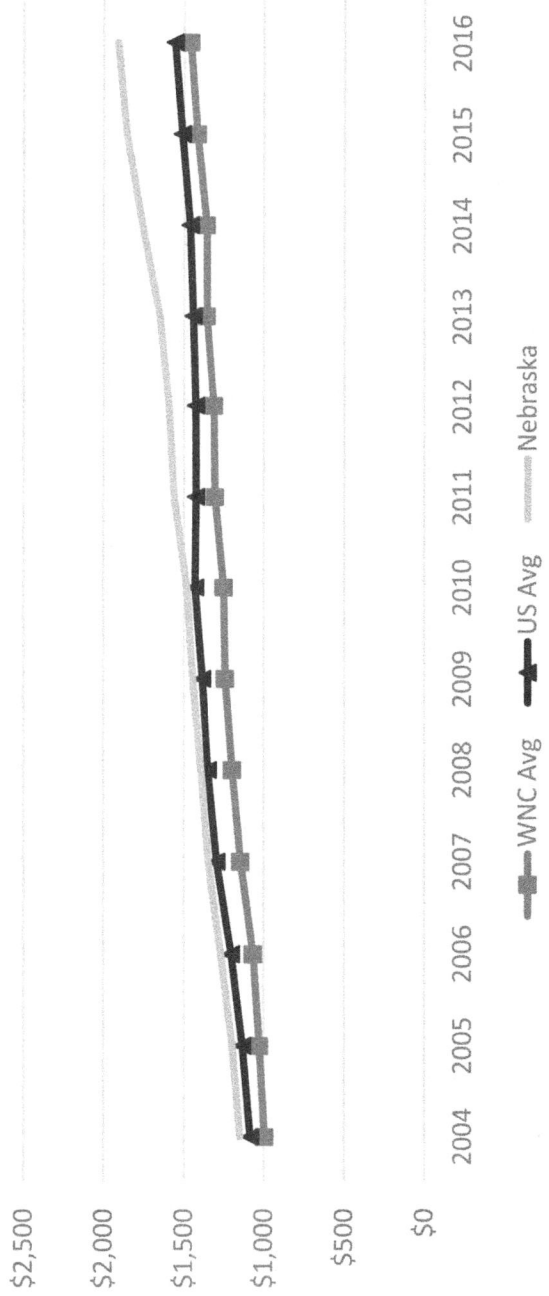

**Fig. 16.** Property tax revenue per capita, United States, West North Central Region, and Nebraska, 2004–16. Source: U.S. Census Bureau. Created by author.

In 2022 this credit was increased and an additional credit for community colleges was added.

As noted earlier, the areas where local spending is high includes schools and highways, which have historically received strong political support. Thus, while most Nebraskans dislike the property tax, they tend to dislike it less than cuts in spending on local schools and highways. The credit is an effort to maintain local control while reducing the burden of the tax. One possibility in the future is a shift toward more financing responsibility for these services to the state.

Nebraska receives revenues from user charges, fines, interest, and miscellaneous sources. Charges for government services are the largest component of this category, with charges for hospitals, state colleges and universities, airports, toll roads, sewerage and solid waste being some of the largest sources of fee revenue. In the 2004–16 time period, Nebraska is slightly above the national average and below the regional average. By 2020 Nebraska dropped slightly below the U.S. average. This is an important revenue source which may be used to replace taxes or fund expenditure increases. At the same time, user charges may create equity problems by placing a burden on lower income people.

The following conclusions can be drawn about Nebraska's revenue patterns:

> Nebraska is significantly above the regional average and slightly below the national average for state and local personal income tax collections.
>
> Corporate income tax revenue is above the national average and the regional average. Revenue from this source is quite volatile.
>
> Sales and excise tax collections are below both the national and regional averages. The state sales tax rate is fourth out of nine in the region. Some states have much higher local sales tax rates. The motor fuels tax is relatively high to support spending on local roads and highways, although the rate decreased since 2020. The cigarette tax and distilled spirits tax are the only state excise tax that are lower than the national median.

Property tax revenues are significantly higher than both the
national and regional average. The trend has increased
faster than the region and the nation. Concerns about the
burden of the tax on agricultural property continue.

In the category of charges, fines, interest, and miscellaneous
revenues, Nebraska was above the national average,
although recently fell below the average.

## Public Debt

Nebraska is very low in state debt outstanding per capita—forty-seventh in
the nation (including DC) and the lowest in the region in 2020. Local debt
outstanding is higher (thirteenth in the nation and fifth in the region). The
state constitution specifies a debt limitation of $100,000 on state govern-
ment, with exceptions for the construction of highways, water conservation construction, and the University of Nebraska, state colleges, and the
State Board of Education. As noted earlier, transportation and education
are favored by longstanding policy. Local debt is high for special districts
and, in particular, electric utilities (types of local governments discussed
in more detail in chapter 8). Once again, Nebraska's public power districts
make it distinctly different from other states. Otherwise, local debt is not
substantially different. An analysis of Nebraska state and local government
debt found that state debt has decreased, while local debt grew by 24.7 percent
in inflation adjusted terms from 2004 to 2011, a moderate rate of increase
(Ebdon and Choo 2014).

### TAX BURDENS

This section presents an analysis of the tax burden on representative Nebraska
families, with comparisons to the nation and the region. It shows both the
distribution of the tax burden at different income levels and the importance of
four different taxes on the family budget. The District of Columbia Office of
Finance does an annual study comparing the tax burdens on families for the
largest city in each state and Washington DC (2017). The following analysis
uses data from the 2020 report. It looks at taxes on a family of three, and
makes assumptions about spending, home values, income, and auto ownership. Four taxes are included: property tax, general sales tax, personal income

tax, and auto taxes. It is a useful comparison of tax burdens by state, and within any state it shows the distribution of the tax burden by income level.

Figure 17 shows Omaha's tax burden compared to the national median and the regional average. Omaha, the representative city for Nebraska, is lower than the nation and higher than the region at the lowest income level, and above both the region and the nation at all four other income levels. Omaha's tax burden is progressive (meaning the tax rate increases as the taxable amount increases) while the national median and regional average are less so. Omaha's tax burden increased over the last four years at all income levels.

Comparing Omaha to the other cities in the region, figure 18 indicates that at most income levels Omaha's tax burden is close to Des Moines and Kansas City. Minneapolis is highly progressive and lower at all income levels than Omaha, while Wichita is proportional (meaning the tax rate is about the same as the taxable base increases or decreases) and lower than Omaha at all levels. Sioux Falls and Fargo are regressive (meaning the tax burden decreases as income increases), with taxes less than half of Omaha at the highest income levels. Sioux Falls is lower at all income levels except the lowest income while Fargo is lower at all income levels. The absence of the personal income tax in South Dakota explains this difference, and while North Dakota has a state personal income tax, it is low.

Figure 19 shows the breakdown for the four taxes for Omaha. The personal income tax is the only progressive tax. The property and auto taxes are basically proportional except at the lowest level. The sales tax is slightly regressive. Combining all taxes, the tax burden in Omaha is progressive, which shows the importance of the personal income tax on the tax burden distribution. If Nebraska were like South Dakota and did not have an income tax but relied more heavily on the sales tax, the overall tax burden would be regressive. As discussed above, the personal income tax was reduced in 2022, while the sales tax stayed the same, likely reducing the progressivity of the state's tax system. It should also be noted that for all but the highest income level, the property tax is highest.

The 2020 national tax burden study conducted by the District of Columbia (2017) leads to the following conclusions.

The Omaha tax burden is higher than the national median except at the lowest income level. The tax burden in Omaha

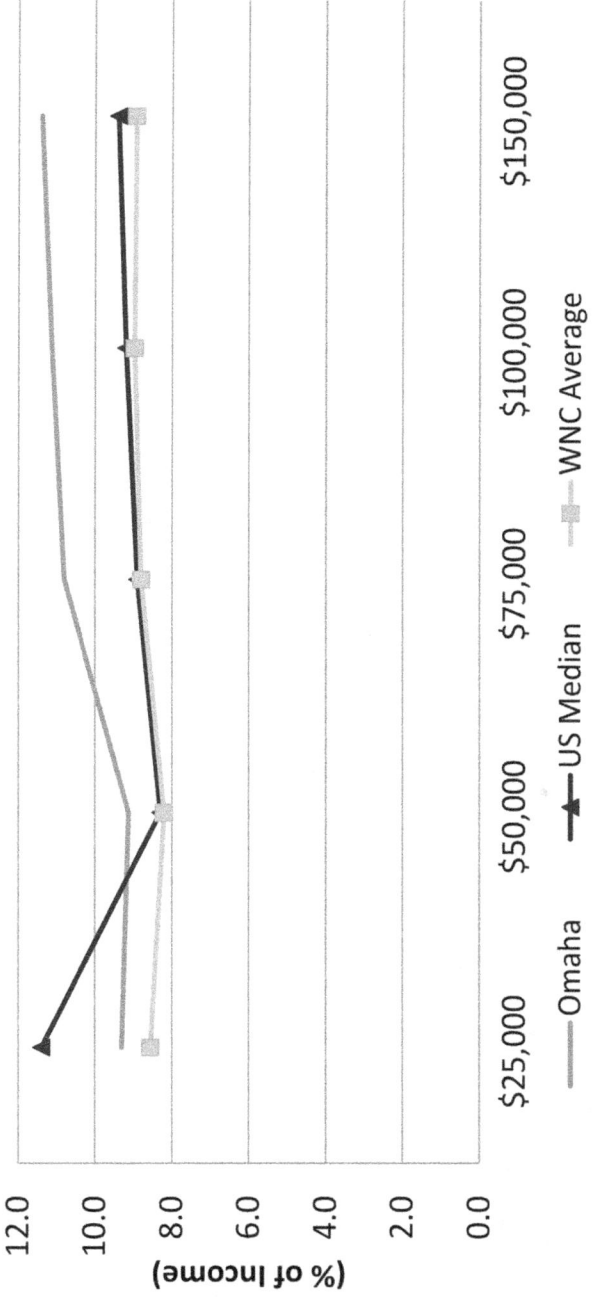

Fig. 17. Tax burden by income, United States, West North Central Region, and Omaha, 2020. Source: Government of the District of Columbia, *2020 Tax Rates and Tax Burdens in the District of Columbia: A Nationwide Comparison* (Washington DC: Government of the District of Columbia, 2022). Created by author.

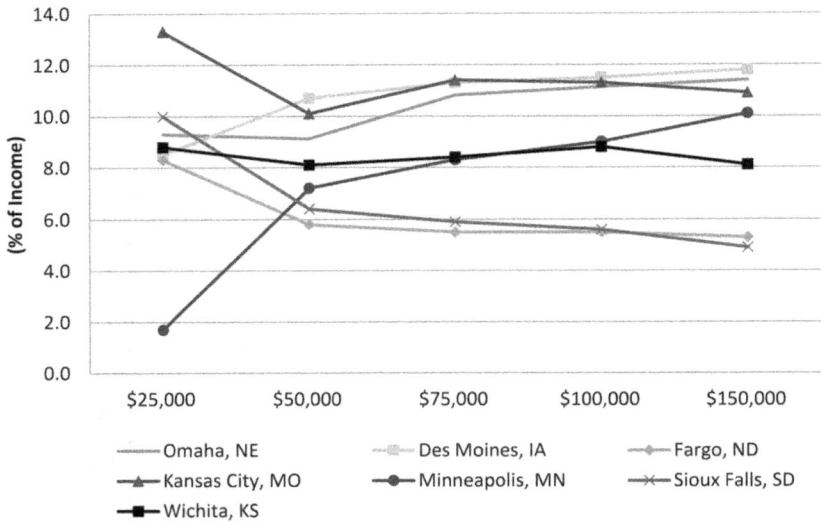

**Fig. 18.** Tax burden by income, West North Central Region, 2020. Source: Government of the District of Columbia, *2020 Tax Rates and Tax Burdens in the District of Columbia: A Nationwide Comparison* (Washington DC: Government of the District of Columbia, 2022). Created by author.

is more progressive than the national and regional tax burden.

Omaha, Kansas City, and Des Moines are the three highest in the region at all income levels except the lowest level. Wichita and Minneapolis taxes are moderate in the region, and Sioux Falls and Fargo are the lowest except at the lowest income level.

Omaha's total tax burden generally is progressive because of the personal income tax.

The degree of reliance on the income tax and the progressivity of that tax are the main determinants of overall progressivity of Omaha's taxes.

The property tax is the highest tax burden except at the highest income level. There are other ways to reduce the regressivity of the property tax, such as the circuit breaker program

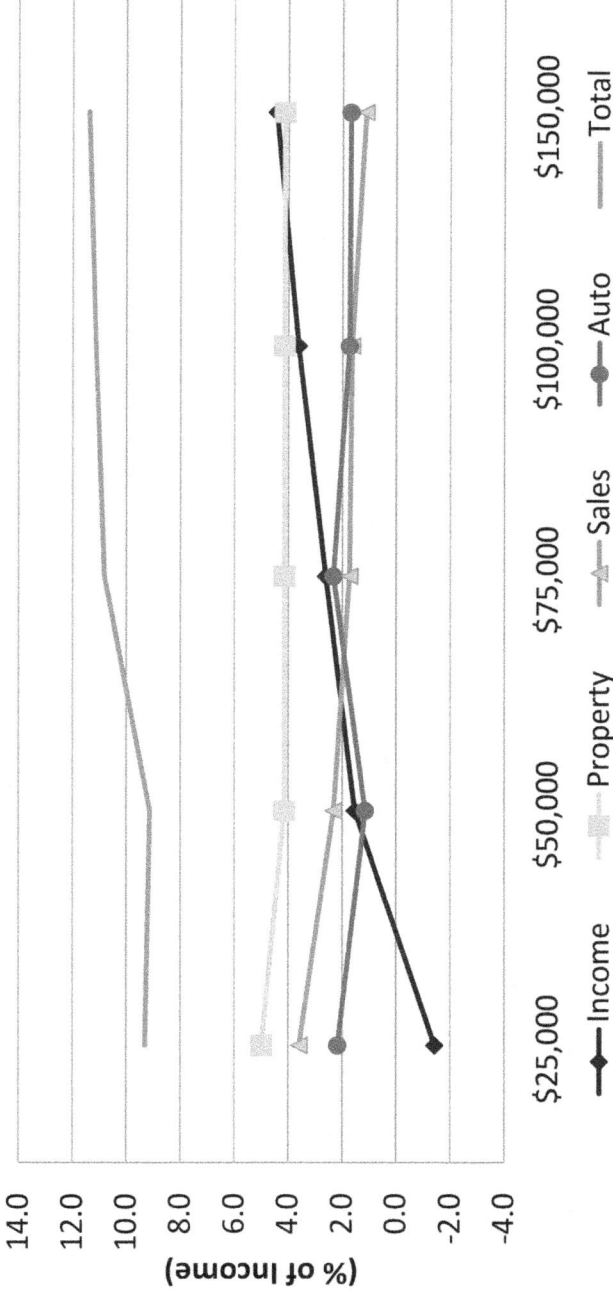

**Fig. 19.** Tax burden by income and type of tax, Omaha, 2020. Source: Government of the District of Columbia, *2020 Tax Rates and Tax Burdens in the District of Columbia: A Nationwide Comparison* (Washington DC: Government of the District of Columbia, 2022). Created by author.

used in some states that provides an income tax refund to taxpayers with low incomes and high property tax burdens. Similarly, the regressivity of the sales tax can be reduced by providing an income tax credit or deduction to large, low-income families. These strategies would reduce the need to rely on the income tax to balance out other regressive taxes.

## CONCLUSIONS

The comparisons of Nebraska tax and fiscal policies to the region and nationally in this chapter point to the following conclusions:

Nebraska has many local governments due to the preference for local control, quality schools, and good roads, all features of the state's political culture. These preferences cause government employment and spending to be higher for these functions. Despite this fact, significant savings are not likely to come from an effort to consolidate local governments.

The presence of all public electric power in Nebraska, another key aspect of its political culture, has a significant effect, causing state spending, public employment, and payroll for this function to be substantially higher.

Overall, government spending in Nebraska is below the national average, and payroll for government employees is generally lower.

Personal income tax revenue in Nebraska is slightly below the national average. Concern about the level of the tax led to a series of rate reductions phased in until 2027. Its progressivity keeps the overall tax burden from being regressive, and it meets the goals of revenue productivity and stability.

The property tax in Nebraska is above the national average and the highest in the region. It is a regressive tax and a burden on low-income taxpayers. Historically, Nebraska is a high property tax state, in large part because of the preference for local control.

The motor-fuels tax supports the demand for highways and
local roads. The corporate income tax and excise taxes on
wine and beer are also above the national median, while
cigarette and tobacco taxes are low.

The overall tax burden is higher and more progressive than
most states in the region and the national average.

## REFERENCES

Ebdon, Carol A., and Byungwoo Cho. 2014. "State and Local Government Debt."
In *Nebraska Legislative Planning Committee 2014 Report: Policy Briefs*, 32–38.
Omaha: University of Nebraska at Omaha Center for Public Affairs Research.
https://digitalcommons.unomaha.edu/cgi/viewcontent.cgi?article=1479&context
=cparpublications.

Federation of Tax Administrators. 2022. Tax Rates/Survey—Tax Rates. https://www
.taxadmin.org/tax-rates.

Government of the District of Columbia. 2017. *Tax Rates and Tax Burdens in the
District of Columbia—A Nationwide Comparison—2016*. Washington DC:
Government of the District of Columbia. https://cfo.dc.gov/sites/default/files/dc
/sites/ocfo/publication/attachments/2016%2051City%20Study.pdf.

Hanson, Russell L., and Eric S. Zeemering, eds. 2021. *Cooperation and Conflict between
State and Local Government*. Lanham MD: Rowman & Littlefield.

Krause, M. A. 1996. *Cost Savings from Consolidating North Dakota's Counties,
Agricultural Economics Report No. 361*. Fargo: North Dakota State University
Department of Agricultural Economics. http://ageconsearch.umn.edu/bitstream
/23321/1/aer361.pdf.

Leland, S. M., and K. Thurmaier, eds. 2010. *City-County Consolidation: Promises Made,
Promises Kept?* Washington DC: Georgetown University Press.

Molnar, Steve. 1996. *Reorganizing Nebraska's Local Government Structure*. Lincoln:
Nebraska Tax Research Council.

———. 1997. *The High Cost of Maintaining Ghost Town Government in Nebraska*.
Lincoln: Nebraska Tax Research Council.

Nebraska Department of Revenue. n.d. "Nebraska Sales and Use Tax FAQs." Accessed
February 1, 2022. https://revenue.nebraska.gov/about/frequently-asked-questions
/nebraska-sales-and-use-tax-faqs.

Nebraska Legislature Committee on Revenue and Legislative Fiscal Office. n.d. "Taxes
in Nebraska." Accessed February 8, 2023. http://www.nebraskalegislature.gov/app
_rev/index.html.

Tax Foundation. 2022. "State and Local Sales Tax Rates, 2022." https://taxfoundation
.org/2022-sales-taxes/#table.

University of South Dakota Department of Political Science and Government Research
Bureau. 1997. *A White Paper Report: County Consolidation in South Dakota*.
Vermillion: University of South Dakota.

U.S. Census Bureau. 2021a. 2017 Census of Governments. https://www.census.gov
/programs-surveys/cog.html.

———. 2021b. Annual Survey of Public Employment and Payroll, 2020. Washington
DC: U.S. Census Bureau. https://www.census.gov/programs-surveys/apes.html.

———. 2021c. Annual Survey of State and Local Government Finances, 2020.
Washington DC: U.S. Census Bureau. https://www.census.gov/programs-surveys
/gov-finances.html.

White, Leonard D. 1933. *Trends in Public Administration*. New York: McGraw-Hill.

# CHAPTER TEN

# The Controversy over Capital Punishment

## A CASE STUDY OF POLITICAL CULTURE

*Christian L. Janousek*

On May 27, 2015, the Nebraska legislature voted 30–19 to abolish the use of the death penalty in the state, overriding the governor's veto issued just a day prior. The landmark vote culminated several decades of debate regarding capital punishment in Nebraska. It can be argued that the issue became a question of policy efficacy. A coalition of Democratic and Republican legislators, in the officially nonpartisan legislature, noted that legal hurdles, cost inefficiencies, moral concerns, and the inconclusiveness of the death penalty as a deterrent for crime among the reasons for their support of the repeal. The following chronicles the circumstances leading to this decision and related implications, highlighting the confluence of purposes, events, and strategies and displaying Nebraska political culture and government in action.

A discussion of capital punishment in Nebraska reflects a complex history. A total of twenty-four individuals have been put to death since the start of executions officially administered by the state in 1903. The majority of these were by electrocution. The electric chair replaced hanging as the method of execution beginning in 1913. Following a Nebraska Supreme Court ruling in 2008 affirming the use of the electric chair unconstitutional, the legislature, in a special session, enacted a bill for lethal injection to become the state's means of capital punishment beginning in 2009. There has been only one execution using lethal injections.

The legislative history of Nebraska's death penalty has been contentious, involving a series of political maneuvers and executive showdowns. In 1979 the Unicameral successfully passed a bill to repeal capital punishment but could not override Governor Charley Thone's veto. A similar fate occurred for a moratorium on death penalty usage passed by the legislature in 1999, the first of its kind among U.S. states, subsequently vetoed by Governor Mike Johanns. In a swell of support in 2007, the Unicameral fell one vote shy of another repeal bill.

True to Nebraska's nonpartisan and independent nature of the Unicameral, and arguably because of its political culture, a mixture of individualism and moralism, the state legislature overrides many vetoes. From 2010 to 2020, for instance, 55 percent of the forty gubernatorial vetoes were overridden (Ballotpedia.org n.d.). In that same time period, forty-three of the other state legislatures overrode 20 percent or less of the vetoes by their governor.

Despite numerous failures to ban the death penalty, including a filibuster to end debate during the 2013 session, the issue remained salient for decades. From 1981 to 2015 a bill was introduced in every legislative session addressing repeal, with each being indefinitely postponed on General File or in committee. Senator Ernie Chambers, the longest serving senator in the legislature and a fierce advocate for abolishment of the death penalty in Nebraska for over forty years, introduced each of the bills.

The death penalty issue arose again in 2015 during a controversial first session of the Unicameral that involved three notable standoffs with newly elected governor Pete Ricketts ending in legislative overrides of gubernatorial vetoes. The primary arguments against the continuation of the death penalty appeared to be policy based, with the relevance of the current methods of capital punishment a key concern. While long disputed as a partisan platform in the arena of national politics, the debate on the death penalty in Nebraska also appealed to more a pragmatic perspective. Notwithstanding a strong conservative majority in the nonpartisan Unicameral, several critical issues contributed to the formation of a bipartisan coalition that supported repeal.

Nebraska did not perform an execution from 1997 to 2018, despite the decree of many death sentences during that period. One reason for this lapse was the expiration of a necessary ingredient for lethal injection, sodium thiopental. This drug had been unavailable in the United States since 2011 and was subsequently deemed unlawful for importation by the U.S. Food and Drug Administration. The Nebraska Department of Correctional Services could not procure the substance. Although Governor Ricketts pledged to obtain the drug, problems remained regarding the legality of its usage. In 2018, nevertheless, the state used lethal injection to execute a condemned man.

Another reason for opposition was the cost efficiency of capital punishment measures as the multitudinous layers of legal appeals and the related expenses of state executions exceeded the costs of life imprisonment. The financial argument coupled with perceptions of government inefficiency and bureaucratic overreach appealed to several conservative legislators. Many of these same legislators also referred to conflicts of morality and religion. Moreover, the state's inability to follow through with death sentences raised further concerns regarding the effectiveness of capital punishment as a crime deterrent and law enforcement policy.

During the debate, citizen perspectives were actively represented from both sides. At the forefront, state interest groups such as the Nebraskans for Alternatives to the Death Penalty and Nebraskans for the Death Penalty promoted their stance through petitions and lobbying. This likewise included intervention by national-level organizations vested in the capital punishment dispute, the American Civil Liberties Union and Conservatives Concerned about the Death Penalty. Although political partisanship from both camps influenced debate, the argument in Nebraska mostly remained focused on issues of practicality, efficacy, and necessity of the current policy.

Senator Ernie Chambers, the passionate advocate for abolishment of capital punishment, introduced the initial repeal bill, as he had done every year he was in the Unicameral. The bill, LB268, replaced the death penalty with a sentence of life without possibility of parole. The Judiciary Committee, a standing committee in the Unicameral, added an amendment for retroactive application to inmates facing capital punishment sentences prior to the enactment of the law, stating that no effective means of carrying out the executions would be plausible if the bill were passed. The committee also eliminated language that would exclude the possibility of parole given that life sentences already disallowed conditional releases under Nebraska state law. The bill advanced from General File to Select File on a 30–13 vote on April 16, 2015, clearing the first of three required votes on a bill by the full Unicameral chamber to become law.

The second vote from Select File to Final Reading was passed on May 15, with a 30–16 margin for repeal. Although this vote included a filibuster by death penalty supporters and an admonishment by Governor Ricketts of an impending veto, the bill maintained the three-fifths majority needed to override a gubernatorial veto. The final vote on LB 268 came on May 20. Prior to the vote, Senator Beau McCoy of Omaha, a staunch opponent of repeal, led a filibuster, a rare circumstance as Final Readings in the legislature generally prohibit further debate. The filibuster ended by a 34–14 vote, and the final vote on repeal, 32–15, added two more votes to the majority.

A week later, on May 26, Governor Ricketts officially signed a veto of the death penalty repeal, noting support from constituents and promising the attainment of the necessary pharmaceuticals for lethal injection. The Republican governor upheld the argument that capital punishment was integral to public safety and representative of the sentiment of most Nebraskans. Along with the attorney general, Governor Ricketts asserted that such a repeal would further weaken the authority of the criminal justice system in the state, already embroiled in criticism over incidences of mismanagement, inefficiency, and bureaucratic failures. Amid this action, two senators defected and sided with Governor Ricketts, bowing to pressure from constituents and an obligation to respect the governor's decision with the caveat of reform to the current policy. Nevertheless, the next day, on May 27, the legislature voted 30–19 to override the veto, maintaining the effort by both Republican and Democratic senators in the nonpartisan legislature to make Nebraska the nineteenth state to ban the death penalty and the first conservative state to eliminate capital punishment since North Dakota in 1973.

The repeal was immediately met with resistance by both lawmakers and citizen groups. Attorney General Doug Peterson raised concerns of unconstitutionality regarding the retroactive component of the bill, suggesting that only the Board of Pardons could alter court-imposed sentences. Several state senators quickly vowed to take measures toward preserving the death penalty, including the formation of civic coalitions with the intent of allowing a statewide vote on capital punishment. Governor Ricketts and his father, TD Ameritrade founder Joe Ricketts, personally donated $200,000 to the citizen group Nebraskans for the Death Penalty, supporting a referendum petition drive.

The referendum process in Nebraska enables citizens to "refer" laws passed by the legislature and place them on the ballot so voters can approve or repeal the legislation. The process provides voters to have the final say on measures passed by the legislature (Nebraska Legislative Research Office 2017). For a referendum that calls for a popular vote on the law and suspends a law from taking effect in the meantime, 10 percent of the registered voters, at the time of the referendum filing, must sign the petition. In addition, signatures must represent 5 percent of the registered voters from at least thirty-eight of the ninety-three counties. The signatures must be submitted within ninety days after the legislative session in which the law was passed has adjourned (Nebraska Legislature 2022).

The petition drive, led by Nebraskans for the Death Penalty, exceeded the requirements, amassing almost 167,000 signatures from 10 percent or more of registered voters in more than seventy counties. The petition was submitted to the Nebraska secretary of state on August 26, one day prior to the deadline, effectively suspending the death penalty repeal until the November 2016 general election.

In the year leading up to election day, the repeal of capital punishment in Nebraska created confusion. This situation evoked an unprecedented set of implications, including the sanction of prosecutors to pursue death sentences during the suspension, the legal status of inmates presently on death row, and the possibility of performing executions in the interim. Governor Ricketts promised to continue the pursuit of lethal injection substances and maintained the ability of the state to carry out death penalties. Both sides of the debate increasingly mobilized efforts toward the referendum vote, redoubling awareness campaigns and grassroots activities.

On November 8, 2016, Nebraskans voted overwhelmingly to overturn the repeal of the legislature and reinstate the death penalty, with over 60 percent of statewide voters supporting the referendum. Among Nebraska's ninety-three counties, in only one—Lancaster County, which contains the state capital of Lincoln—was the vote in favor of retaining the repeal, albeit by a narrow margin (52 percent to 48 percent). In many counties, support for retaining the death penalty as an option for criminal punishment exceeded 80 percent. Total statewide voter turnout for the election approached 70 percent, a dramatically high turnout even in a presidential election year.

Following the vote, Governor Ricketts vowed to act on extant death row sentences and to ensure the capacity of the state to perform executions, asserting that the will of the people had been unequivocally represented by the referendum vote. In the 2016 elections, two other states, Oklahoma and California, also voted to maintain the death penalty in their respective states.

The process of banning the death penalty by the legislature and the subsequent repeal of this law by voters in Nebraska illustrates several central and enduring attributes of the state's political culture, the actions of governmental institutions, and the development of public policy. Every stage of this event, from the initial procedural movements in the Unicameral to the final decisions of the voters, displays the overarching themes and crux of the state's unique approach to public policy and governmental operations.

In all, this is an excellent example of Nebraska's interplay of political culture and governance: intermittent progressivism dually monitored by fierce independence and nonpartisan pragmatism all within the context of individualistic localization, conservative underpinnings, and liberalized direct government. These fundamental values and ideals remain enshrined in the resiliently populist template of Nebraska politics, resonant of the stoic edifice adorning the main entry to the state capitol, "The salvation of the state is watchfulness in the citizen."

## REFERENCES

Ballotpedia.org. n.d. "Veto Overrides in State Legislatures." Accessed February 8, 2023. https://ballotpedia.org/Veto_overrides_in_state_legislatures.

Nebraska Legislative Research Office. 2017. "Initiative and Referendum in Nebraska: A Legislative Research Office Backgrounder." Lincoln: Nebraska Legislative Research Office.

Nebraska State Legislature. 2022. *2022–2023 Nebraska Blue Book.* Lincoln: Nebraska State Legislature.

# Appendix

## THE NEBRASKA JUDICIARY

*Christian L. Janousek*

### INTRODUCTION

The Nebraska state judicial branch, as per the Nebraska Constitution (Article V, Section 1) distinguishes the authority of judicial powers among the supreme court, court of appeals, district and county courts, and other courts created by the state legislature, with administrative authority over all courts assigned to the supreme court by constitutional amendment in 1970. The Nebraska Supreme Court originated as a territorial tribunal in 1854, prior to Nebraska's established statehood. Following the constitutional provisions of 1866 and 1875, the supreme court consisted of a chief justice and three judges, which was expanded by a 1920 constitutional amendment to six judges elected by district. A 1962 constitutional amendment approved by voters instituted a merit plan for judicial selection (Nebraska State Constitution, Article V, Section 21), contributing to the present configuration of six associate justices selected from six districts by gubernatorial appointment, with the chief justice selected at large. The governor also selects the six judges of the court of appeals from the same districts, with the chief judge appointed by the supreme court. Judges in Nebraska must be U.S. citizens, at least thirty years of age, and have been lawyers in the state for a minimum of five years (Nebraska Legislature n.d.; Nebraska Supreme Court n.d.).

## NEBRASKA COURT STRUCTURE

The Nebraska Supreme Court is the highest appellate court and regulates the practice of law within the state over all inferior courts. In addition to specified cases for which the Supreme Court has original authority, a 1990 constitutional amendment guarantees appeal to the supreme court for cases regarding the death penalty, life imprisonment, or constitutional questions. The supreme court also supplies administration leadership for the state judicial system and appoints the state court administrator. In oversight of state legal practice, the Supreme Court determines admission of applicants to the Nebraska State Bar Association. A variety of supreme court officers assist with administrative duties and functions.

The court of appeals, established in 1991, is the next intermediate appellate court and hears all appealed cases other than those of guaranteed appeal to the Supreme Court. To expedite the appeals process, the court of appeals comprises two panels of three judges. Petitioned cases from the court of appeals are reviewed by the supreme court, which may also grant cases to bypass the court of appeals and move directly to the supreme court docket. A denial of petition by the supreme court provides for the final ruling by the court of appeals. The clerk and reporter of the supreme court serve in this same capacity for the court of appeals.

Formed by the state constitution of 1875, Nebraska district courts operate from twelve districts across the state. District courts are trial courts of general jurisdiction that preside over felony, domestic relations, and civil cases, while also acting as an appellate court for county courts and administrative agencies. A 1920 constitutional amendment instructs that district court judges aid the supreme court when needed. Clerks of the district court, an elected county officer, supervise administrative tasks of the district courts.

Under a 1970 constitutional amendment, the judicial system was restructured for an integration of local courts, which delineated the current guidelines for county courts. County courts likewise attend the twelve state districts and handle a range of civil, criminal, domestic, and small claims cases as well as preliminary hearings for felony cases. County courts exist in every county within the state. A clerk magistrate in each county assists with administration of the courts, except in Douglas, Lancaster, and Sarpy Counties, which have judicial administrators.

Two other specialized courts officiate within this structure. The separate juvenile courts, located only in Douglas, Lancaster, and Sarpy Counties, handle cases of neglected, dependent, and delinquent children. These courts have concurrent jurisdiction with district courts. In counties without juvenile courts, county courts fulfill this purpose. The other, the workers' compensation court, established in 1935, addresses all related claims and enforcement of the Nebraska Workers' Compensation Act. These courts manage all cases involving worker compensation benefits and have statewide jurisdiction. Appeals from workers' compensation court may be taken to the court of appeals.

### POLITICAL CULTURE:
### JUDICIAL UNIFICATION AND OVERSIGHT

In 1970 legislation was approved for a constitutional amendment toward reorganization of the Nebraska court structure, the first major reform to the state's judicial branch since its founding in 1867. Prior to the reformation, Nebraska courts had historically embraced a localized and fragmented arrangement, representative of the strong individualistic and populist cultures of government within the state. The amendment introduced a number of significant changes to the court system with the intent of increased uniformity, centralization, and professionalism. Notably, the supreme court was given administrative authority over all other courts, an elimination of justice courts and elected justices of the peace, a consolidation and restructuring of regional and local courts, and the institution of a state court administrator office. These reforms have led to a more unified and integrated court system throughout the state (Sittig 1984).

Likewise consistent with the fervent political culture of Nebraska to maintain citizen control and responsiveness in governance, all court judges were originally elected to office and are generally required to reside in the districts for which they serve. Since a 1962 constitutional amendment approved by voters, the selection process of judges in Nebraska has been shifted to a merit-based appointment procedure following the general constructs of the Missouri Plan (Sittig 1984). In this practice a judicial nominating commission of members from the district, with four lawyers selected by the Nebraska State Bar Association and four citizen appointees chosen by the governor, recommends at least two qualified candidates for consideration of the vacancy. A non-voting member of the supreme court chairs the commission. The recommendations are provided to the governor for a decision on appointment. If the governor does not make an appointment within sixty days of the recommendation, the chief justice selects the nominee. This process extends to all judge selections in state courts. However, preserving a continued accountability to the electorate, appointed judges are subject to a retention vote in the first general election that occurs after three years in office and every six years thereafter.

To ensure supplementary public oversight for appointed judges, two additional judicial commissions contribute to the selection and retention of judgeships. The Judicial Resources Commission, comprising state citizens, judges, and attorneys, makes recommendations to the state legislature regarding the status of judicial vacancies and judicial district boundaries and the number of district judgeships. Correspondingly, the Commission on Judicial Qualifications, formed in 1966 by a constitutional amendment approved by Nebraska voters, investigates complaints filed against presiding judges and may recommend disciplinary actions and order formal hearings. The Commission on Judicial Qualifications also includes state citizens, judges, and attorneys.

### REFERENCES

Nebraska State Legislature. n.d. *Nebraska Blue Book*. Lincoln: Nebraska State Legislature. Several editions of the *Nebraska Blue Book* were referenced and are one of two primary sources of the information provided in this appendix.

Nebraska Supreme Court. n.d. "State of Nebraska Judicial Branch." Accessed February 13, 2023. https://supremecourt.nebraska.gov/. This website is one of two primary sources of the information provided in this appendix.

Sittig, Robert. 1984. "The Judiciary." In *Nebraska Government and Politics*, edited by Robert D. Miewald, 87–103. Lincoln: University of Nebraska Press.

# Suggestions for Further Reading

The following list compiles a selection of further readings and resources regarding Nebraska politics and government. This list is not meant to be exhaustive. Rather, it is a small grouping of carefully chosen research works and resources presented by the authors of this book for the novice reader or interested scholar, student, or citizen, offering a broader range and more in-depth perspective of Nebraska's history, literature, political culture, and governmental institutions. The University of Nebraska Press has many books on Nebraska in addition to the ones listed below. A detailed listing of a variety of sources available for further study of Nebraska politics and government may also be found in each chapter's references.

## NEBRASKA GOVERNMENT, POLITICS, AND INSTITUTIONS

Berens, Charlyne. 2005. *One House: The Unicameral's Progressive Vision for Nebraska.* Lincoln: University of Nebraska Press.

Haley, Alex, and Attallah Shabazz Malcolm X. 1965. *The Autobiography of Malcom X, as Told to Alex Haley.* New York: Grove.

Kazin, Michael. 2006. *A Godly Hero: The Life of William Jennings Bryan.* New York: Alfred A. Knopf.

Krane, Dale, Platon N. Rigos, and Melvin B. Hill Jr., eds. 2001. *Home Rule in America: A Fifty-State Handbook.* Washington DC: CQ Press.

Miewald, Robert D., ed. 1984. *Nebraska Government and Politics.* Lincoln: University of Nebraska Press.

Miewald, Robert D., and Peter J. Longo. 1993. *The Nebraska State Constitution: A Reference Guide.* Westport CT: Greenwood Press.

Norris, George W. 2009. *Fighting Liberal: The Autobiography of George W. Norris.* 2nd ed. Lincoln: University of Nebraska Press.

## NEBRASKA HISTORY

Hickey, Donald R., Susan A. Wunder, and John R. Wunder. 2007. *Nebraska Moments.* Lincoln: University of Nebraska Press.

Johnsgard, Paul A. 1984. *The Platte: Channels in Time.* Lincoln: University of Nebraska Press.

Luebke, Frederick C. 2005. *Nebraska: An Illustrated History.* 2nd ed. Lincoln: University of Nebraska Press.

Naugle, Ronald C., John J. Montag, and James C. Olson. 2015. *History of Nebraska.* 4th ed. Lincoln: University of Nebraska Press.

Potter, James E. 2013. *Standing Firmly by the Flag: Nebraska Territory and the Civil War, 1861–1867.* Lincoln: University of Nebraska Press.

Starita, Joe. 2009. *I Am a Man: Chief Standing Bear's Journey for Justice.* New York: Macmillan.

## NEBRASKA LITERATURE AND CULTURE

Aldrich, Bess Streeter. (1935) 1985. *Spring Came On Forever.* Lincoln: University of Nebraska Press.

Cather, Willa. (1918) 2013. *My Antonia.* Lincoln: University of Nebraska Press.

Kloefkorn, William. 2010. *Nebraska: This Place, These People.* Norfolk NE: Nebraska Life.

Kooser, Ted. 2002. *Local Wonders: Season in the Bohemian Alps.* Lincoln: University of Nebraska Press.

Morris, Wright. (1948) 1999. *The Home Place.* Lincoln: University of Nebraska Press.

Neihardt, John G. (1932) 2014. *Black Elk Speaks.* Lincoln: University of Nebraska Press.

Pound, Louise. (1918) 2006. *Nebraska Folklore.* Lincoln: University of Nebraska Press.

Sandoz, Mari. (1935) 2005. *Old Jules.* 3rd ed. Lincoln: University of Nebraska Press.

## STATE OF NEBRASKA ONLINE RESOURCES

History Nebraska. https://history.nebraska.gov/.

*Nebraska Blue Book.* http://nebraskalegislature.gov/about/blue-book.php.

Nebraska Office of the Governor. https://governor.nebraska.gov/.

Nebraska State Government. http://www.nebraska.gov/.

Nebraska State Legislature. http://nebraskalegislature.gov/index.php.

University of Nebraska Press. https://www.nebraskapress.unl.edu/.

# Contributors

JOHN BARTLE, PhD, is a distinguished professor of public administration and dean emeritus of the College of Public Affairs and Community Service at the University of Nebraska at Omaha. He received his PhD in public policy and management from the Ohio State University. His research areas are public financial policy, budgeting, sustainable development, and state and local government.

ROBERT BLAIR, PhD, is a professor emeritus in the School of Public Administration at the University of Nebraska at Omaha. He received his PhD in political science from the University of Nebraska–Lincoln. His research and teaching specializations include public policy, economic development, and comparative professional local government management.

JEROME DEICHERT is director emeritus for the Center for Public Affairs Research at the University of Nebraska at Omaha. He is a past member and chair of the Nebraska Economic Forecasting Advisory Board and past manager of the Nebraska State Data Center, with expertise in Nebraska data and trends. He received his MA in economics from the University of Nebraska–Lincoln.

DIANE L. DUFFIN, PhD, is a professor of political science in the Department of Political Science at the University of Nebraska at Kearney. Her teaching and research interests include American government institutions and politics. Her PhD is from the University of Missouri–St. Louis.

CAROL EBDON, PhD, is a professor emeritus of public administration in the School of Public Administration at the University of Nebraska at Omaha. She received her PhD in public administration from the State University of New York at Albany. Her teaching and research focused on public budgeting, financial management, and local government administration.

JAMES HARROLD, PhD, is an instructor in the School of Public Administration at the University of Nebraska at Omaha. His research interests include public budgeting and finance, policy and federal defense budgets, and public sector pensions. His PhD in public administration is from the University of Nebraska at Omaha.

CHRISTIAN L. JANOUSEK, JD, PhD, is an assistant professor in the Department of Political Science and International Relations at Creighton University. His research focuses on state and local government, professional management, public policy, and political culture. He received his PhD in public administration from the University of Nebraska at Omaha and his JD in law from the Creighton University School of Law.

PETER LONGO, JD, PhD, is a professor in the Department of Political Science at the University of Nebraska at Kearney. He has a PhD in political science from the University of Nebraska–Lincoln and a JD from the University of Nebraska College of Law. His teaching and research areas are constitutional law, civil rights and liberties, and environmental policy.

The late ROBERT D. MIEWALD, PhD, was a long-time professor of political science at the University of Nebraska–Lincoln. He is the editor of the first edition of this volume. His research and teaching interests included the study of Nebraska politics and government.

ANTHONY SCHUTZ is associate dean for faculty and an associate professor at the University of Nebraska College of Law. He received a JD, with highest distinction, from the University of Nebraska College of Law. His teaching and research interests include agricultural law, environmental and natural resources law, and state and local government.

# Index

*Page numbers in italics refer to illustrations.*

*West Virginia Politics and
Government, third edition*
By Richard A. Brisbin Jr., John C.
Kilwein, and L. Christopher Plein

*Wisconsin Politics and
Government: America's
Laboratory of Democracy*
By James K. Conant

To order or obtain more information on these or other University of Nebraska Press titles, visit nebraskapress.unl.edu.